BEN REILLY: THE SCARLET SPIDER

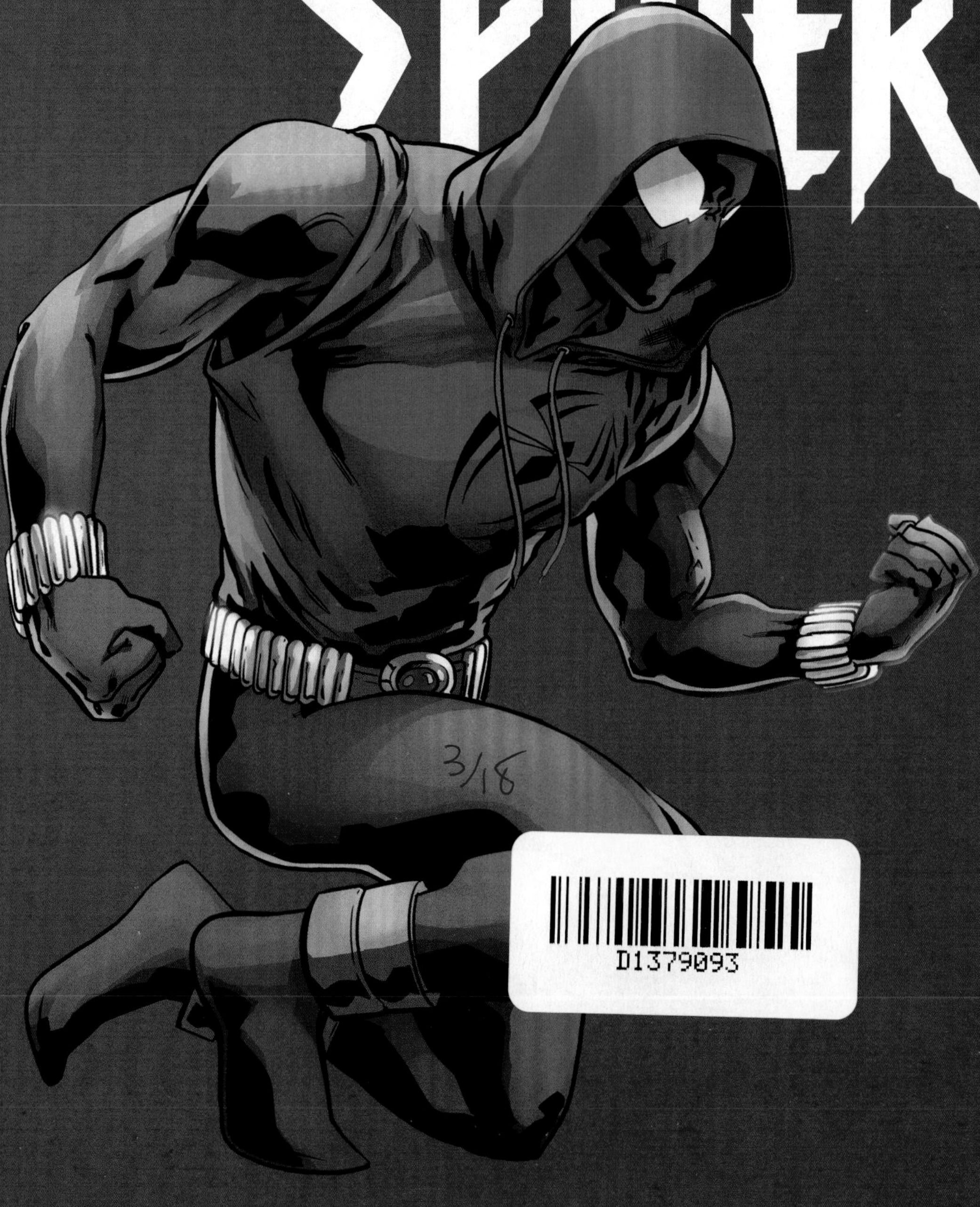

BEN REILLY:
THE SCARLET SPIDER

DEATH'S STING

PETER DAVID
WRITER

WILL SLINEY
ARTIST

JASON KEITH WITH
ANDREW CROSSLEY [#8]
COLOR ARTISTS

VC's JOE CARAMAGNA
LETTERER

MARK BAGLEY, JOHN DELL & JASON KEITH [#6];
MARK BAGLEY, SCOTT HANNA & PAUL MOUNTS [#7];
MARK BAGLEY, SCOTT HANNA & ANDREW CROSSLEY [#8]; AND
MARK BAGLEY, ANDREW HENNESSY & JAY DAVID RAMOS [#9]
COVER ART

ALLISON STOCK
ASSISTANT EDITOR

DEVIN LEWIS
EDITOR

NICK LOWE
EXECUTIVE EDITOR

COLLECTION EDITOR: MARK D. BEAZLEY
ASSISTANT EDITOR: CAITLIN O'CONNELL
ASSOCIATE MANAGING EDITOR: KATERI WOODY
SENIOR EDITOR, SPECIAL PROJECTS: JENNIFER GRÜNWALD
VP PRODUCTION & SPECIAL PROJECTS: JEFF YOUNGQUIST
SVP PRINT, SALES & MARKETING: DAVID GABRIEL
BOOK DESIGNER: ADAM DEL RE

EDITOR IN CHIEF: C.B. CEBULSKI
CHIEF CREATIVE OFFICER: JOE QUESADA
PRESIDENT: DAN BUCKLEY
EXECUTIVE PRODUCER: ALAN FINE

BEN REILLY: SCARLET SPIDER VOL. 2 — DEATH'S STING. Contains material originally published in magazine form as BEN REILLY: SCARLET SPIDER #6-9 and SLINGERS #0. First printing 2018. ISBN 978-0-7851-9459-0. Published by MARVEL WORLDWIDE, INC., a subsidiary of MARVEL ENTERTAINMENT, LLC. OFFICE OF PUBLICATION: 135 West 50th Street, New York, NY 10020. Copyright © 2018 MARVEL No similarity between any of the names, characters, persons, and/or institutions in this magazine with those of any living or dead person or institution is intended, and any such similarity which may exist is purely coincidental. Printed in Canada. DAN BUCKLEY, President, Marvel Entertainment; JOE QUESADA, Chief Creative Officer; TOM BREVOORT, SVP of Publishing; DAVID BOGART, SVP of Business Affairs & Operations, Publishing & Partnership; DAVID GABRIEL, SVP of Sales & Marketing, Publishing; JEFF YOUNGQUIST, VP of Production & Special Projects; DAN CARR, Executive Director of Publishing Technology; ALEX MORALES, Director of Publishing Operations; SUSAN CRESPI, Production Manager; STAN LEE, Chairman Emeritus. For information regarding advertising in Marvel Comics or on Marvel.com, please contact Vit DeBellis, Custom Solutions & Integrated Advertising Manager, at vdebellis@marvel.com. For Marvel subscription inquiries, please call 888-511-5480. Manufactured between 12/8/2017 and 1/9/2018 by SOLISCO PRINTERS, SCOTT, QC, CANADA.

10 9 8 7 6 5 4 3 2 1

Years ago, Miles Warren, one of Peter Parker's college professors, stole a sample of Peter's genetic material and used it to create a perfect clone of **SPIDER-MAN**. With all of Peter's memories, the clone fled. Created, not born, and without an identity of his own, he gave himself a new name and made his own way in the world as **BEN REILLY: THE SCARLET SPIDER!**

Ben Reilly has been lying low in Las Vegas. Fortunately, he has found an unlikely ally in Cassandra Mercury, owner of the **MERCURY RISING** casino.

Mercury's young daughter, Abigail, has been afflicted with a rare medical condition. In exchange for a place to stay and the equipment necessary to conduct his research, Reilly has offered to search for a cure for the deadly disease.

Meanwhile, Kaine, another clone of Peter Parker, has been tailing Ben for weeks, and the two recently came to blows. After learning of Ben's efforts to cure Abigail, Kaine begrudgingly offered a truce: as long as Abigail remains alive and Ben is working to cure her, Kaine will let him live...

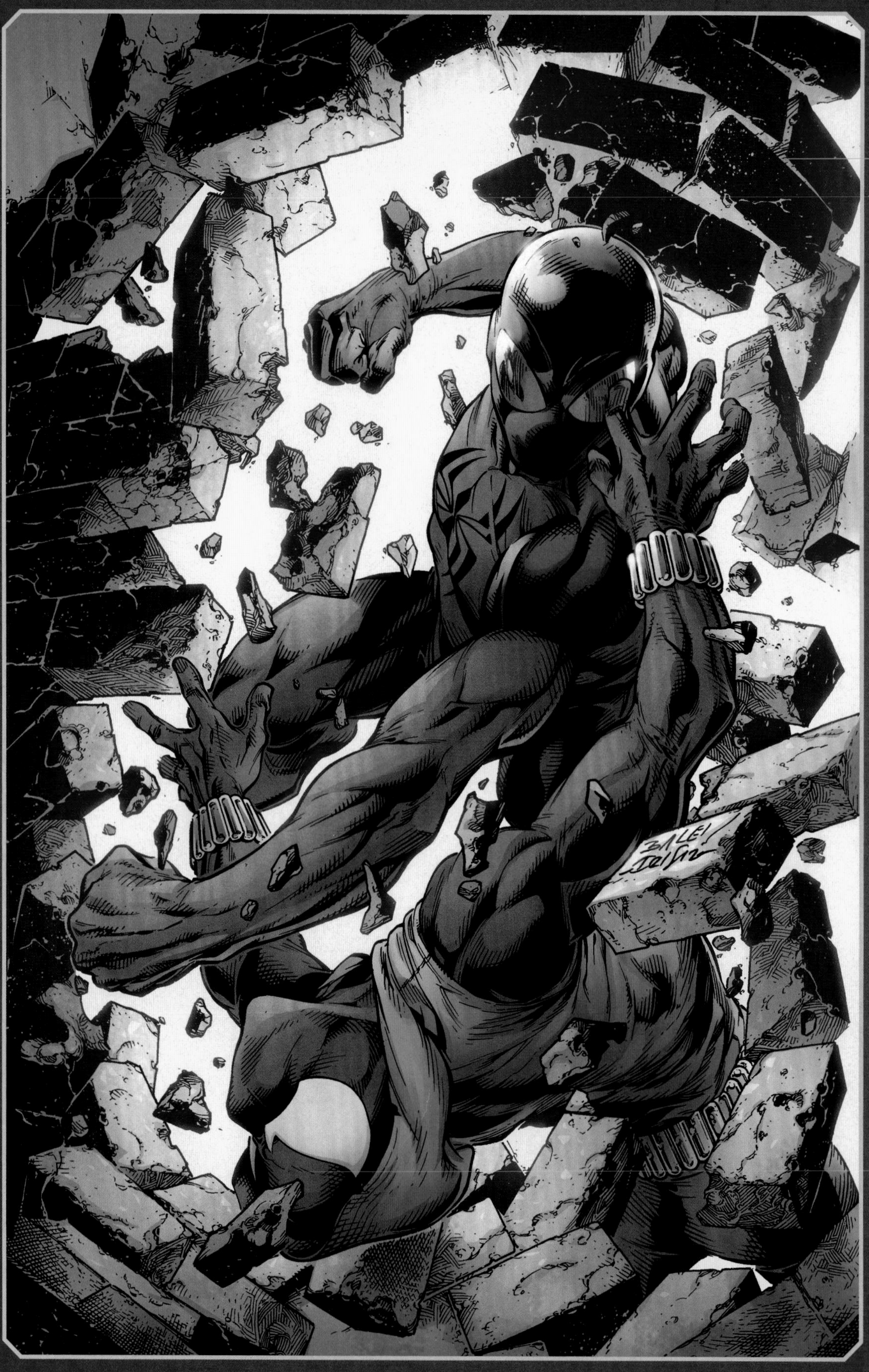

6

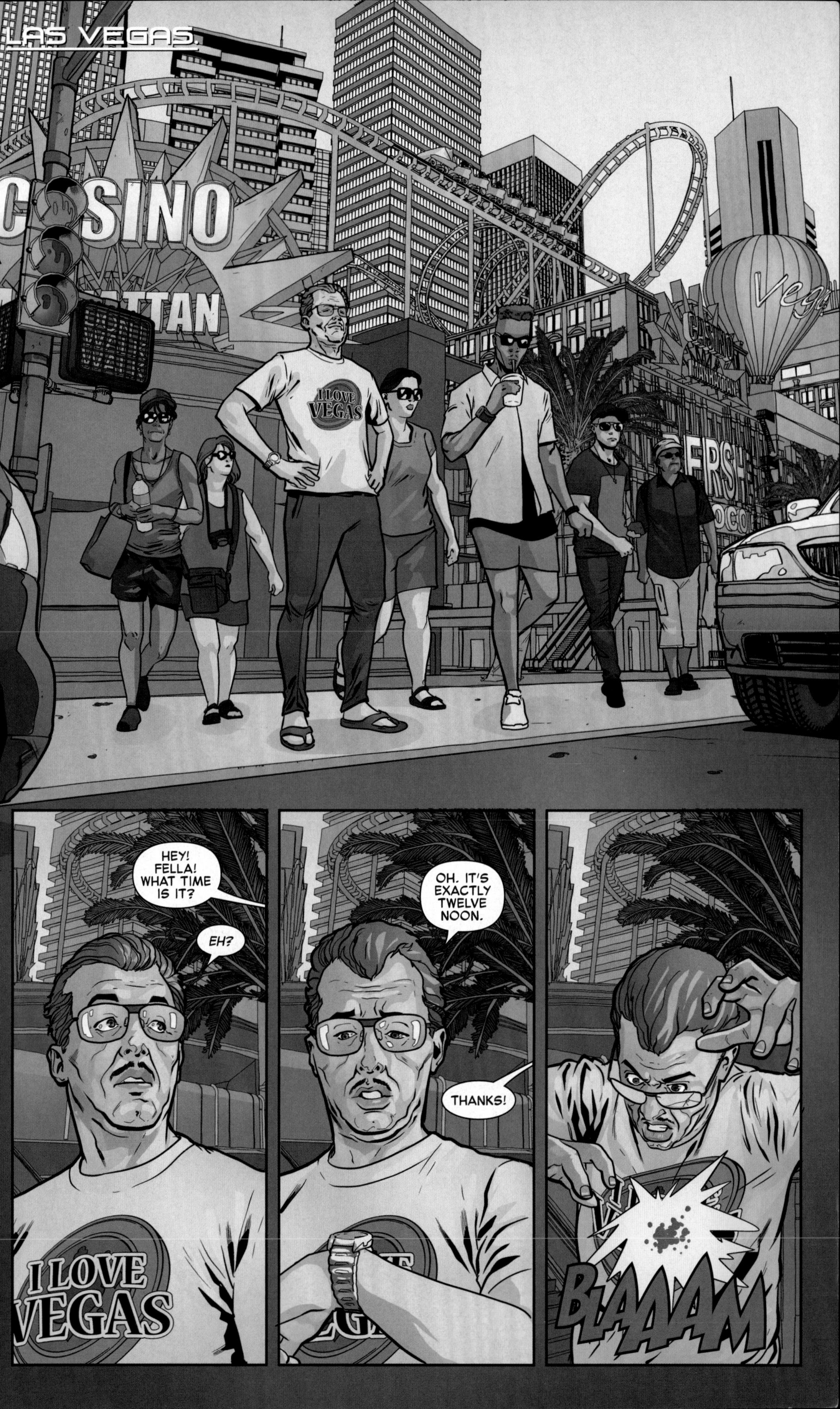

LAS VEGAS.
HEY! FELLA! WHAT TIME IS IT?
EH?
OH. IT'S EXACTLY TWELVE NOON.
THANKS!
BLAAAM

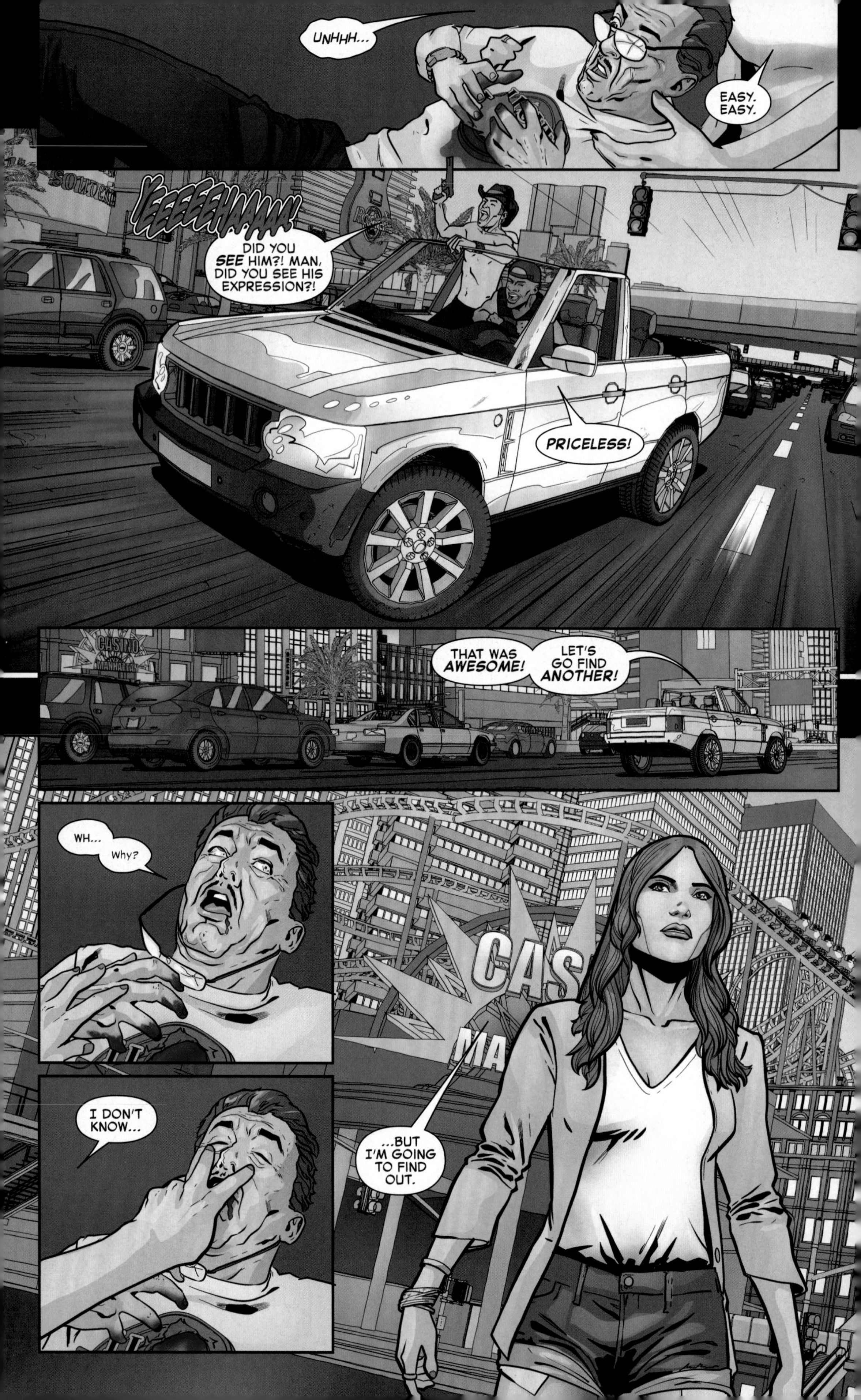
UNHHH...
EASY. EASY.
YEEEEEHAAAA!
DID YOU SEE HIM?! MAN, DID YOU SEE HIS EXPRESSION?!
PRICELESS!
THAT WAS AWESOME!
LET'S GO FIND ANOTHER!
WH...
Why?
I DON'T KNOW...
...BUT I'M GOING TO FIND OUT.

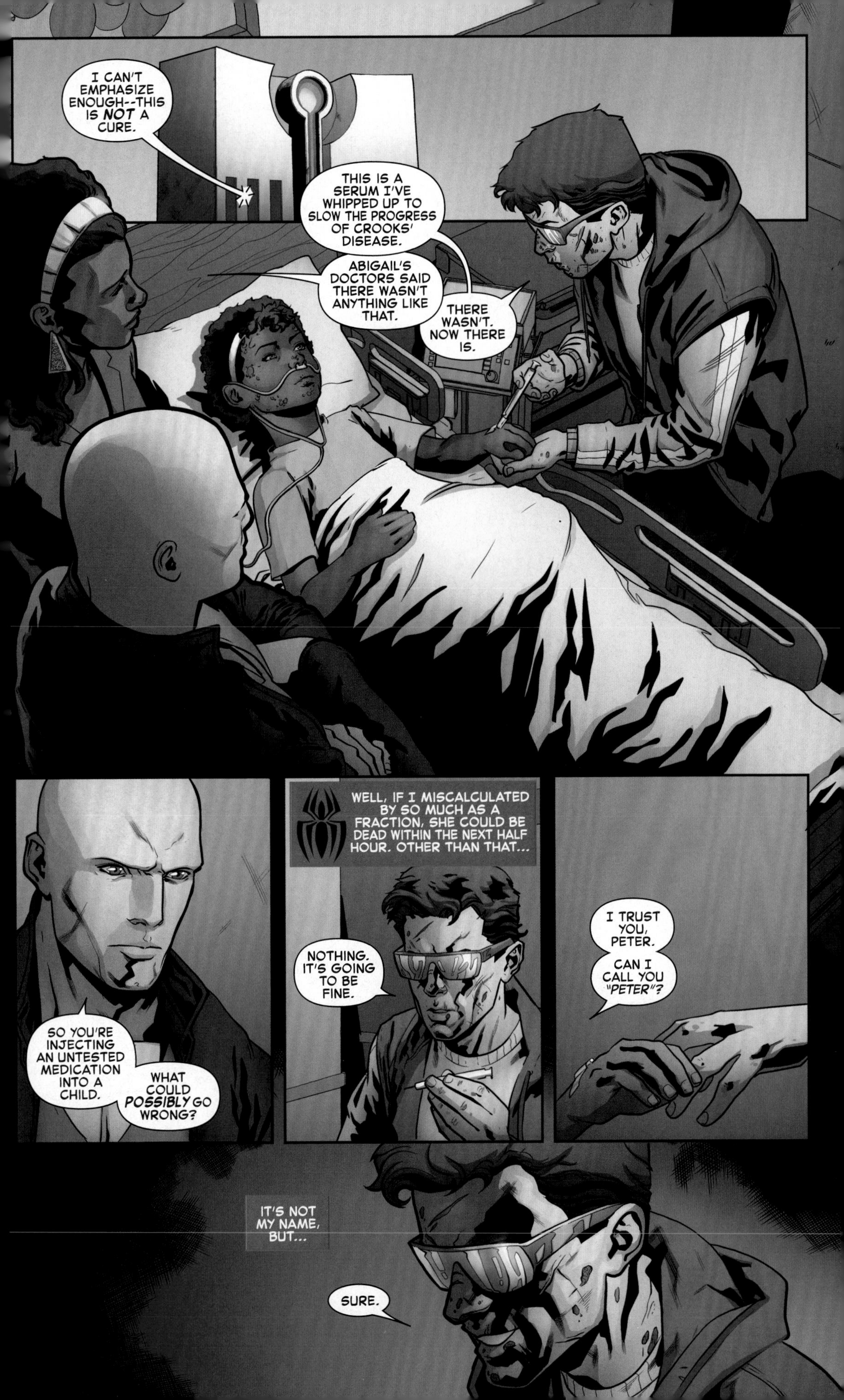
I CAN'T EMPHASIZE ENOUGH--THIS IS NOT A CURE.
THIS IS A SERUM I'VE WHIPPED UP TO SLOW THE PROGRESS OF CROOKS' DISEASE.
ABIGAIL'S DOCTORS SAID THERE WASN'T ANYTHING LIKE THAT.
THERE WASN'T. NOW THERE IS.
SO YOU'RE INJECTING AN UNTESTED MEDICATION INTO A CHILD.
WHAT COULD POSSIBLY GO WRONG?
WELL, IF I MISCALCULATED BY SO MUCH AS A FRACTION, SHE COULD BE DEAD WITHIN THE NEXT HALF HOUR. OTHER THAN THAT...
NOTHING. IT'S GOING TO BE FINE.
I TRUST YOU, PETER.
CAN I CALL YOU "PETER"?
IT'S NOT MY NAME, BUT...
SURE.

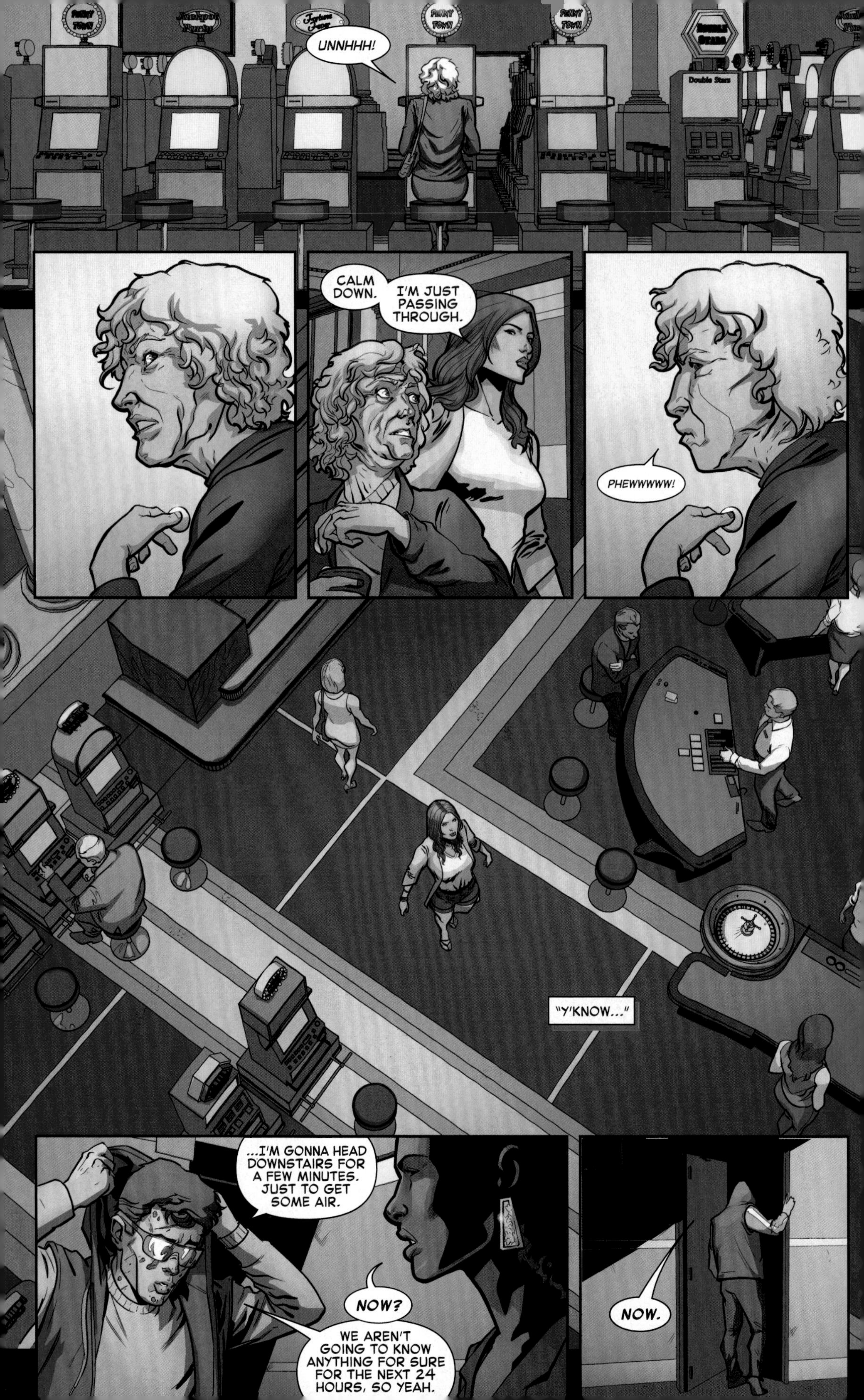

PENNY TOWN
Jackpot Party
Fortune Fever
PENNY TOWN
PENNY TOWN
DOUBLE STARS
Double Stars
UNNHHH!
CALM DOWN.
I'M JUST PASSING THROUGH.
PHEWWWWW!
"Y'KNOW..."
...I'M GONNA HEAD DOWNSTAIRS FOR A FEW MINUTES. JUST TO GET SOME AIR.
NOW?
WE AREN'T GOING TO KNOW ANYTHING FOR SURE FOR THE NEXT 24 HOURS, SO YEAH.
NOW.

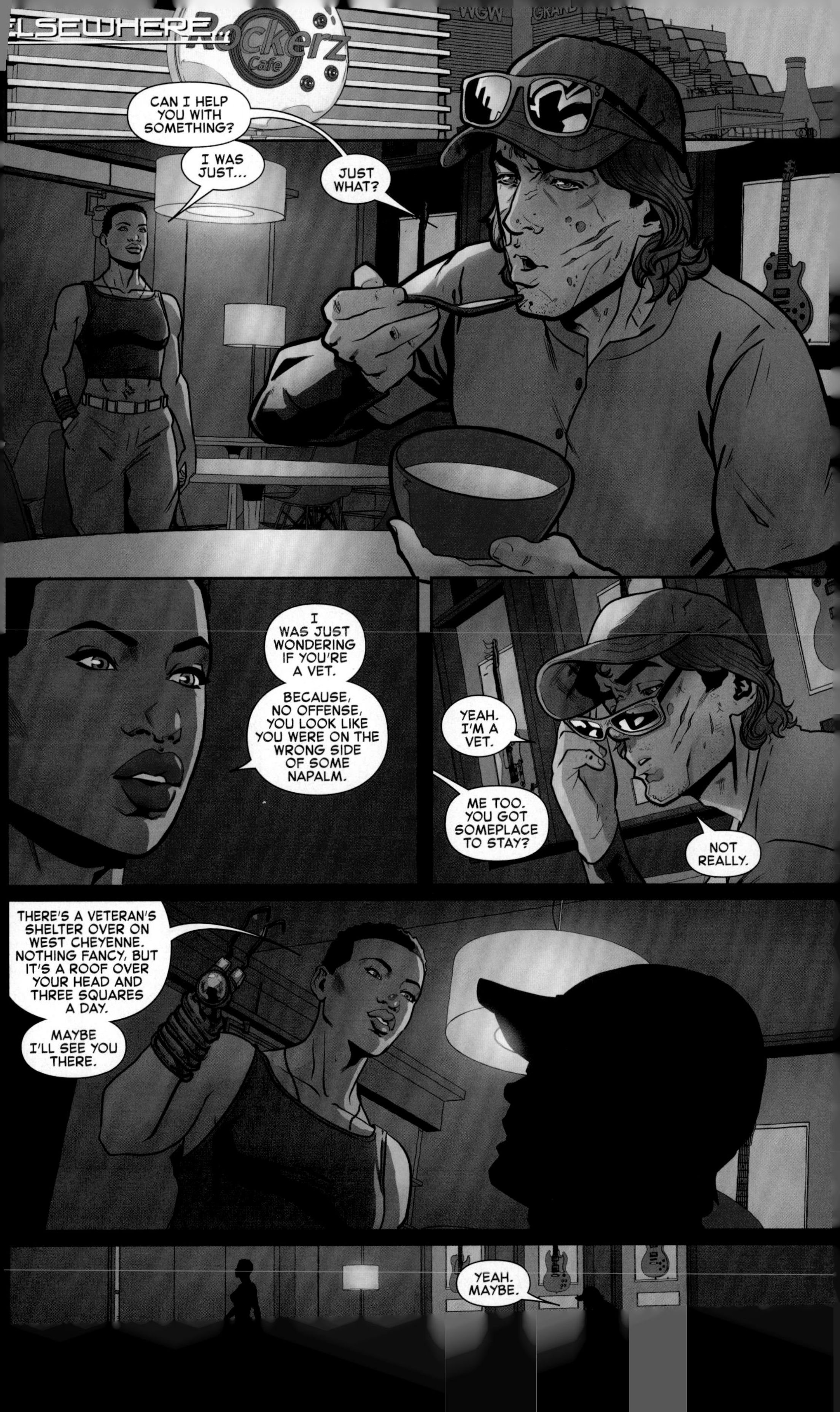
ELSEWHERE...
Rockerz Cafe
CAN I HELP YOU WITH SOMETHING?
I WAS JUST...
JUST WHAT?
I WAS JUST WONDERING IF YOU'RE A VET.
BECAUSE, NO OFFENSE, YOU LOOK LIKE YOU WERE ON THE WRONG SIDE OF SOME NAPALM.
YEAH. I'M A VET.
ME TOO. YOU GOT SOMEPLACE TO STAY?
NOT REALLY.
THERE'S A VETERAN'S SHELTER OVER ON WEST CHEYENNE. NOTHING FANCY, BUT IT'S A ROOF OVER YOUR HEAD AND THREE SQUARES A DAY.
MAYBE I'LL SEE YOU THERE.
YEAH. MAYBE.

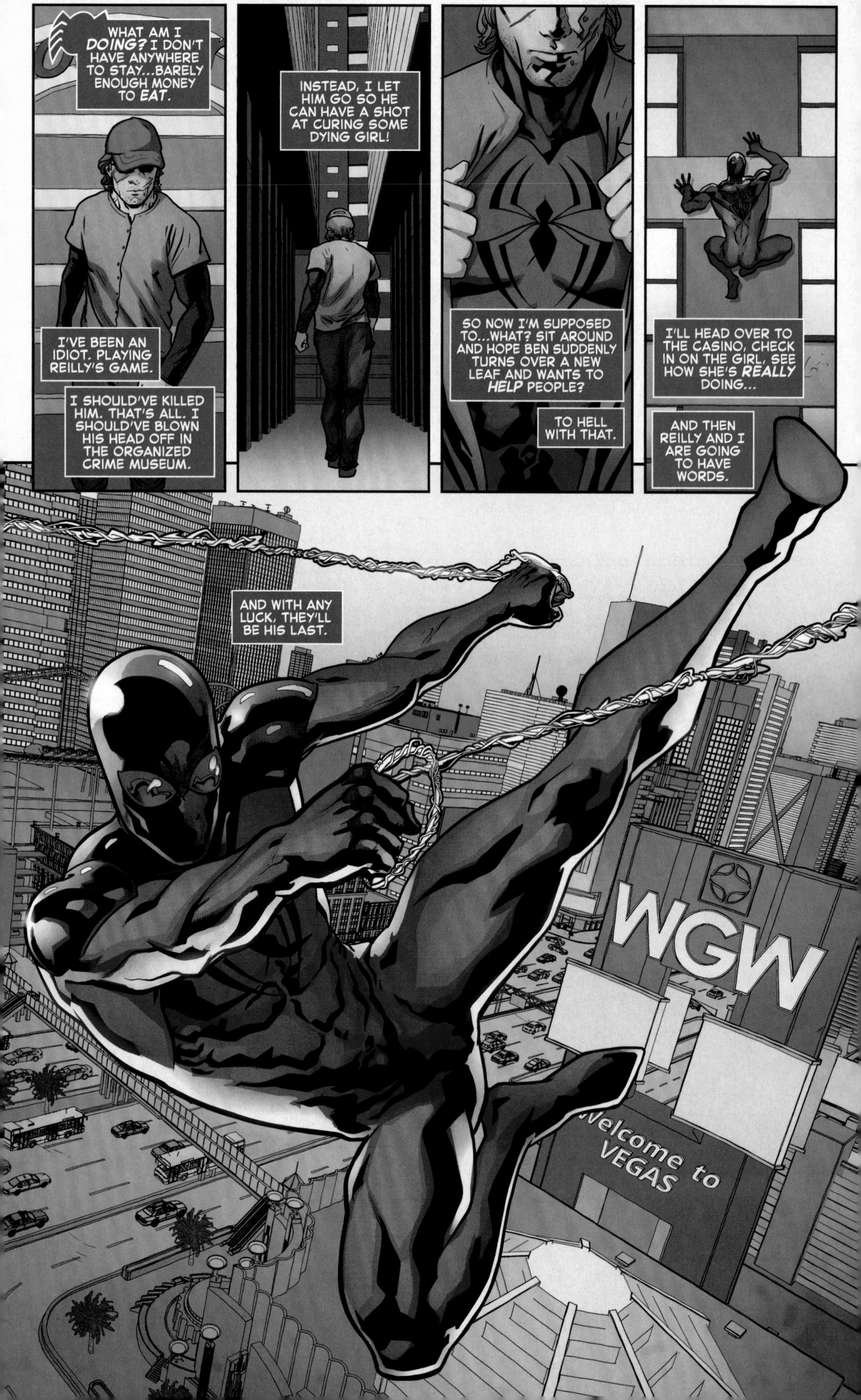

WHAT AM I DOING? I DON'T HAVE ANYWHERE TO STAY...BARELY ENOUGH MONEY TO EAT.
I'VE BEEN AN IDIOT. PLAYING REILLY'S GAME.
I SHOULD'VE KILLED HIM. THAT'S ALL. I SHOULD'VE BLOWN HIS HEAD OFF IN THE ORGANIZED CRIME MUSEUM.
INSTEAD, I LET HIM GO SO HE CAN HAVE A SHOT AT CURING SOME DYING GIRL!
SO NOW I'M SUPPOSED TO...WHAT? SIT AROUND AND HOPE BEN SUDDENLY TURNS OVER A NEW LEAF AND WANTS TO HELP PEOPLE?
TO HELL WITH THAT.
I'LL HEAD OVER TO THE CASINO, CHECK IN ON THE GIRL, SEE HOW SHE'S REALLY DOING...
AND THEN REILLY AND I ARE GOING TO HAVE WORDS.
AND WITH ANY LUCK, THEY'LL BE HIS LAST.
WGW
Welcome to VEGAS

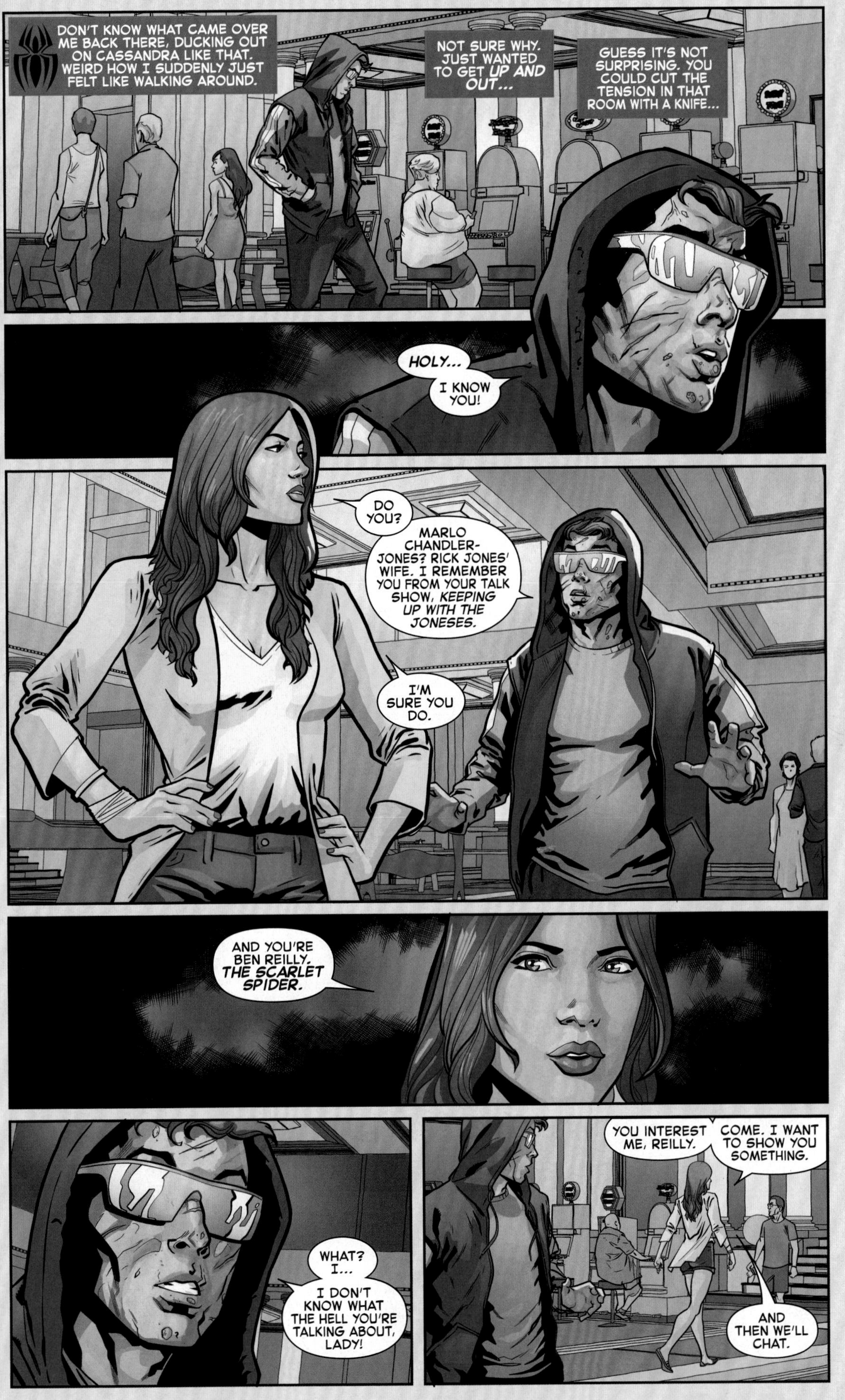

DON'T KNOW WHAT CAME OVER ME BACK THERE, DUCKING OUT ON CASSANDRA LIKE THAT. WEIRD HOW I SUDDENLY JUST FELT LIKE WALKING AROUND.
NOT SURE WHY. JUST WANTED TO GET *UP AND OUT*...
GUESS IT'S NOT SURPRISING. YOU COULD CUT THE TENSION IN THAT ROOM WITH A KNIFE...
HOLY...
I KNOW YOU!
DO YOU?
MARLO CHANDLER-JONES? RICK JONES' WIFE. I REMEMBER YOU FROM YOUR TALK SHOW, *KEEPING UP WITH THE JONESES.*
I'M SURE YOU DO.
AND YOU'RE BEN REILLY. ***THE SCARLET SPIDER.***
WHAT? I...
I DON'T KNOW WHAT THE HELL YOU'RE TALKING ABOUT, LADY!
YOU INTEREST ME, REILLY.
COME. I WANT TO SHOW YOU SOMETHING.
AND THEN WE'LL CHAT.

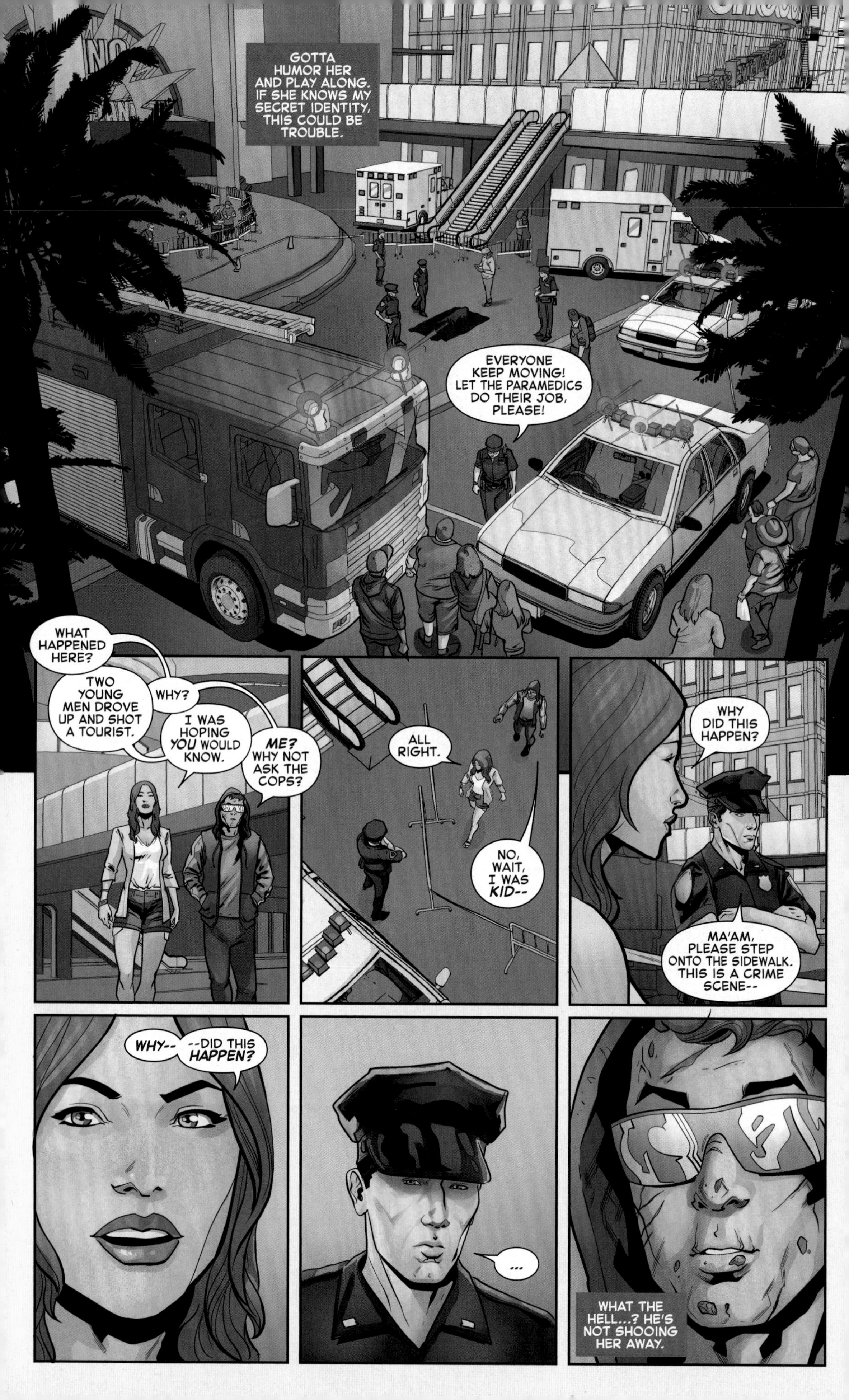
GOTTA HUMOR HER AND PLAY ALONG. IF SHE KNOWS MY SECRET IDENTITY, THIS COULD BE TROUBLE.
EVERYONE KEEP MOVING! LET THE PARAMEDICS DO THEIR JOB, PLEASE!
WHAT HAPPENED HERE?
TWO YOUNG MEN DROVE UP AND SHOT A TOURIST.
WHY?
I WAS HOPING YOU WOULD KNOW.
ME? WHY NOT ASK THE COPS?
ALL RIGHT.
NO, WAIT, I WAS KID--
WHY DID THIS HAPPEN?
MA'AM, PLEASE STEP ONTO THE SIDEWALK. THIS IS A CRIME SCENE--
WHY--
--DID THIS HAPPEN?
...
WHAT THE HELL...? HE'S NOT SHOOING HER AWAY.

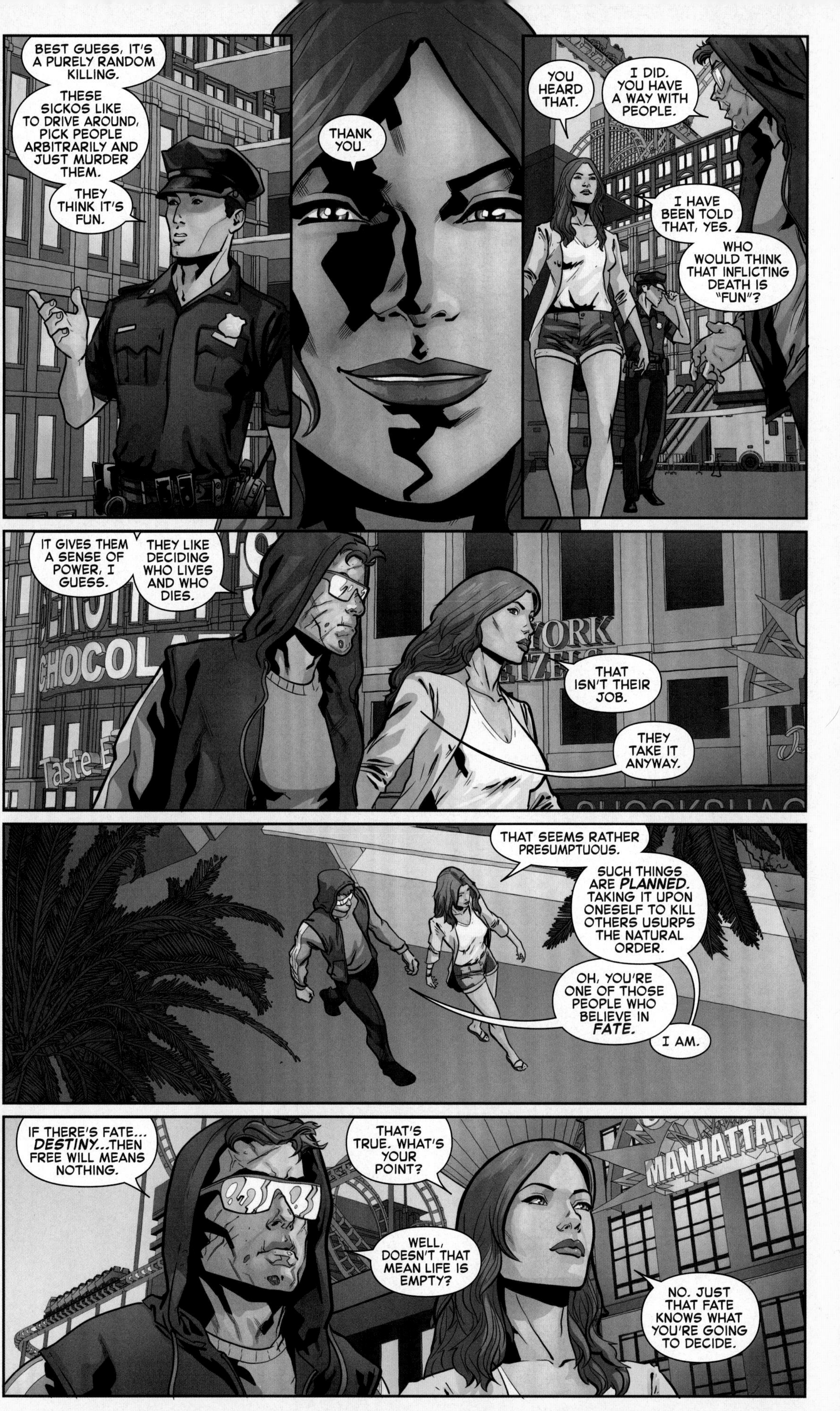
BEST GUESS, IT'S A PURELY RANDOM KILLING.
THESE SICKOS LIKE TO DRIVE AROUND, PICK PEOPLE ARBITRARILY AND JUST MURDER THEM.
THEY THINK IT'S FUN.
THANK YOU.
YOU HEARD THAT.
I DID. YOU HAVE A WAY WITH PEOPLE.
I HAVE BEEN TOLD THAT, YES.
WHO WOULD THINK THAT INFLICTING DEATH IS "FUN"?
IT GIVES THEM A SENSE OF POWER, I GUESS.
THEY LIKE DECIDING WHO LIVES AND WHO DIES.
CHOCOL
YORK
THAT ISN'T THEIR JOB.
THEY TAKE IT ANYWAY.
THAT SEEMS RATHER PRESUMPTUOUS.
SUCH THINGS ARE ***PLANNED.*** TAKING IT UPON ONESELF TO KILL OTHERS USURPS THE NATURAL ORDER.
OH, YOU'RE ONE OF THOSE PEOPLE WHO BELIEVE IN ***FATE.***
I AM.
IF THERE'S FATE... ***DESTINY...*** THEN FREE WILL MEANS NOTHING.
THAT'S TRUE. WHAT'S YOUR POINT?
MANHATTAN
WELL, DOESN'T THAT MEAN LIFE IS EMPTY?
NO. JUST THAT FATE KNOWS WHAT YOU'RE GOING TO DECIDE.

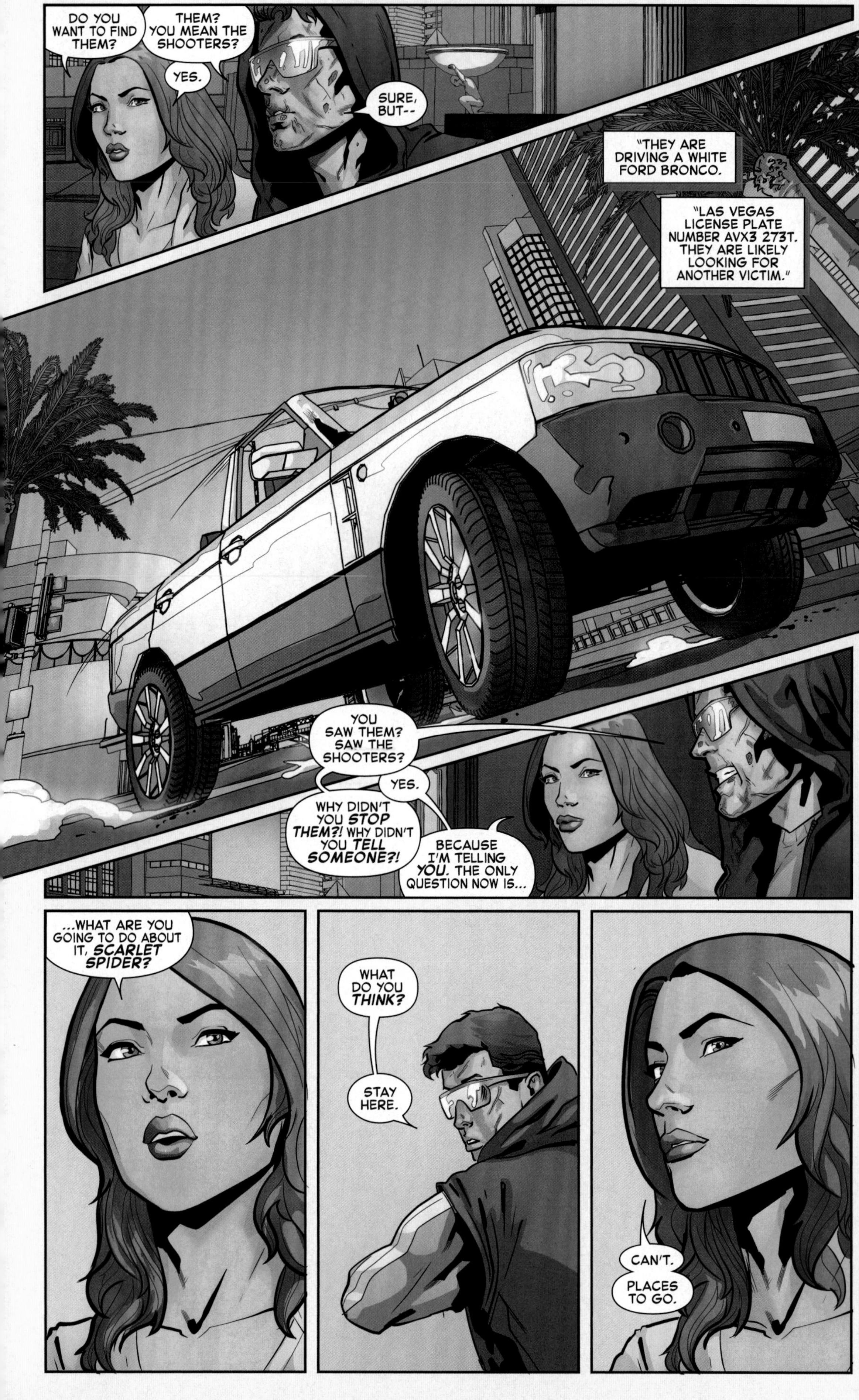
DO YOU WANT TO FIND THEM?
THEM? YOU MEAN THE SHOOTERS?
YES.
SURE, BUT--
"THEY ARE DRIVING A WHITE FORD BRONCO.
"LAS VEGAS LICENSE PLATE NUMBER AVX3 273T. THEY ARE LIKELY LOOKING FOR ANOTHER VICTIM."
YOU SAW THEM? SAW THE SHOOTERS?
YES.
WHY DIDN'T YOU STOP THEM?! WHY DIDN'T YOU TELL SOMEONE?!
BECAUSE I'M TELLING YOU. THE ONLY QUESTION NOW IS...
...WHAT ARE YOU GOING TO DO ABOUT IT, SCARLET SPIDER?
WHAT DO YOU THINK?
STAY HERE.
CAN'T.
PLACES TO GO.

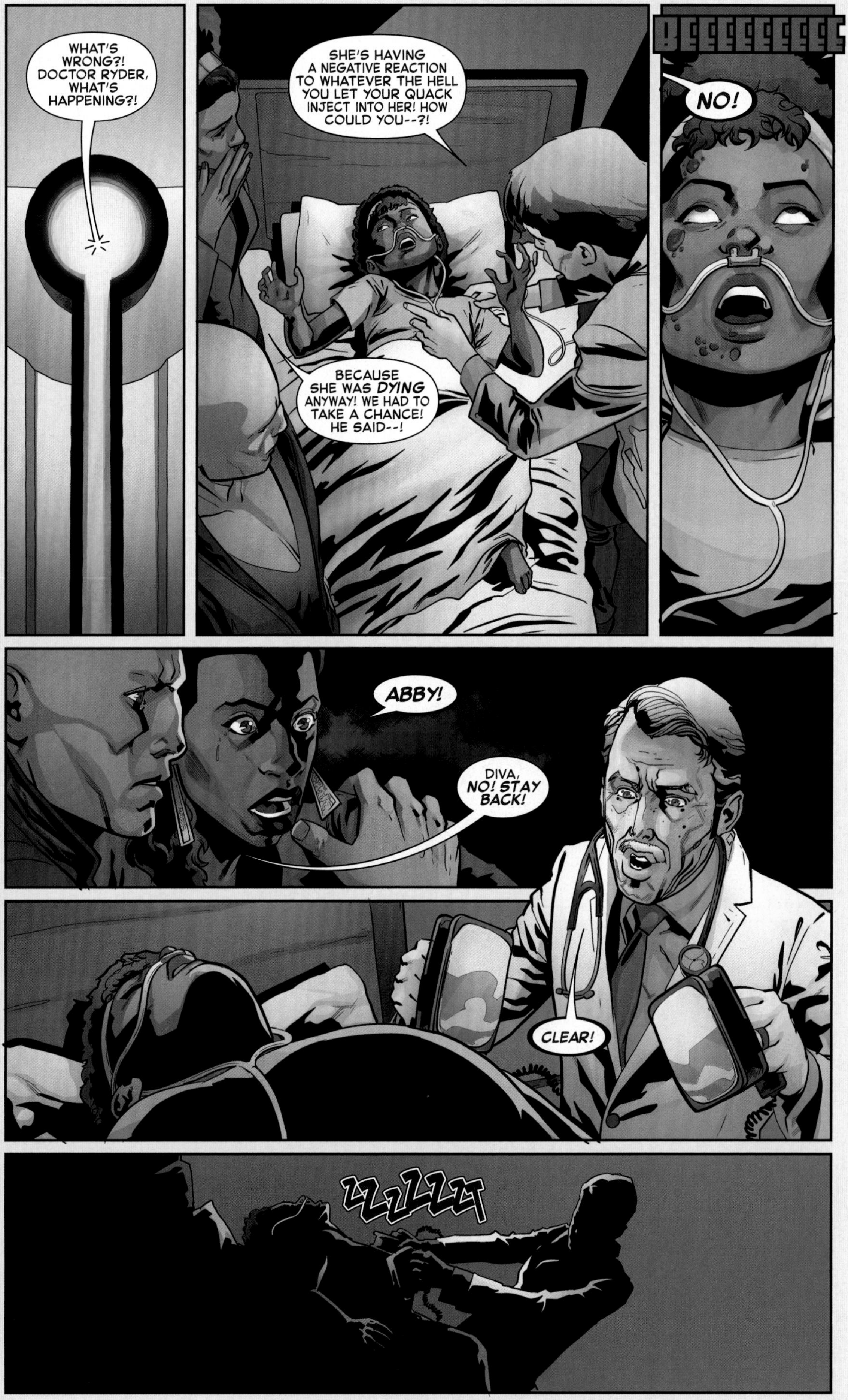
WHAT'S WRONG?! DOCTOR RYDER, WHAT'S HAPPENING?!
SHE'S HAVING A NEGATIVE REACTION TO WHATEVER THE HELL YOU LET YOUR QUACK INJECT INTO HER! HOW COULD YOU--?!
BECAUSE SHE WAS DYING ANYWAY! WE HAD TO TAKE A CHANCE! HE SAID--!
BEEEEEEEEE
NO!
ABBY!
DIVA, NO! STAY BACK!
CLEAR!
ZZZZZZT

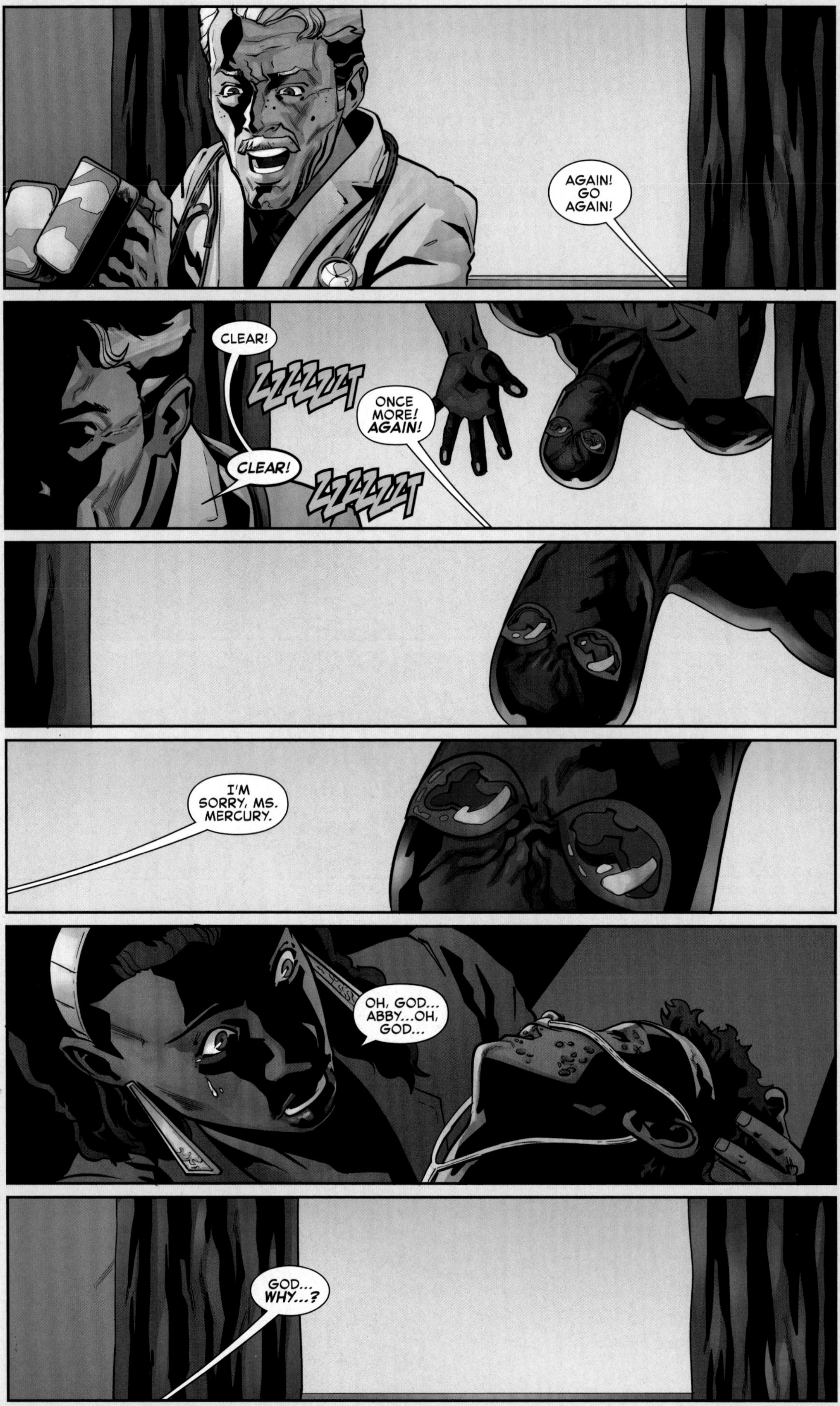
AGAIN! GO AGAIN!
CLEAR!
ZZZZZZT
ONCE MORE! AGAIN!
CLEAR!
ZZZZZZT
I'M SORRY, MS. MERCURY.
OH, GOD... ABBY...OH, GOD...
GOD... WHY...?

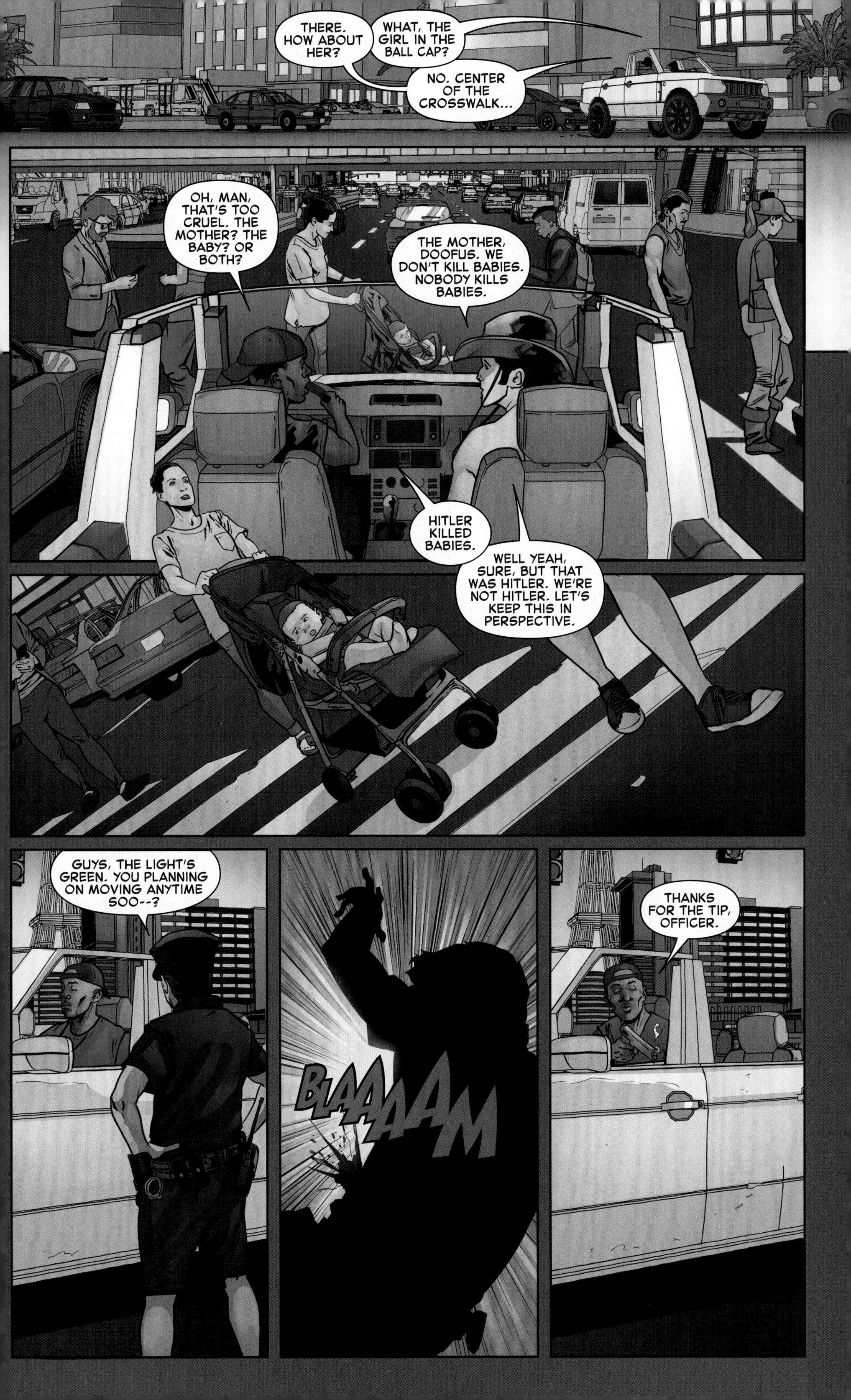
THERE. HOW ABOUT HER?
WHAT, THE GIRL IN THE BALL CAP?
NO. CENTER OF THE CROSSWALK...
OH, MAN, THAT'S TOO CRUEL. THE MOTHER? THE BABY? OR BOTH?
THE MOTHER, DOOFUS. WE DON'T KILL BABIES. NOBODY KILLS BABIES.
HITLER KILLED BABIES.
WELL YEAH, SURE, BUT THAT WAS HITLER. WE'RE NOT HITLER. LET'S KEEP THIS IN PERSPECTIVE.
GUYS, THE LIGHT'S GREEN. YOU PLANNING ON MOVING ANYTIME SOO--?
BLAAAAAM
THANKS FOR THE TIP, OFFICER.

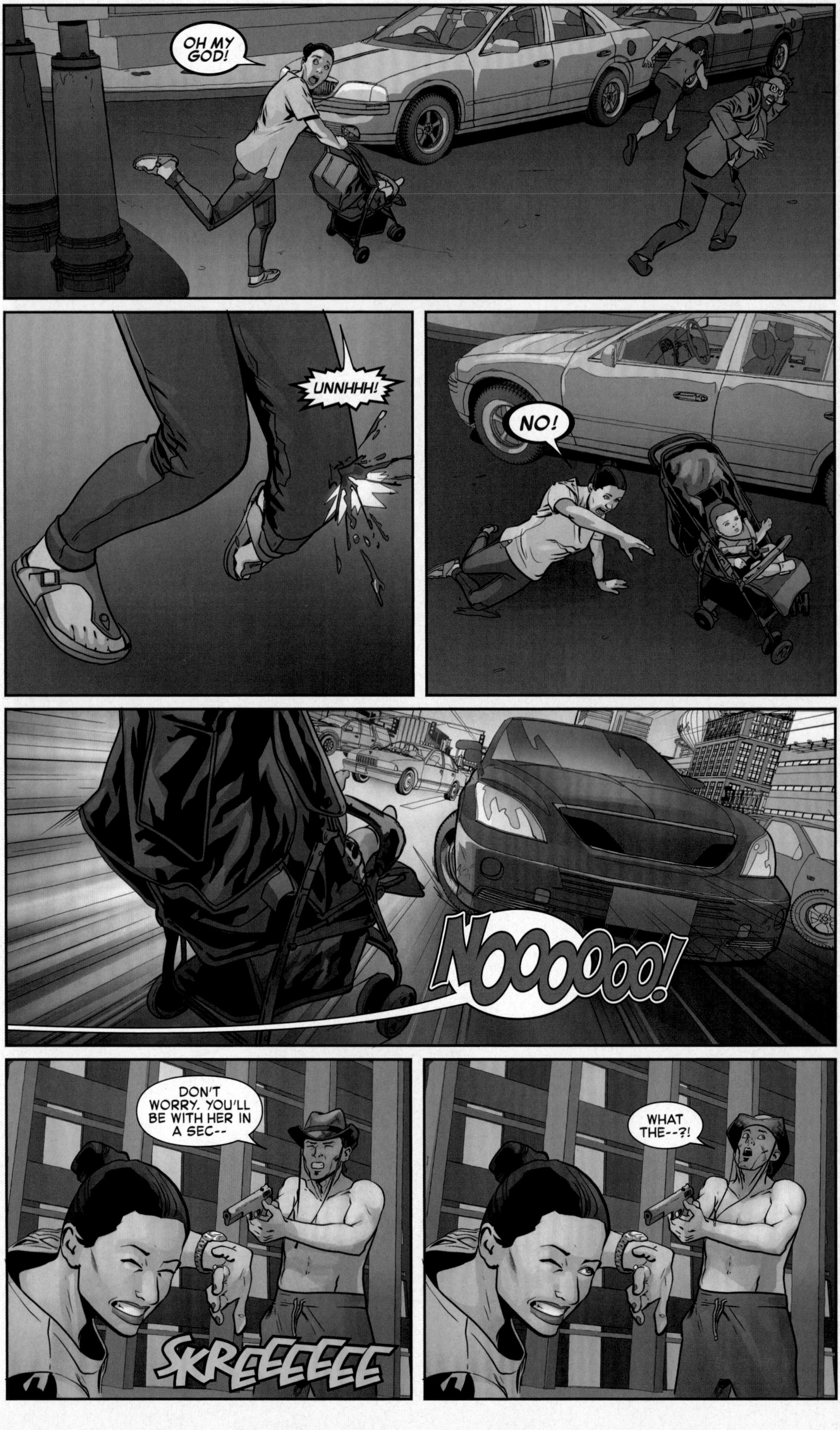
OH MY GOD!
UNNHHH!
NO!
NOOOOOO!
DON'T WORRY. YOU'LL BE WITH HER IN A SEC--
SKREEEEEEE
WHAT THE--?!

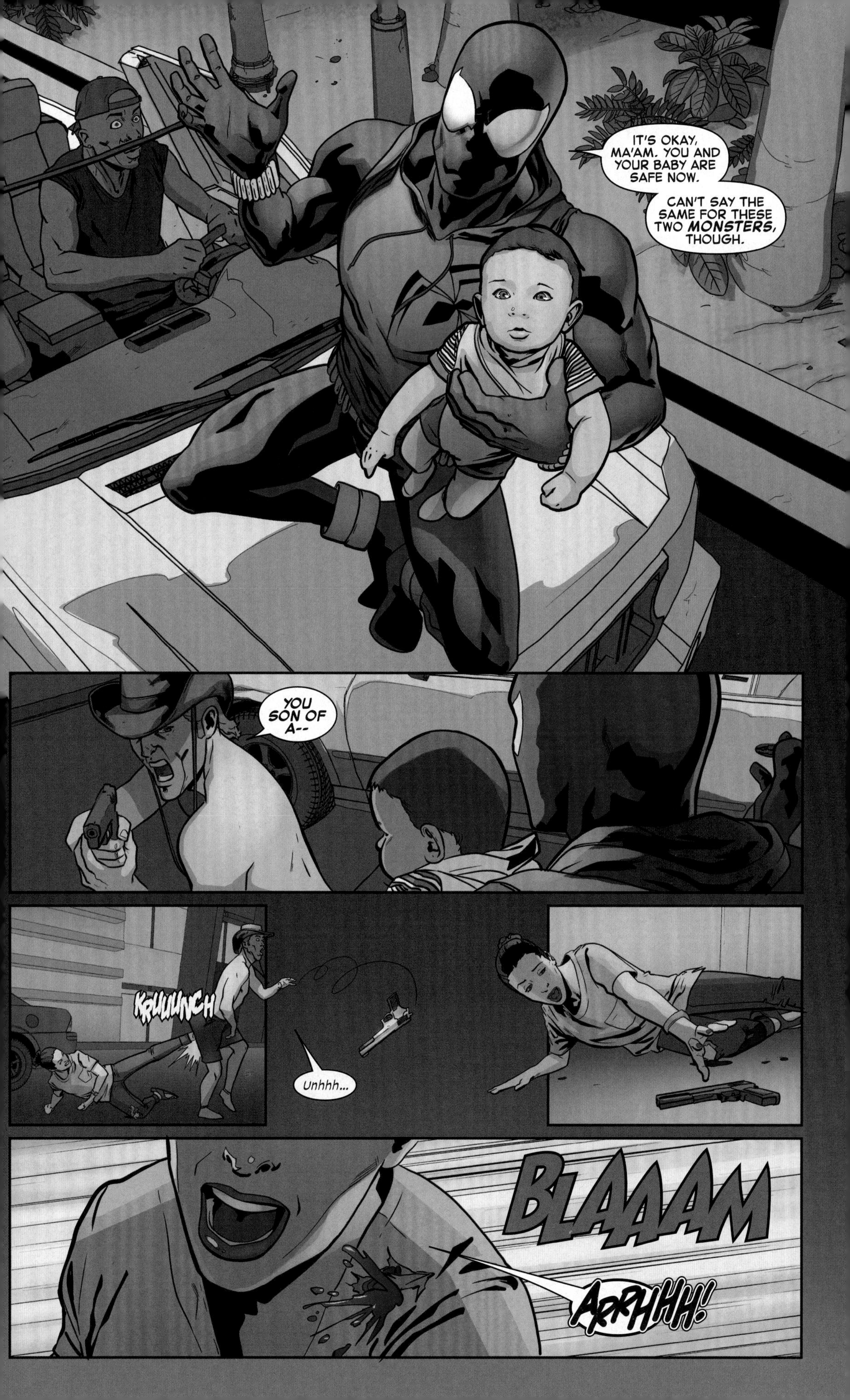
IT'S OKAY, MA'AM. YOU AND YOUR BABY ARE SAFE NOW.
CAN'T SAY THE SAME FOR THESE TWO MONSTERS, THOUGH.
YOU SON OF A--
KRUUUNCH
Unhhh...
BLAAAM
ARRHHH!

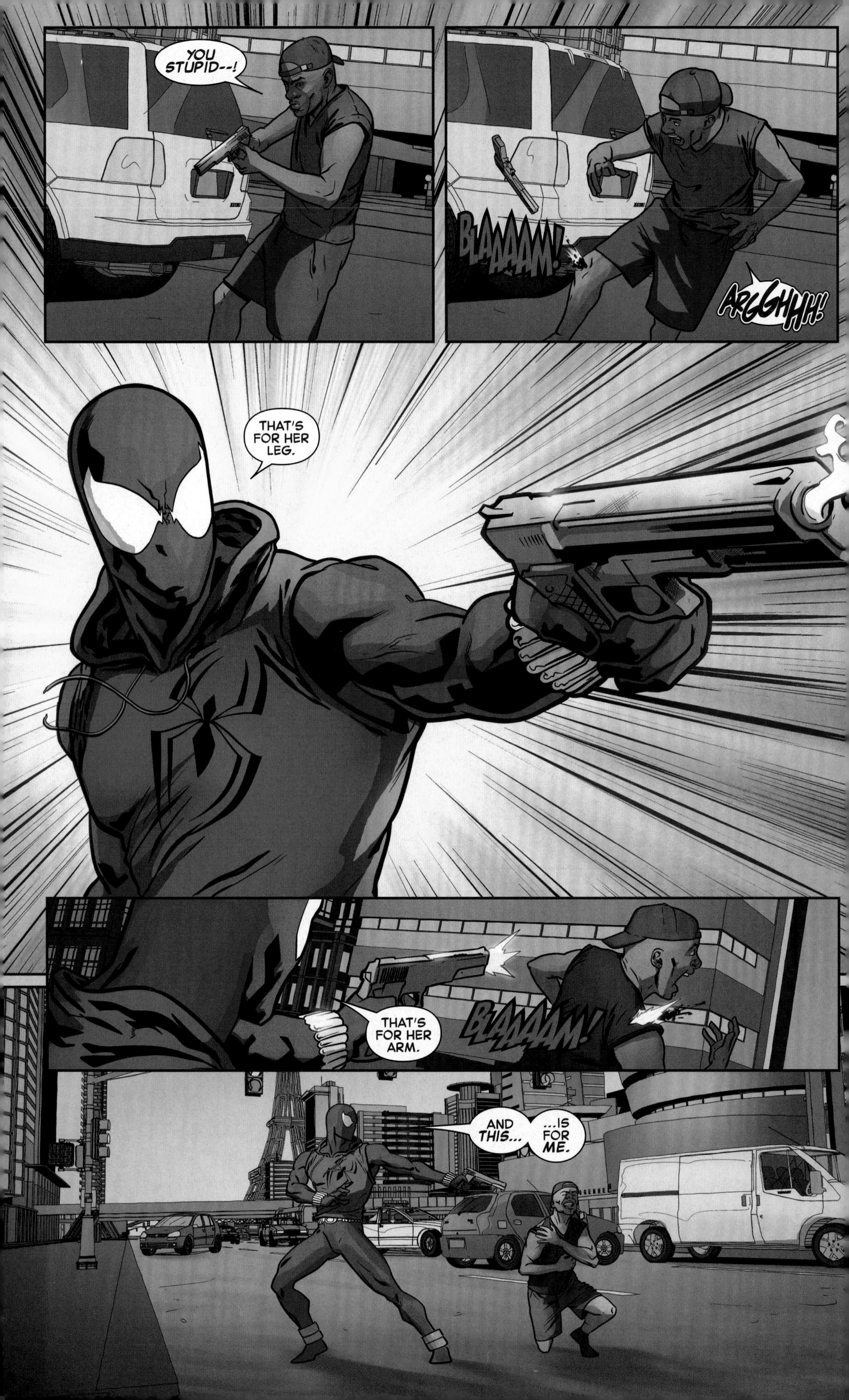
YOU STUPID--!
BLAAAAM!
ARGGHHH!
THAT'S FOR HER LEG.
THAT'S FOR HER ARM.
BLAAAAM!
AND THIS...
...IS FOR ME.

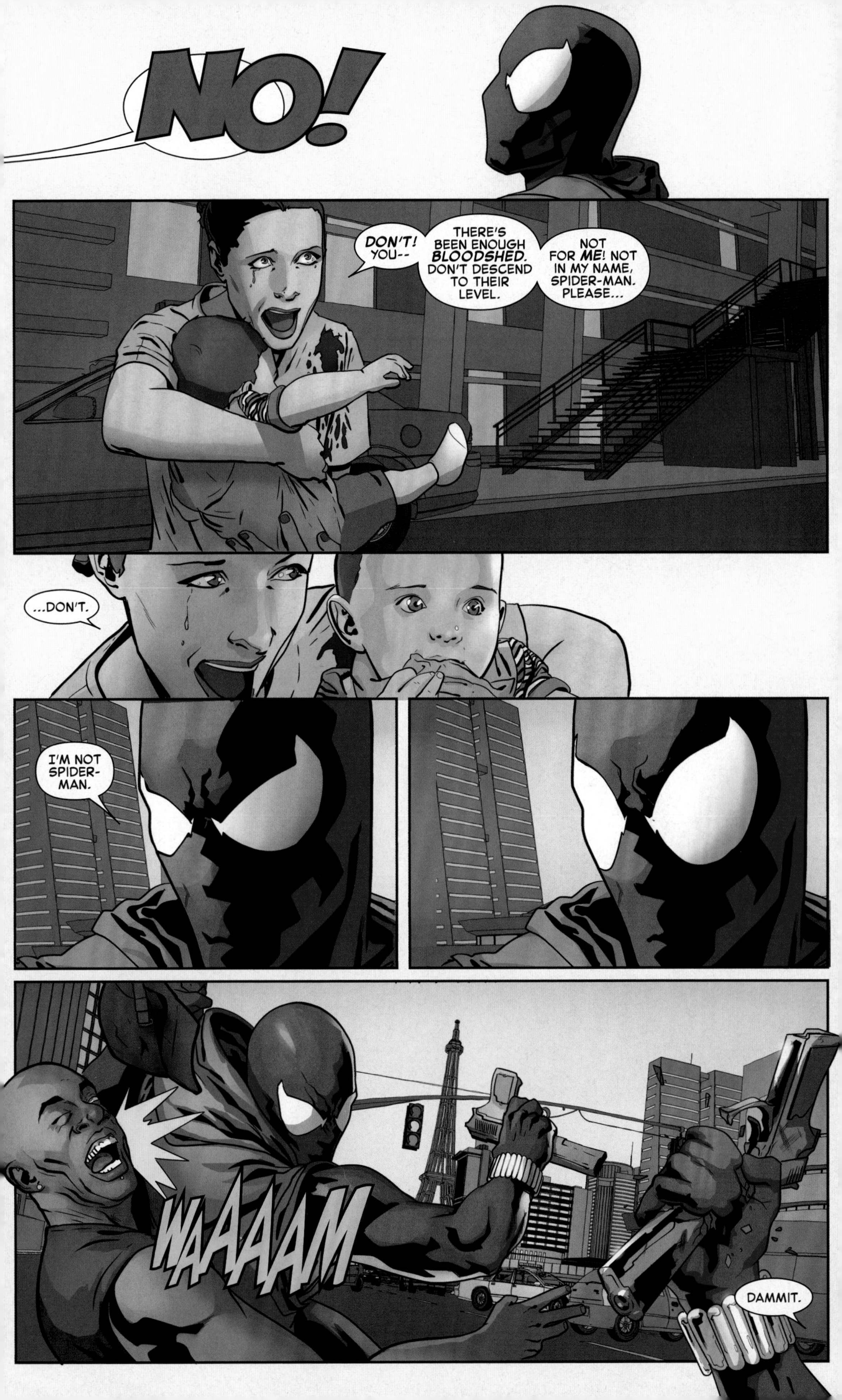
NO!
DON'T! YOU--
THERE'S BEEN ENOUGH BLOODSHED. DON'T DESCEND TO THEIR LEVEL.
NOT FOR ME! NOT IN MY NAME, SPIDER-MAN. PLEASE...
...DON'T.
I'M NOT SPIDER-MAN.
WAAAAM
DAMMIT.

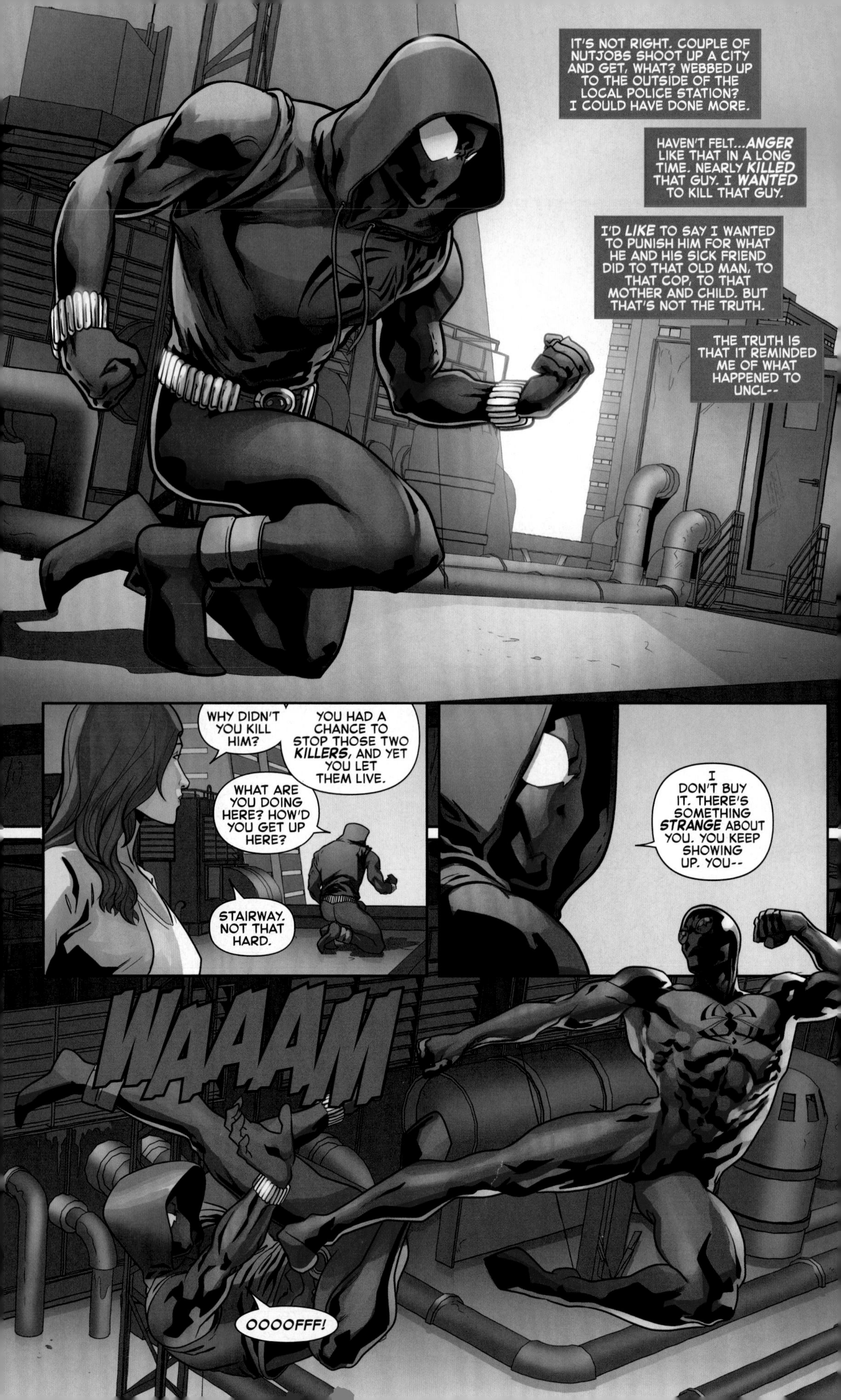

IT'S NOT RIGHT. COUPLE OF NUTJOBS SHOOT UP A CITY AND GET, WHAT? WEBBED UP TO THE OUTSIDE OF THE LOCAL POLICE STATION? I COULD HAVE DONE MORE.
HAVEN'T FELT...ANGER LIKE THAT IN A LONG TIME. NEARLY KILLED THAT GUY. I WANTED TO KILL THAT GUY.
I'D LIKE TO SAY I WANTED TO PUNISH HIM FOR WHAT HE AND HIS SICK FRIEND DID TO THAT OLD MAN, TO THAT COP, TO THAT MOTHER AND CHILD. BUT THAT'S NOT THE TRUTH.
THE TRUTH IS THAT IT REMINDED ME OF WHAT HAPPENED TO UNCL--
WHY DIDN'T YOU KILL HIM?
YOU HAD A CHANCE TO STOP THOSE TWO KILLERS, AND YET YOU LET THEM LIVE.
WHAT ARE YOU DOING HERE? HOW'D YOU GET UP HERE?
STAIRWAY. NOT THAT HARD.
I DON'T BUY IT. THERE'S SOMETHING STRANGE ABOUT YOU. YOU KEEP SHOWING UP. YOU--
WAAAM
OOOOFFF!

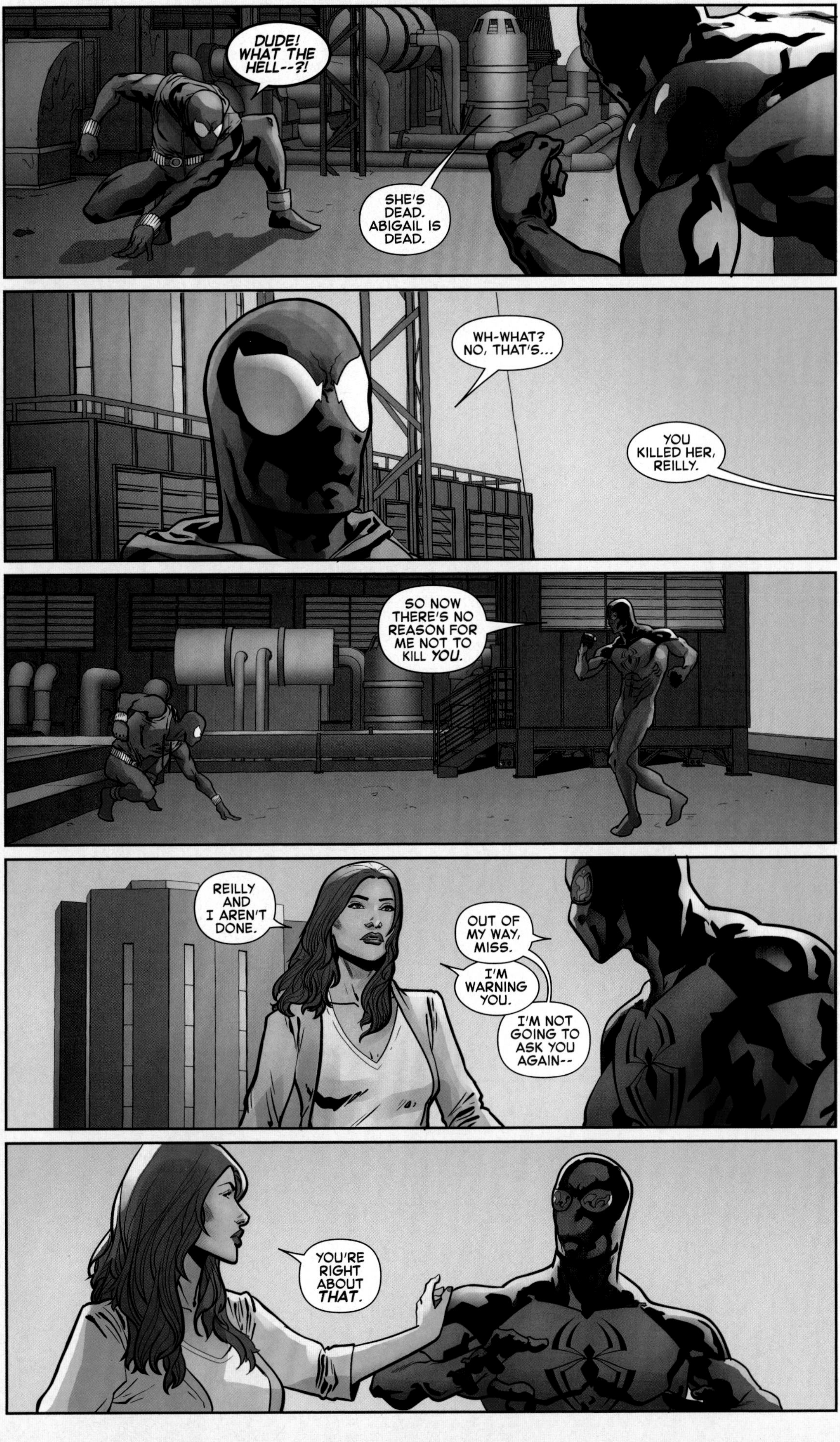
DUDE! WHAT THE HELL--?!
SHE'S DEAD. ABIGAIL IS DEAD.
WH-WHAT? NO, THAT'S...
YOU KILLED HER, REILLY.
SO NOW THERE'S NO REASON FOR ME NOT TO KILL YOU.
REILLY AND I AREN'T DONE.
OUT OF MY WAY, MISS.
I'M WARNING YOU.
I'M NOT GOING TO ASK YOU AGAIN--
YOU'RE RIGHT ABOUT THAT.

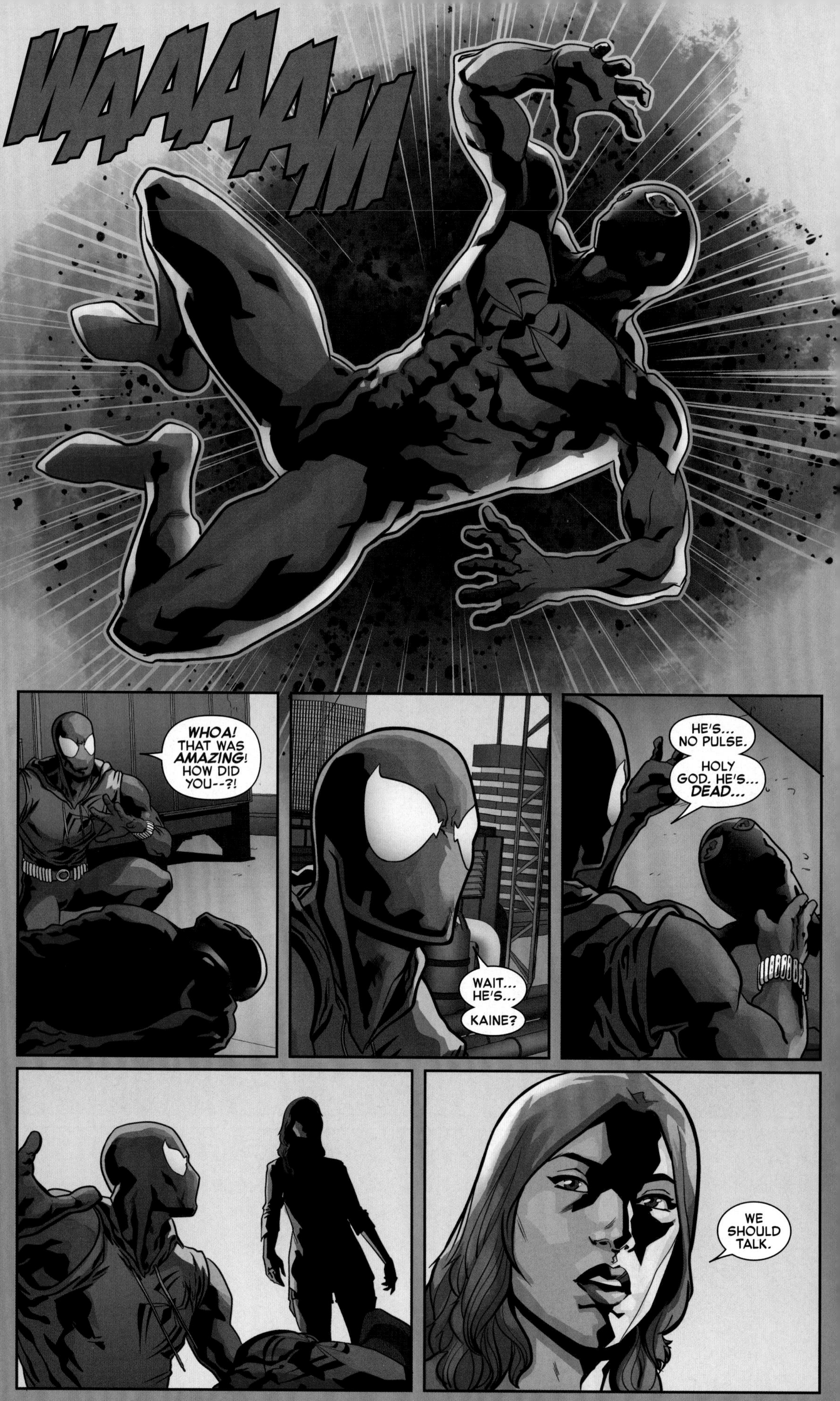
WAAAAAM
WHOA! THAT WAS AMAZING! HOW DID YOU--?!
WAIT... HE'S...
KAINE?
HE'S... NO PULSE.
HOLY GOD. HE'S... DEAD...
WE SHOULD TALK.

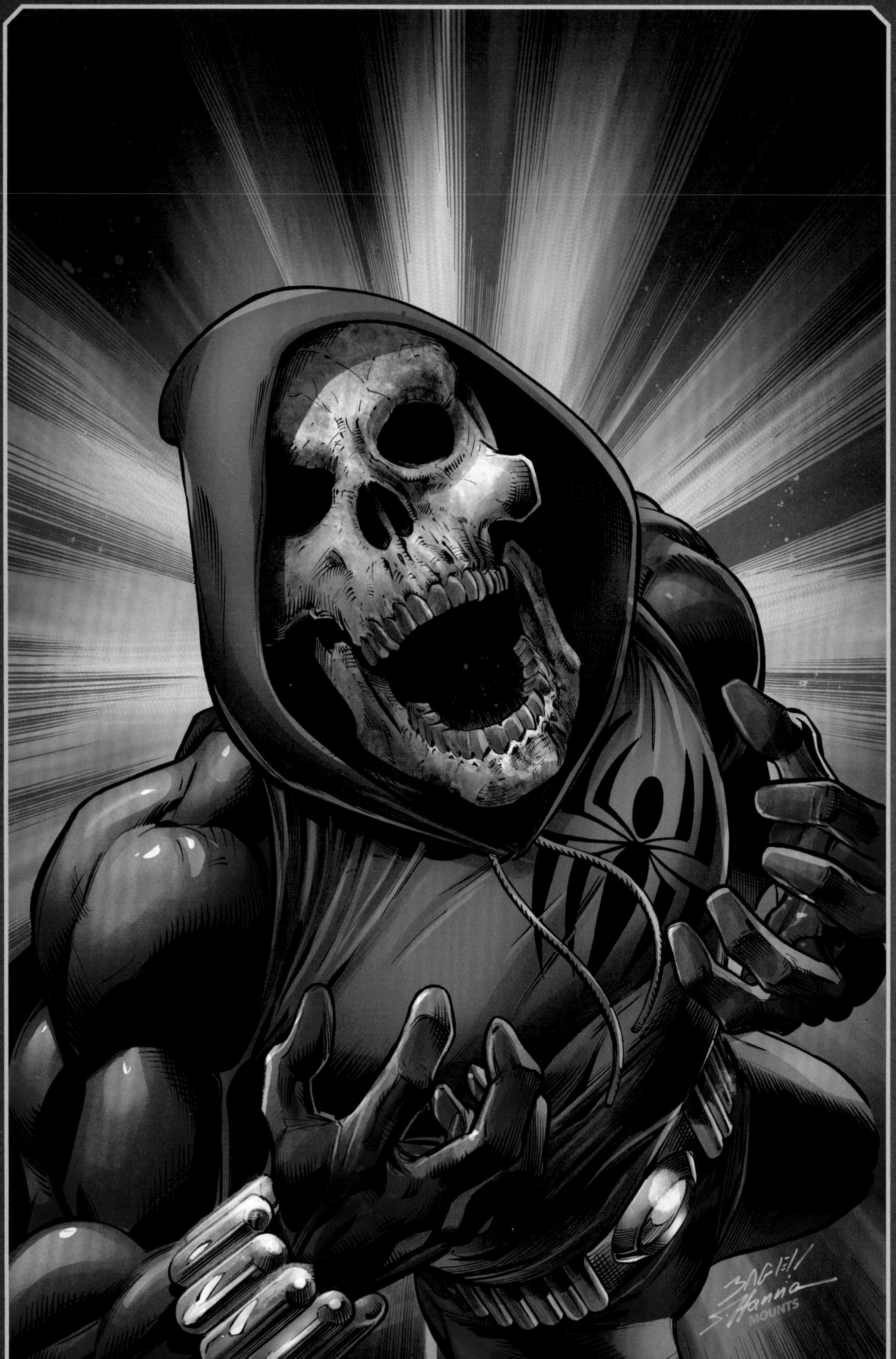

7

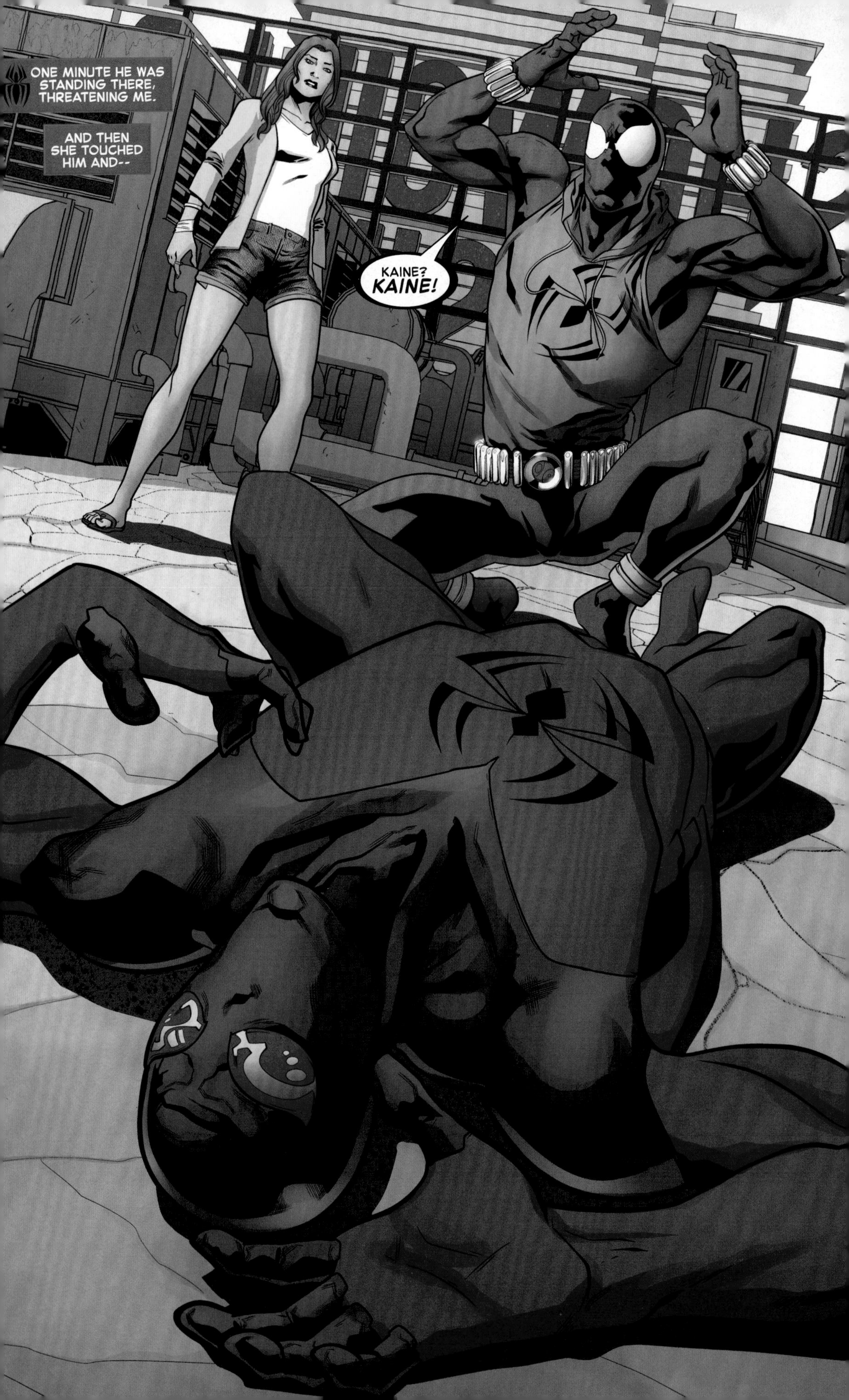
ONE MINUTE HE WAS STANDING THERE, THREATENING ME.
AND THEN SHE TOUCHED HIM AND--
KAINE? KAINE!

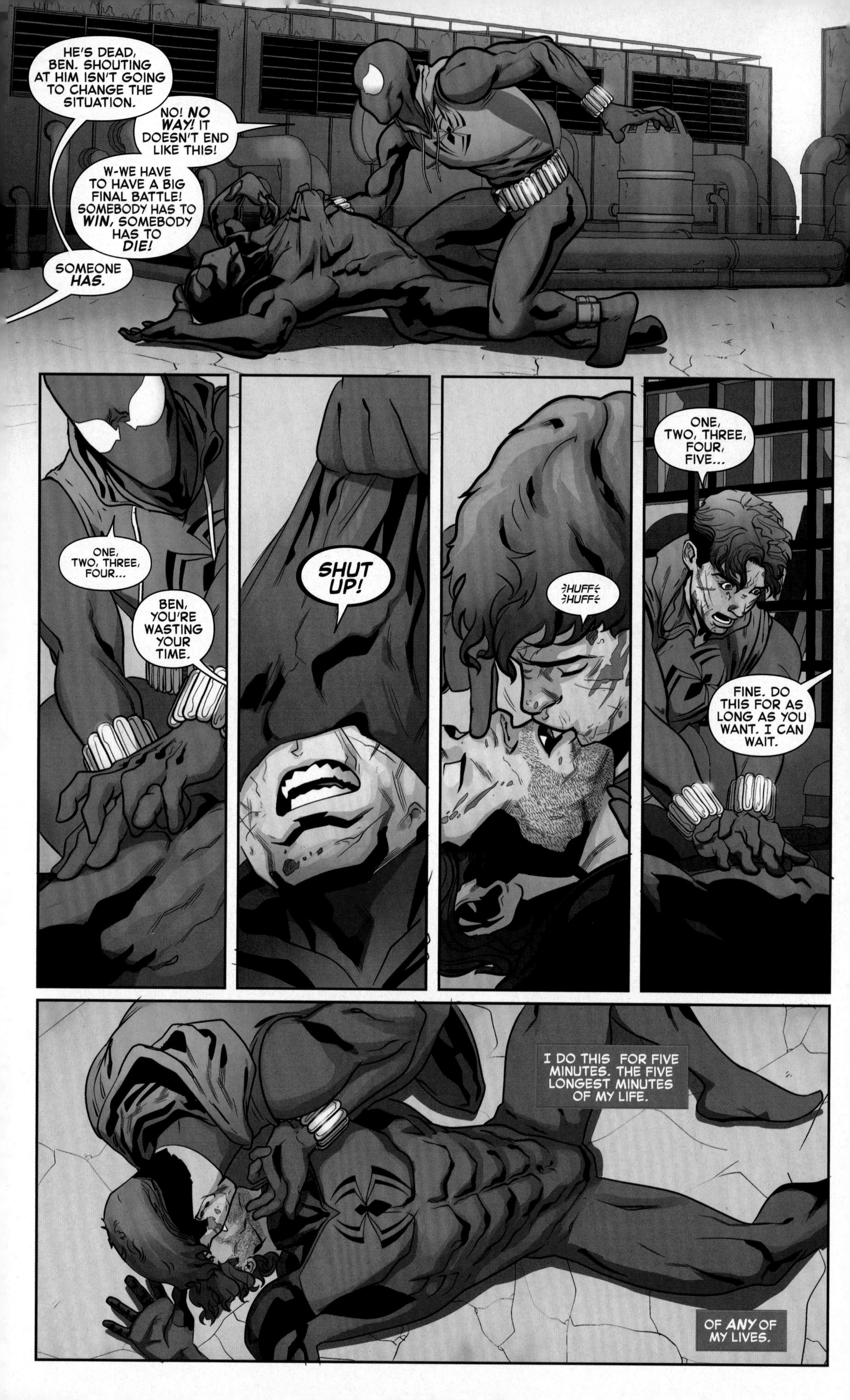
HE'S DEAD, BEN. SHOUTING AT HIM ISN'T GOING TO CHANGE THE SITUATION.
NO! NO WAY! IT DOESN'T END LIKE THIS!
W-WE HAVE TO HAVE A BIG FINAL BATTLE! SOMEBODY HAS TO WIN, SOMEBODY HAS TO DIE!
SOMEONE HAS.
ONE, TWO, THREE, FOUR...
BEN, YOU'RE WASTING YOUR TIME.
SHUT UP!
HUFF HUFF
ONE, TWO, THREE, FOUR, FIVE...
FINE. DO THIS FOR AS LONG AS YOU WANT. I CAN WAIT.
I DO THIS FOR FIVE MINUTES. THE FIVE LONGEST MINUTES OF MY LIFE.
OF ANY OF MY LIVES.

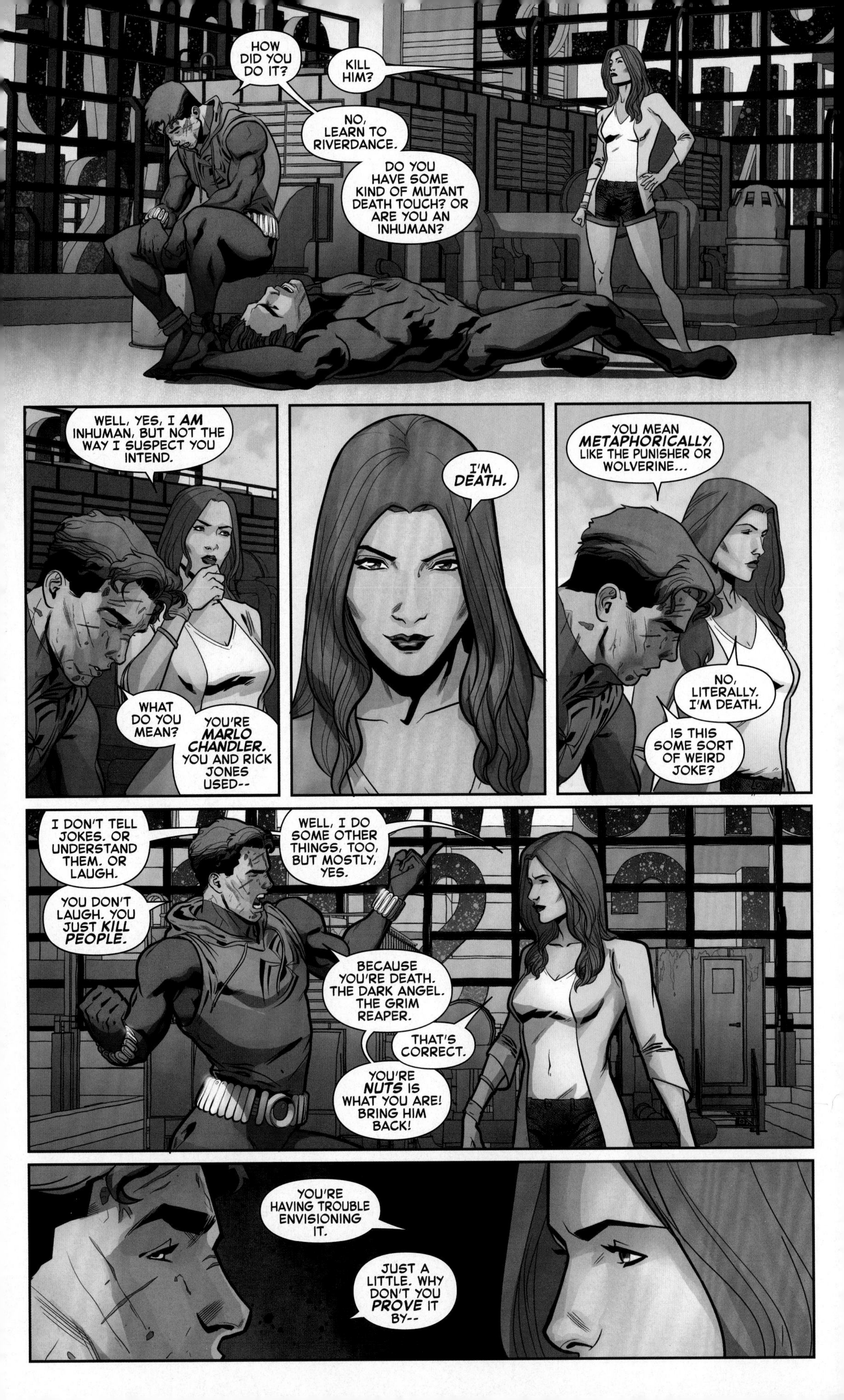
HOW DID YOU DO IT?
KILL HIM?
NO, LEARN TO RIVERDANCE.
DO YOU HAVE SOME KIND OF MUTANT DEATH TOUCH? OR ARE YOU AN INHUMAN?
WELL, YES, I AM INHUMAN, BUT NOT THE WAY I SUSPECT YOU INTEND.
WHAT DO YOU MEAN?
YOU'RE MARLO CHANDLER. YOU AND RICK JONES USED--
I'M DEATH.
YOU MEAN METAPHORICALLY, LIKE THE PUNISHER OR WOLVERINE...
NO, LITERALLY. I'M DEATH.
IS THIS SOME SORT OF WEIRD JOKE?
I DON'T TELL JOKES. OR UNDERSTAND THEM. OR LAUGH.
YOU DON'T LAUGH. YOU JUST KILL PEOPLE.
WELL, I DO SOME OTHER THINGS, TOO, BUT MOSTLY, YES.
BECAUSE YOU'RE DEATH. THE DARK ANGEL. THE GRIM REAPER.
THAT'S CORRECT.
YOU'RE NUTS IS WHAT YOU ARE! BRING HIM BACK!
YOU'RE HAVING TROUBLE ENVISIONING IT.
JUST A LITTLE. WHY DON'T YOU PROVE IT BY--

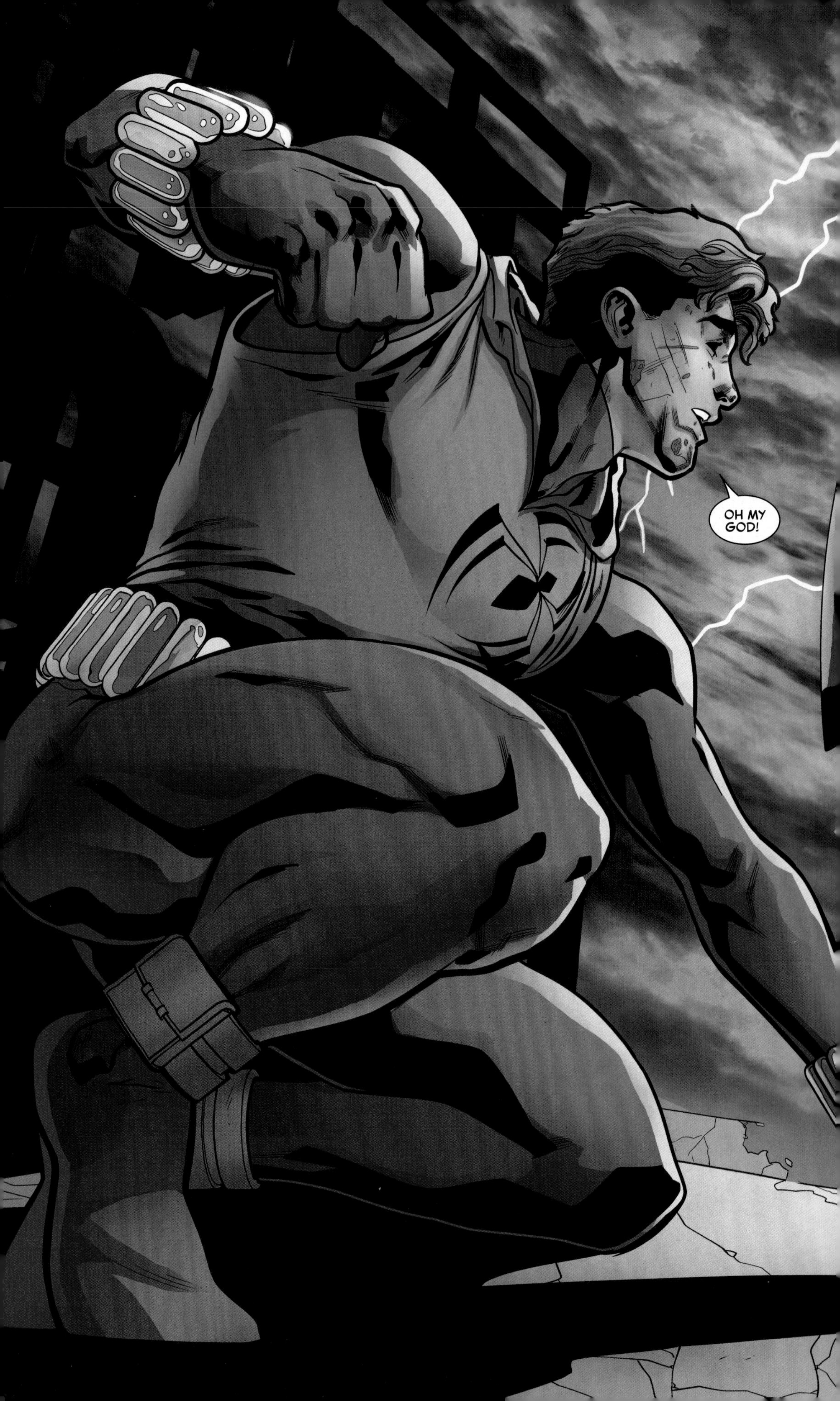
OH MY GOD!

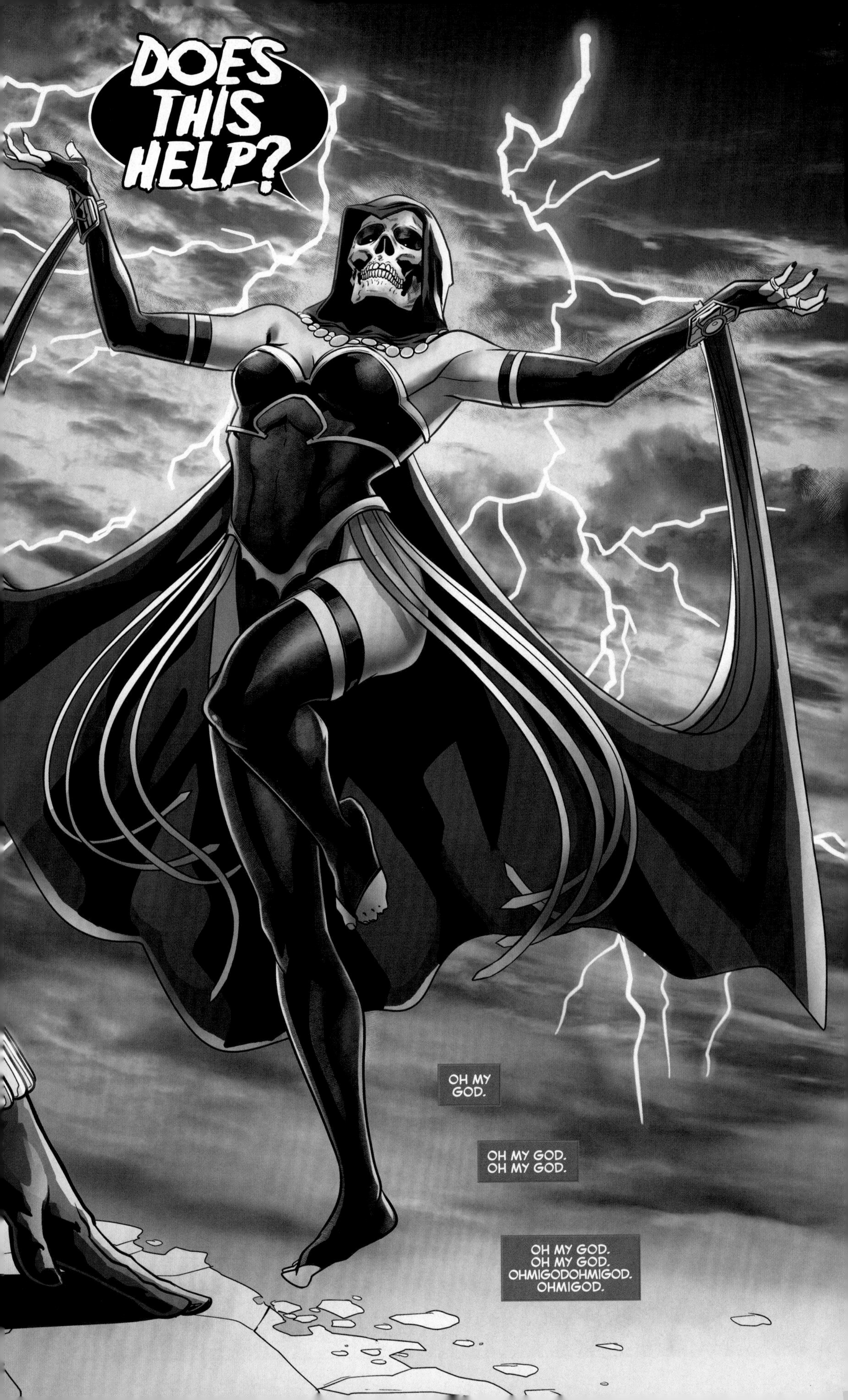
DOES THIS HELP?
OH MY GOD.
OH MY GOD. OH MY GOD.
OH MY GOD. OH MY GOD. OHMIGODOHMIGOD. OHMIGOD.

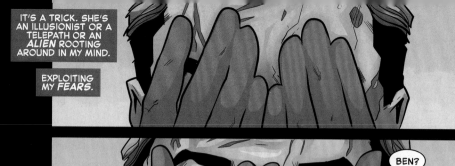

IT'S A TRICK. SHE'S AN ILLUSIONIST OR A TELEPATH OR AN *ALIEN* ROOTING AROUND IN MY MIND.

EXPLOITING MY *FEARS*.

BEN?

BEN, IT'S OKAY. YOU CAN LOOK NOW.

SEE? ALL BETTER.

SO... YOU'RE *DEATH.*

YES.

THE *COSMIC ENTITY.*

DEATH.

THAT'S RIGHT.

WOW. YOU *REALLY* SUCK.

I GET THAT A LOT.

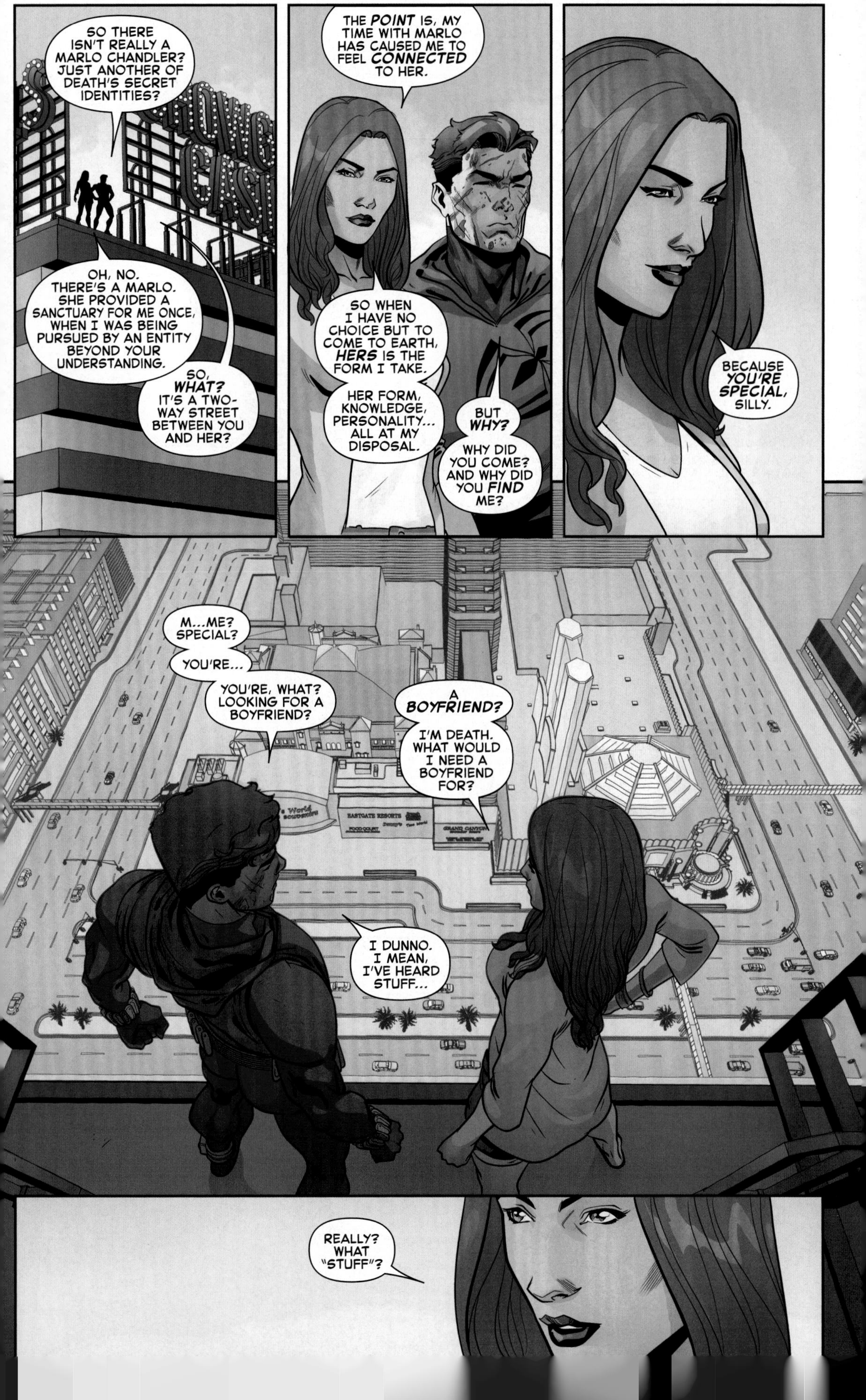
SO THERE ISN'T REALLY A MARLO CHANDLER? JUST ANOTHER OF DEATH'S SECRET IDENTITIES?
OH, NO. THERE'S A MARLO. SHE PROVIDED A SANCTUARY FOR ME ONCE, WHEN I WAS BEING PURSUED BY AN ENTITY BEYOND YOUR UNDERSTANDING.
SO, WHAT? IT'S A TWO-WAY STREET BETWEEN YOU AND HER?
THE POINT IS, MY TIME WITH MARLO HAS CAUSED ME TO FEEL CONNECTED TO HER.
SO WHEN I HAVE NO CHOICE BUT TO COME TO EARTH, HERS IS THE FORM I TAKE.
HER FORM, KNOWLEDGE, PERSONALITY... ALL AT MY DISPOSAL.
BUT WHY?
WHY DID YOU COME? AND WHY DID YOU FIND ME?
BECAUSE YOU'RE SPECIAL, SILLY.
M...ME? SPECIAL?
YOU'RE...
YOU'RE, WHAT? LOOKING FOR A BOYFRIEND?
A BOYFRIEND?
I'M DEATH. WHAT WOULD I NEED A BOYFRIEND FOR?
I DUNNO. I MEAN, I'VE HEARD STUFF...
REALLY? WHAT "STUFF"?

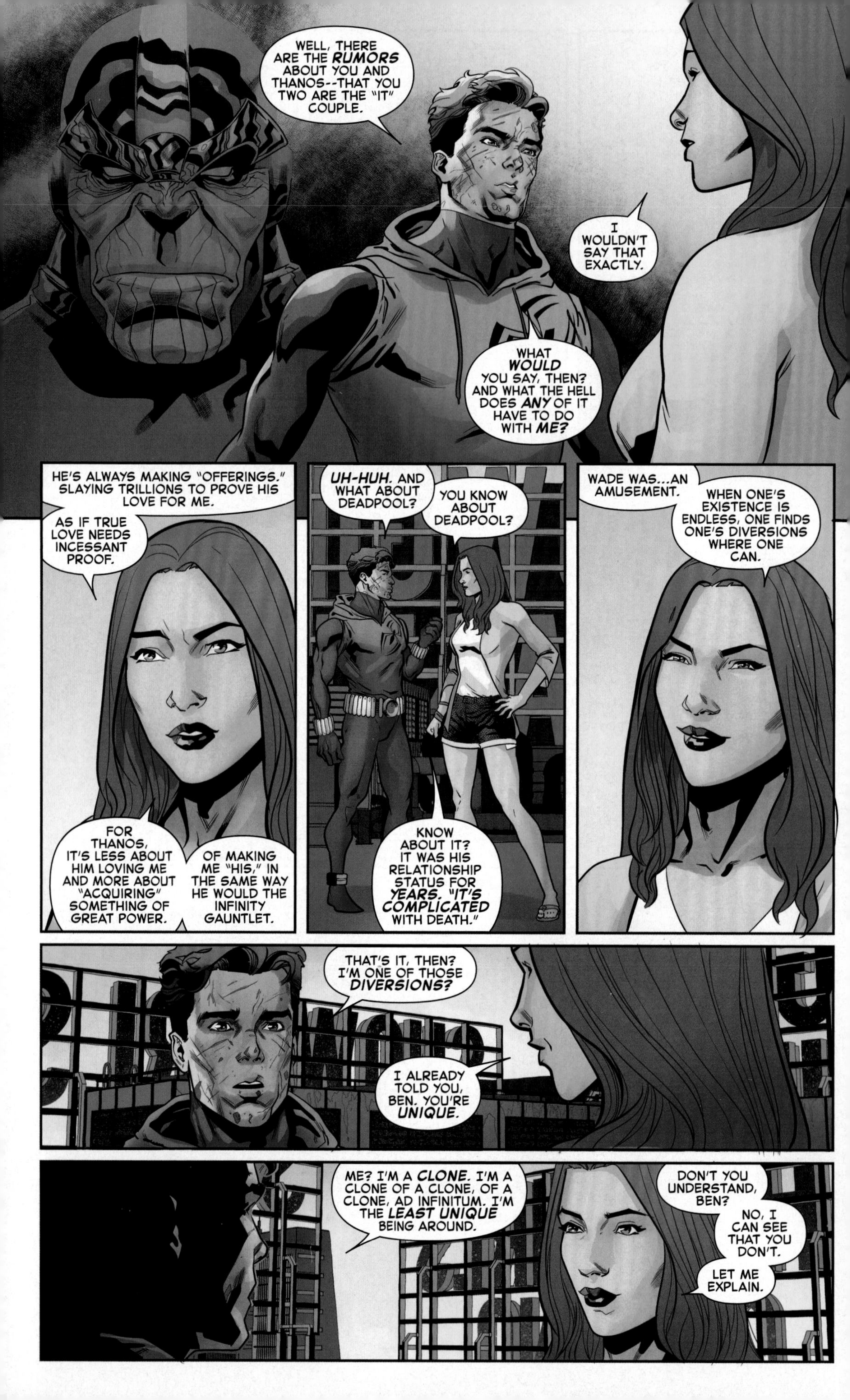
WELL, THERE ARE THE RUMORS ABOUT YOU AND THANOS--THAT YOU TWO ARE THE "IT" COUPLE.
I WOULDN'T SAY THAT EXACTLY.
WHAT WOULD YOU SAY, THEN? AND WHAT THE HELL DOES ANY OF IT HAVE TO DO WITH ME?
HE'S ALWAYS MAKING "OFFERINGS." SLAYING TRILLIONS TO PROVE HIS LOVE FOR ME.
AS IF TRUE LOVE NEEDS INCESSANT PROOF.
FOR THANOS, IT'S LESS ABOUT HIM LOVING ME AND MORE ABOUT "ACQUIRING" SOMETHING OF GREAT POWER.
OF MAKING ME "HIS," IN THE SAME WAY HE WOULD THE INFINITY GAUNTLET.
UH-HUH. AND WHAT ABOUT DEADPOOL?
YOU KNOW ABOUT DEADPOOL?
KNOW ABOUT IT? IT WAS HIS RELATIONSHIP STATUS FOR YEARS. "IT'S COMPLICATED WITH DEATH."
WADE WAS...AN AMUSEMENT.
WHEN ONE'S EXISTENCE IS ENDLESS, ONE FINDS ONE'S DIVERSIONS WHERE ONE CAN.
THAT'S IT, THEN? I'M ONE OF THOSE DIVERSIONS?
I ALREADY TOLD YOU, BEN. YOU'RE UNIQUE.
ME? I'M A CLONE. I'M A CLONE OF A CLONE, OF A CLONE, AD INFINITUM. I'M THE LEAST UNIQUE BEING AROUND.
DON'T YOU UNDERSTAND, BEN?
NO, I CAN SEE THAT YOU DON'T.
LET ME EXPLAIN.

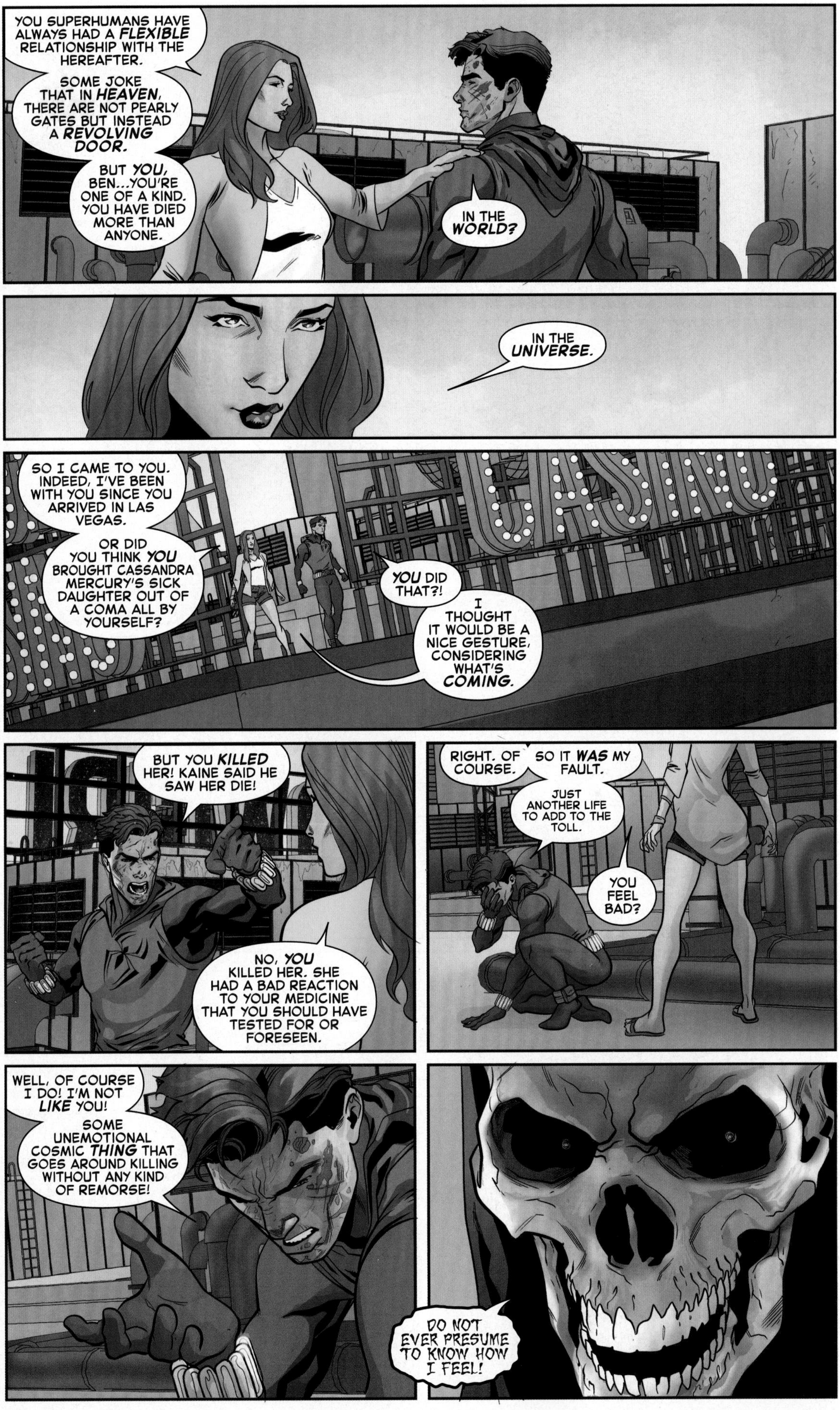
YOU SUPERHUMANS HAVE ALWAYS HAD A FLEXIBLE RELATIONSHIP WITH THE HEREAFTER.
SOME JOKE THAT IN HEAVEN, THERE ARE NOT PEARLY GATES BUT INSTEAD A REVOLVING DOOR.
BUT YOU, BEN...YOU'RE ONE OF A KIND. YOU HAVE DIED MORE THAN ANYONE.
IN THE WORLD?
IN THE UNIVERSE.
SO I CAME TO YOU. INDEED, I'VE BEEN WITH YOU SINCE YOU ARRIVED IN LAS VEGAS.
OR DID YOU THINK YOU BROUGHT CASSANDRA MERCURY'S SICK DAUGHTER OUT OF A COMA ALL BY YOURSELF?
YOU DID THAT?!
I THOUGHT IT WOULD BE A NICE GESTURE, CONSIDERING WHAT'S COMING.
BUT YOU KILLED HER! KAINE SAID HE SAW HER DIE!
NO, YOU KILLED HER. SHE HAD A BAD REACTION TO YOUR MEDICINE THAT YOU SHOULD HAVE TESTED FOR OR FORESEEN.
RIGHT. OF COURSE.
SO IT WAS MY FAULT.
JUST ANOTHER LIFE TO ADD TO THE TOLL.
YOU FEEL BAD?
WELL, OF COURSE I DO! I'M NOT LIKE YOU!
SOME UNEMOTIONAL COSMIC THING THAT GOES AROUND KILLING WITHOUT ANY KIND OF REMORSE!
DO NOT EVER PRESUME TO KNOW HOW I FEEL!

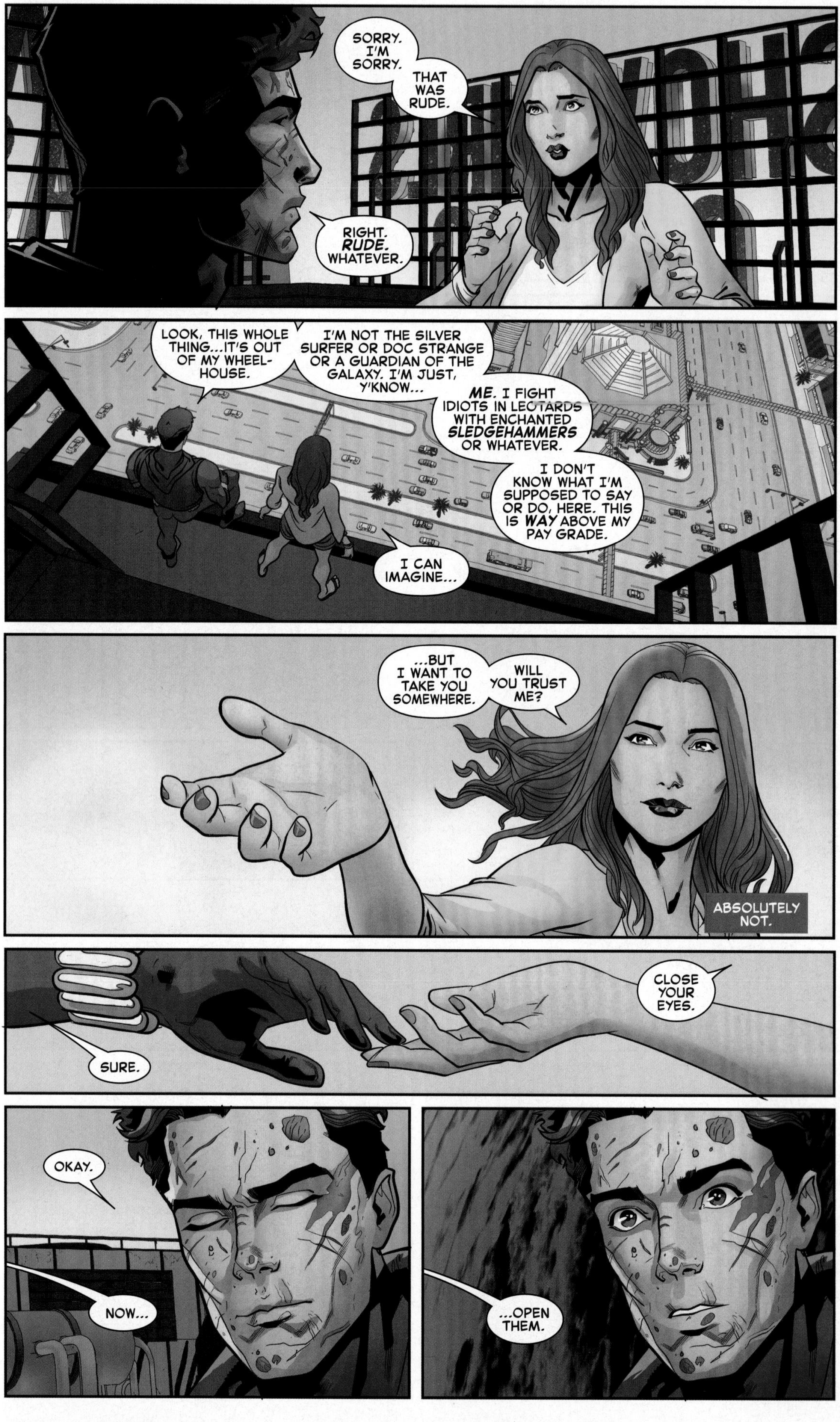
SORRY. I'M SORRY.
THAT WAS RUDE.
RIGHT. RUDE. WHATEVER.
LOOK, THIS WHOLE THING...IT'S OUT OF MY WHEEL-HOUSE.
I'M NOT THE SILVER SURFER OR DOC STRANGE OR A GUARDIAN OF THE GALAXY. I'M JUST, Y'KNOW...
ME. I FIGHT IDIOTS IN LEOTARDS WITH ENCHANTED SLEDGEHAMMERS OR WHATEVER.
I DON'T KNOW WHAT I'M SUPPOSED TO SAY OR DO, HERE. THIS IS WAY ABOVE MY PAY GRADE.
I CAN IMAGINE...
...BUT I WANT TO TAKE YOU SOMEWHERE.
WILL YOU TRUST ME?
ABSOLUTELY NOT.
CLOSE YOUR EYES.
SURE.
OKAY.
NOW...
...OPEN THEM.

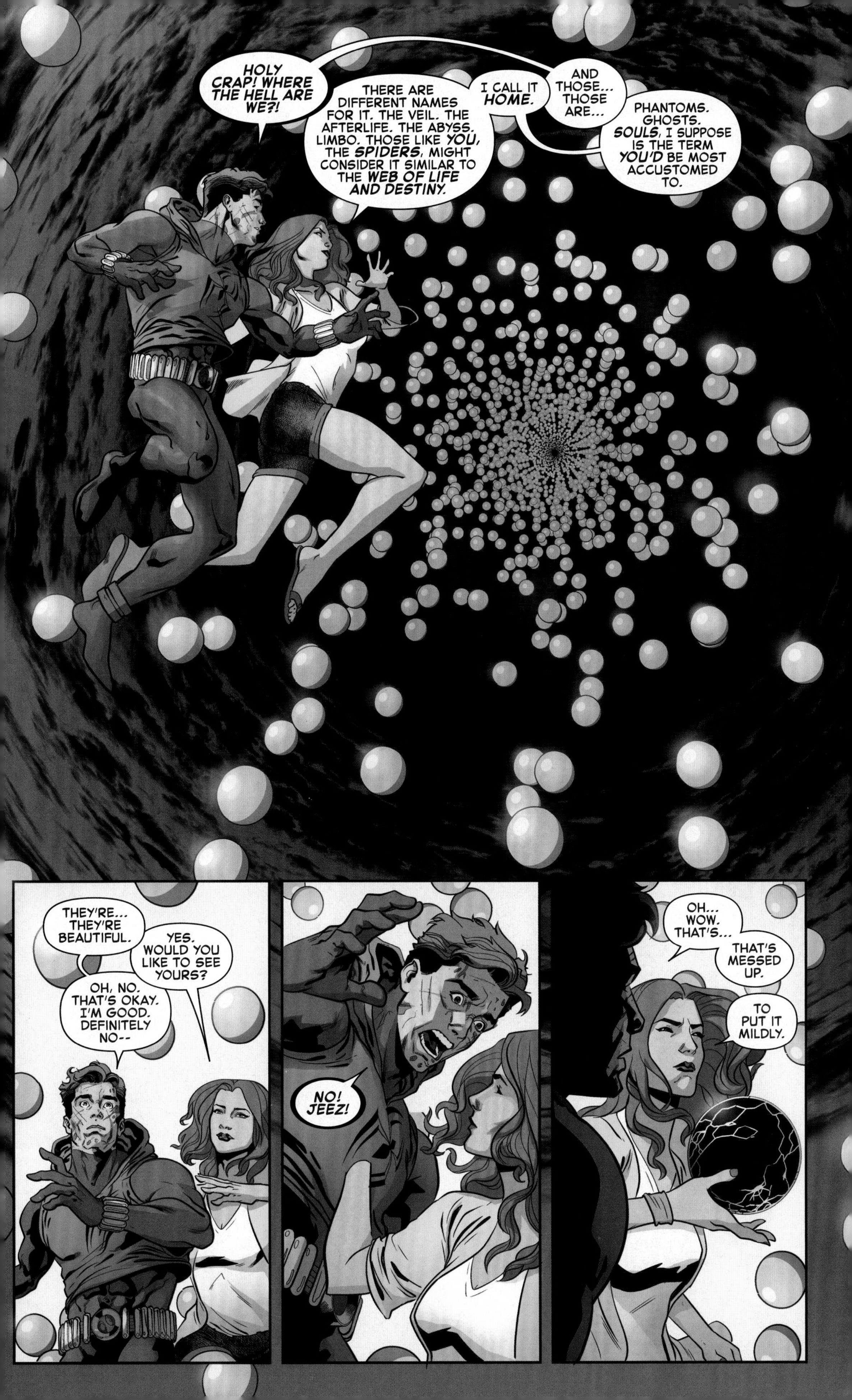
HOLY CRAP! WHERE THE HELL ARE WE?!
THERE ARE DIFFERENT NAMES FOR IT. THE VEIL. THE AFTERLIFE. THE ABYSS. LIMBO. THOSE LIKE YOU, THE SPIDERS, MIGHT CONSIDER IT SIMILAR TO THE WEB OF LIFE AND DESTINY.
I CALL IT HOME.
AND THOSE... THOSE ARE...
PHANTOMS. GHOSTS. SOULS, I SUPPOSE IS THE TERM YOU'D BE MOST ACCUSTOMED TO.
THEY'RE... THEY'RE BEAUTIFUL.
YES. WOULD YOU LIKE TO SEE YOURS?
OH, NO. THAT'S OKAY. I'M GOOD. DEFINITELY NO--
NO! JEEZ!
OH... WOW. THAT'S...
THAT'S MESSED UP.
TO PUT IT MILDLY.

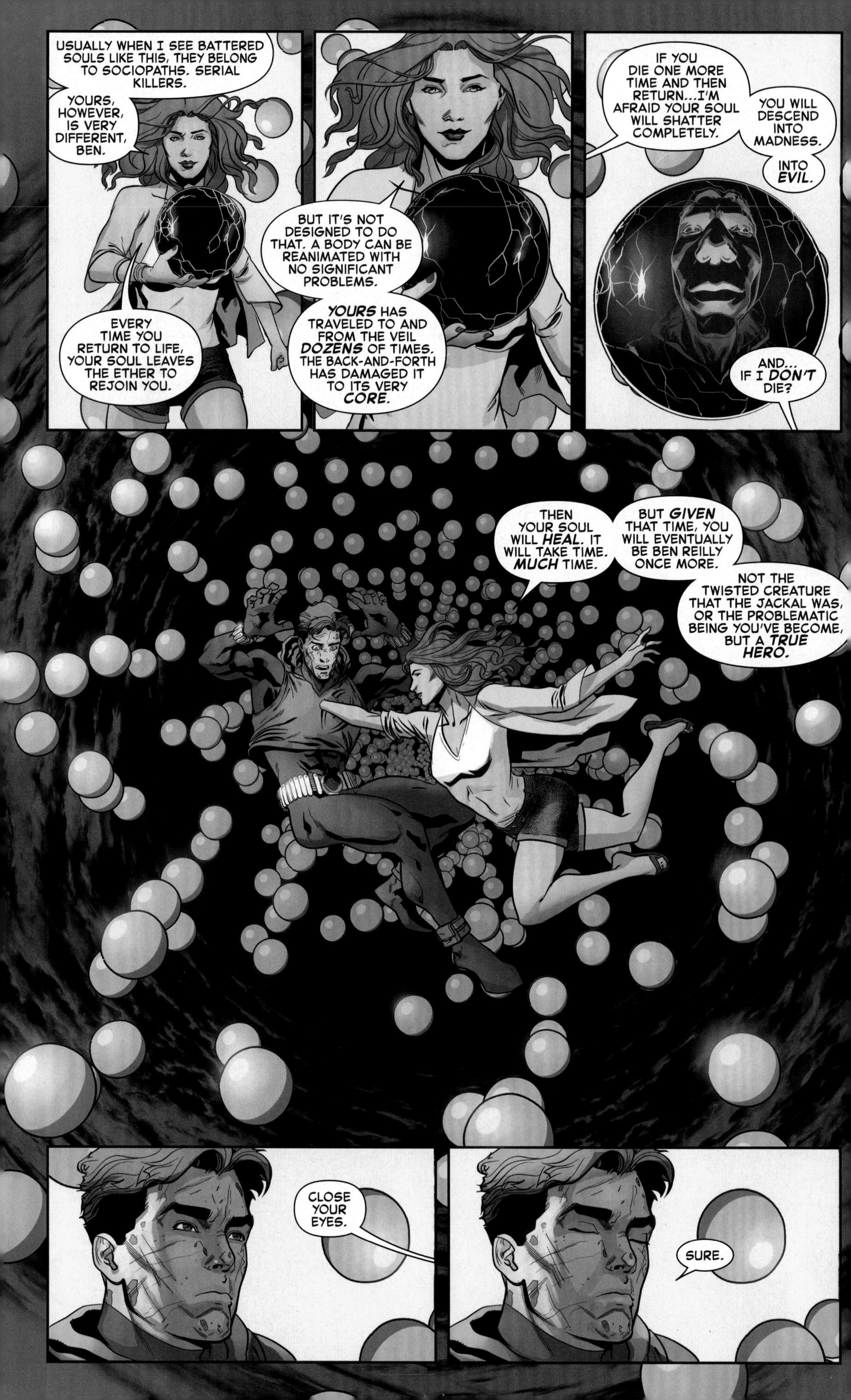
USUALLY WHEN I SEE BATTERED SOULS LIKE THIS, THEY BELONG TO SOCIOPATHS. SERIAL KILLERS.
YOURS, HOWEVER, IS VERY DIFFERENT, BEN.
EVERY TIME YOU RETURN TO LIFE, YOUR SOUL LEAVES THE ETHER TO REJOIN YOU.
BUT IT'S NOT DESIGNED TO DO THAT. A BODY CAN BE REANIMATED WITH NO SIGNIFICANT PROBLEMS.
YOURS HAS TRAVELED TO AND FROM THE VEIL *DOZENS* OF TIMES. THE BACK-AND-FORTH HAS DAMAGED IT TO ITS VERY *CORE*.
IF YOU DIE ONE MORE TIME AND THEN RETURN...I'M AFRAID YOUR SOUL WILL SHATTER COMPLETELY.
YOU WILL DESCEND INTO MADNESS.
INTO *EVIL*.
AND... IF I *DON'T* DIE?
THEN YOUR SOUL WILL *HEAL*. IT WILL TAKE TIME. *MUCH* TIME.
BUT *GIVEN* THAT TIME, YOU WILL EVENTUALLY BE BEN REILLY ONCE MORE.
NOT THE TWISTED CREATURE THAT THE JACKAL WAS, OR THE PROBLEMATIC BEING YOU'VE BECOME, BUT A *TRUE HERO*.
CLOSE YOUR EYES.
SURE.

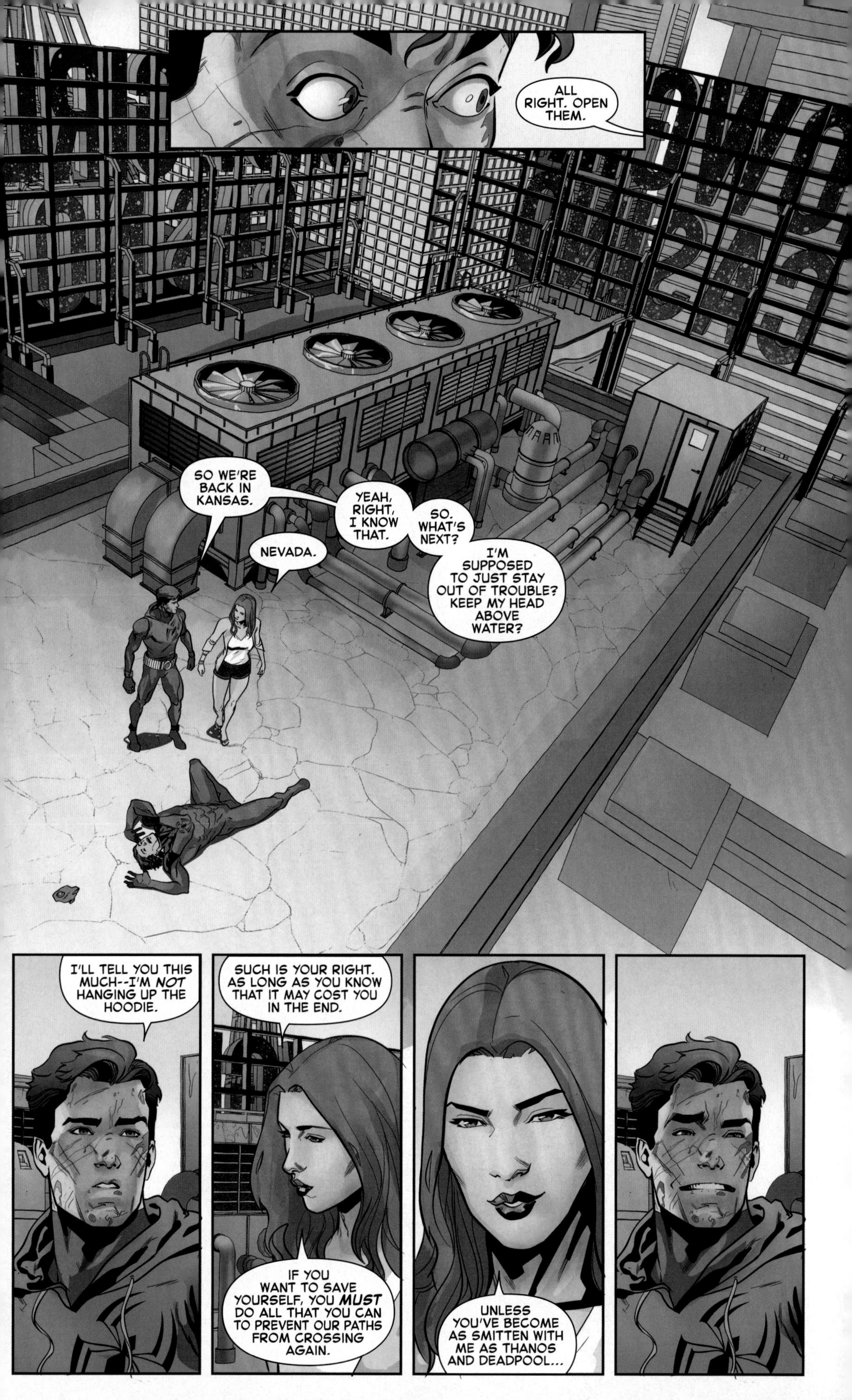

ALL RIGHT. OPEN THEM.
SO WE'RE BACK IN KANSAS.
NEVADA.
YEAH, RIGHT, I KNOW THAT.
SO. WHAT'S NEXT?
I'M SUPPOSED TO JUST STAY OUT OF TROUBLE? KEEP MY HEAD ABOVE WATER?
I'LL TELL YOU THIS MUCH--I'M *NOT* HANGING UP THE HOODIE.
SUCH IS YOUR RIGHT. AS LONG AS YOU KNOW THAT IT MAY COST YOU IN THE END.
IF YOU WANT TO SAVE YOURSELF, YOU ***MUST*** DO ALL THAT YOU CAN TO PREVENT OUR PATHS FROM CROSSING AGAIN.
UNLESS YOU'VE BECOME AS SMITTEN WITH ME AS THANOS AND DEADPOOL...

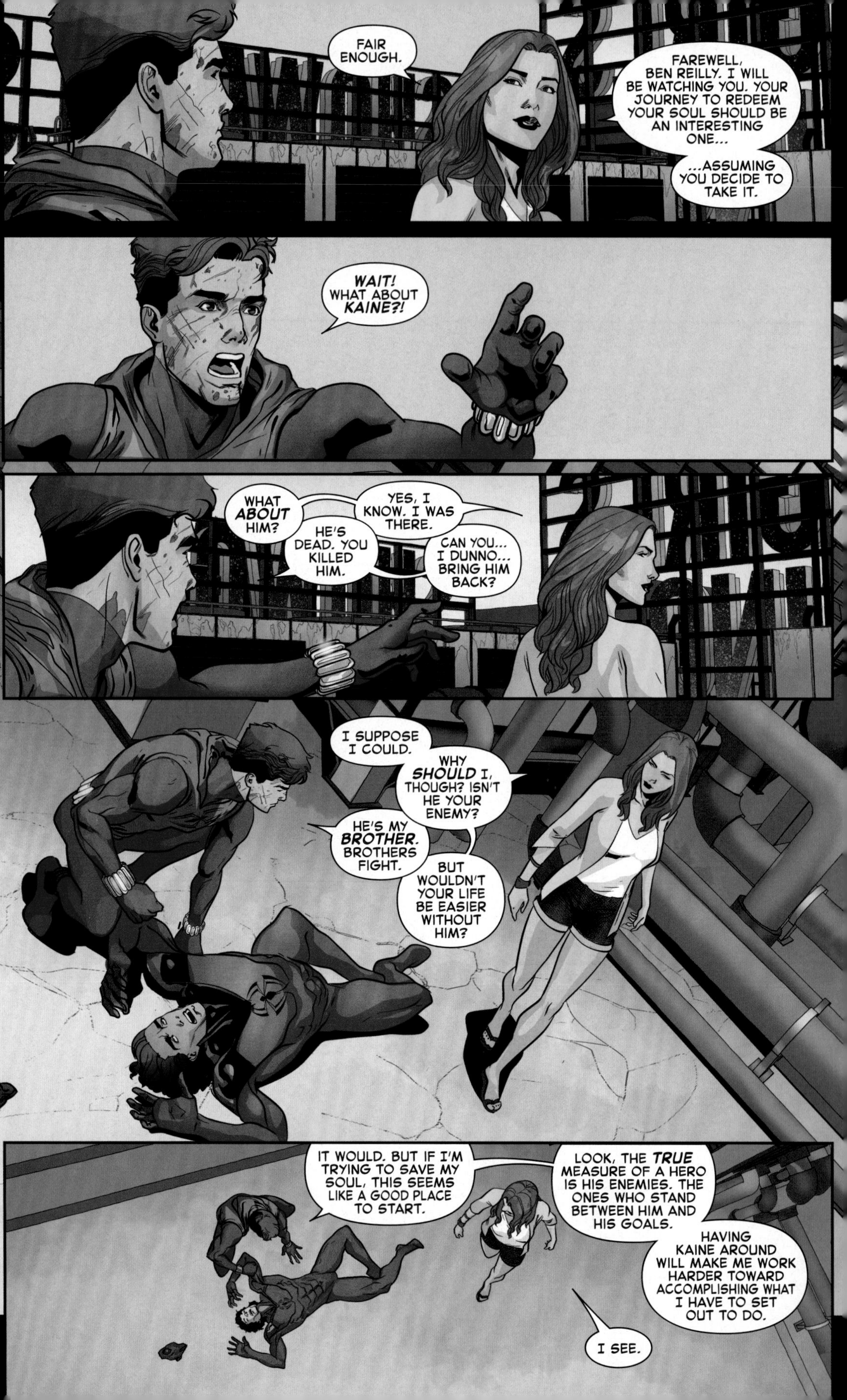
FAIR ENOUGH.
FAREWELL, BEN REILLY. I WILL BE WATCHING YOU. YOUR JOURNEY TO REDEEM YOUR SOUL SHOULD BE AN INTERESTING ONE...
...ASSUMING YOU DECIDE TO TAKE IT.
WAIT! WHAT ABOUT KAINE?!
WHAT ABOUT HIM?
YES, I KNOW. I WAS THERE.
HE'S DEAD. YOU KILLED HIM.
CAN YOU... I DUNNO... BRING HIM BACK?
I SUPPOSE I COULD.
WHY SHOULD I, THOUGH? ISN'T HE YOUR ENEMY?
HE'S MY BROTHER. BROTHERS FIGHT.
BUT WOULDN'T YOUR LIFE BE EASIER WITHOUT HIM?
IT WOULD. BUT IF I'M TRYING TO SAVE MY SOUL, THIS SEEMS LIKE A GOOD PLACE TO START.
LOOK, THE TRUE MEASURE OF A HERO IS HIS ENEMIES. THE ONES WHO STAND BETWEEN HIM AND HIS GOALS.
HAVING KAINE AROUND WILL MAKE ME WORK HARDER TOWARD ACCOMPLISHING WHAT I HAVE TO SET OUT TO DO.
I SEE.

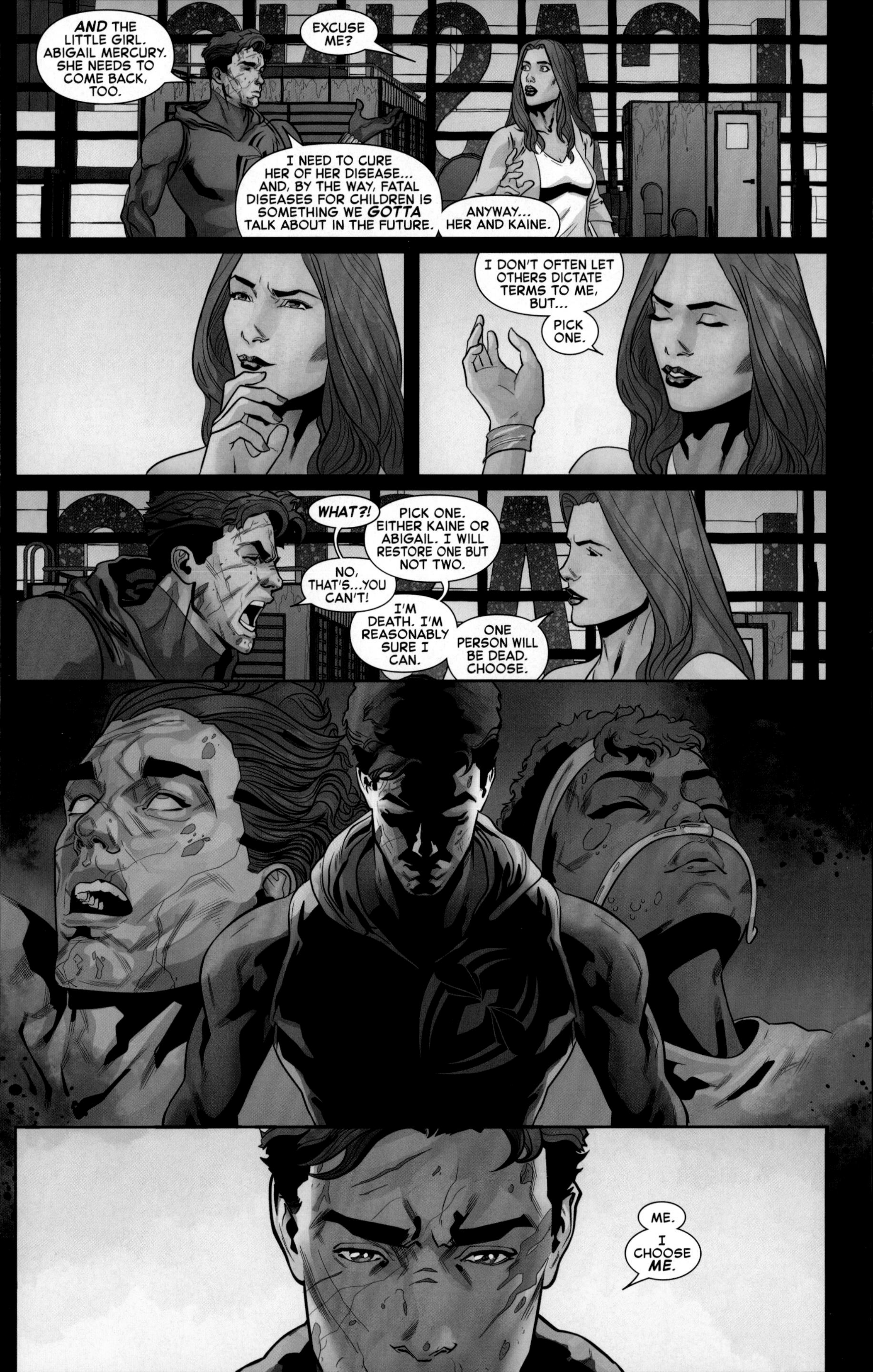
AND THE LITTLE GIRL. ABIGAIL MERCURY. SHE NEEDS TO COME BACK, TOO.
EXCUSE ME?
I NEED TO CURE HER OF HER DISEASE... AND, BY THE WAY, FATAL DISEASES FOR CHILDREN IS SOMETHING WE GOTTA TALK ABOUT IN THE FUTURE.
ANYWAY... HER AND KAINE.
I DON'T OFTEN LET OTHERS DICTATE TERMS TO ME, BUT...
PICK ONE.
WHAT?!
PICK ONE. EITHER KAINE OR ABIGAIL. I WILL RESTORE ONE BUT NOT TWO.
NO, THAT'S...YOU CAN'T!
I'M DEATH. I'M REASONABLY SURE I CAN.
ONE PERSON WILL BE DEAD. CHOOSE.
ME. I CHOOSE ME.

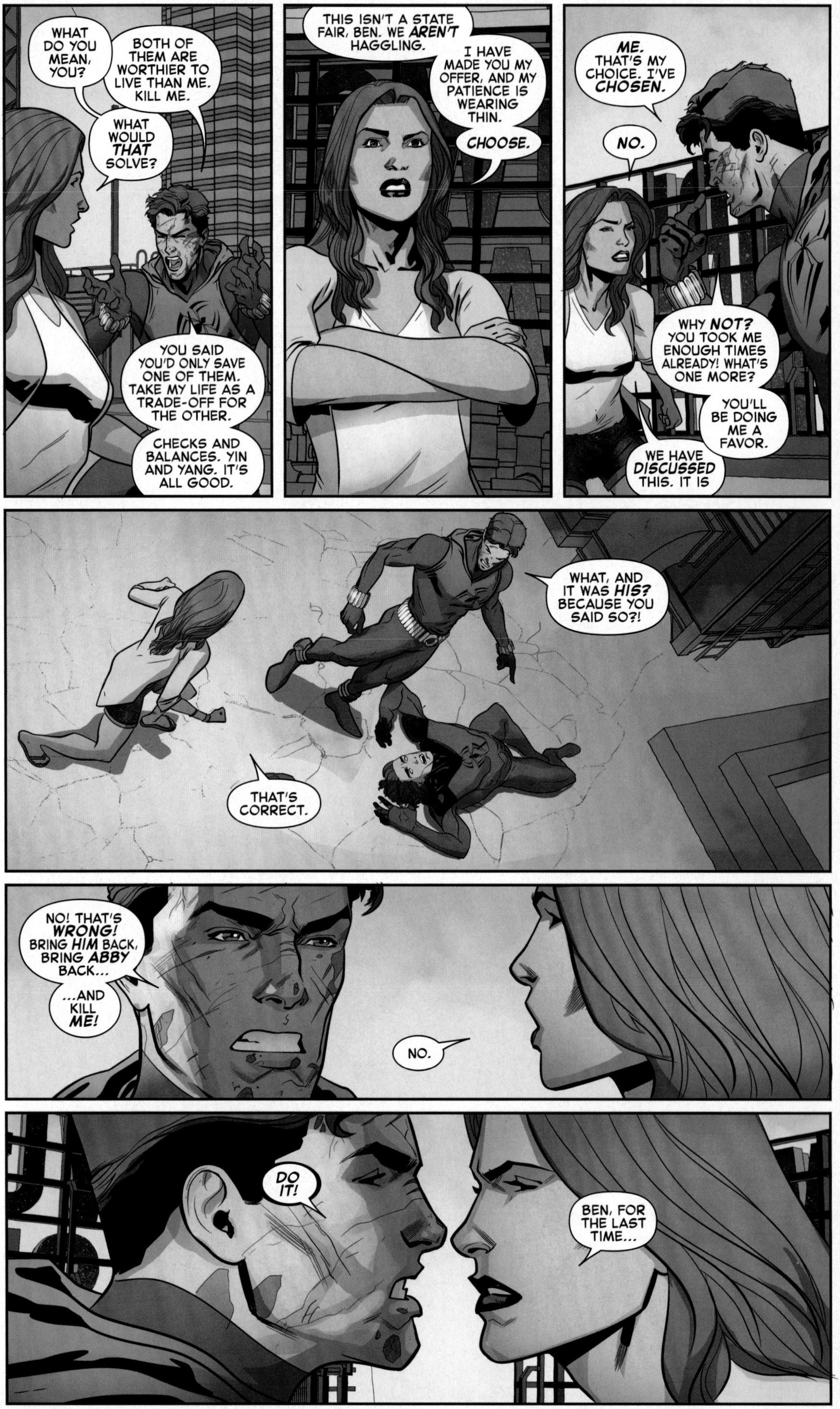
WHAT DO YOU MEAN, YOU?
BOTH OF THEM ARE WORTHIER TO LIVE THAN ME. KILL ME.
WHAT WOULD THAT SOLVE?
YOU SAID YOU'D ONLY SAVE ONE OF THEM. TAKE MY LIFE AS A TRADE-OFF FOR THE OTHER.
CHECKS AND BALANCES. YIN AND YANG. IT'S ALL GOOD.
THIS ISN'T A STATE FAIR, BEN. WE AREN'T HAGGLING.
I HAVE MADE YOU MY OFFER, AND MY PATIENCE IS WEARING THIN.
CHOOSE.
ME. THAT'S MY CHOICE. I'VE CHOSEN.
NO.
WHY NOT? YOU TOOK ME ENOUGH TIMES ALREADY! WHAT'S ONE MORE?
YOU'LL BE DOING ME A FAVOR.
WE HAVE DISCUSSED THIS. IT IS
WHAT, AND IT WAS HIS? BECAUSE YOU SAID SO?!
THAT'S CORRECT.
NO! THAT'S WRONG! BRING HIM BACK, BRING ABBY BACK...
...AND KILL ME!
NO.
DO IT!
BEN, FOR THE LAST TIME...

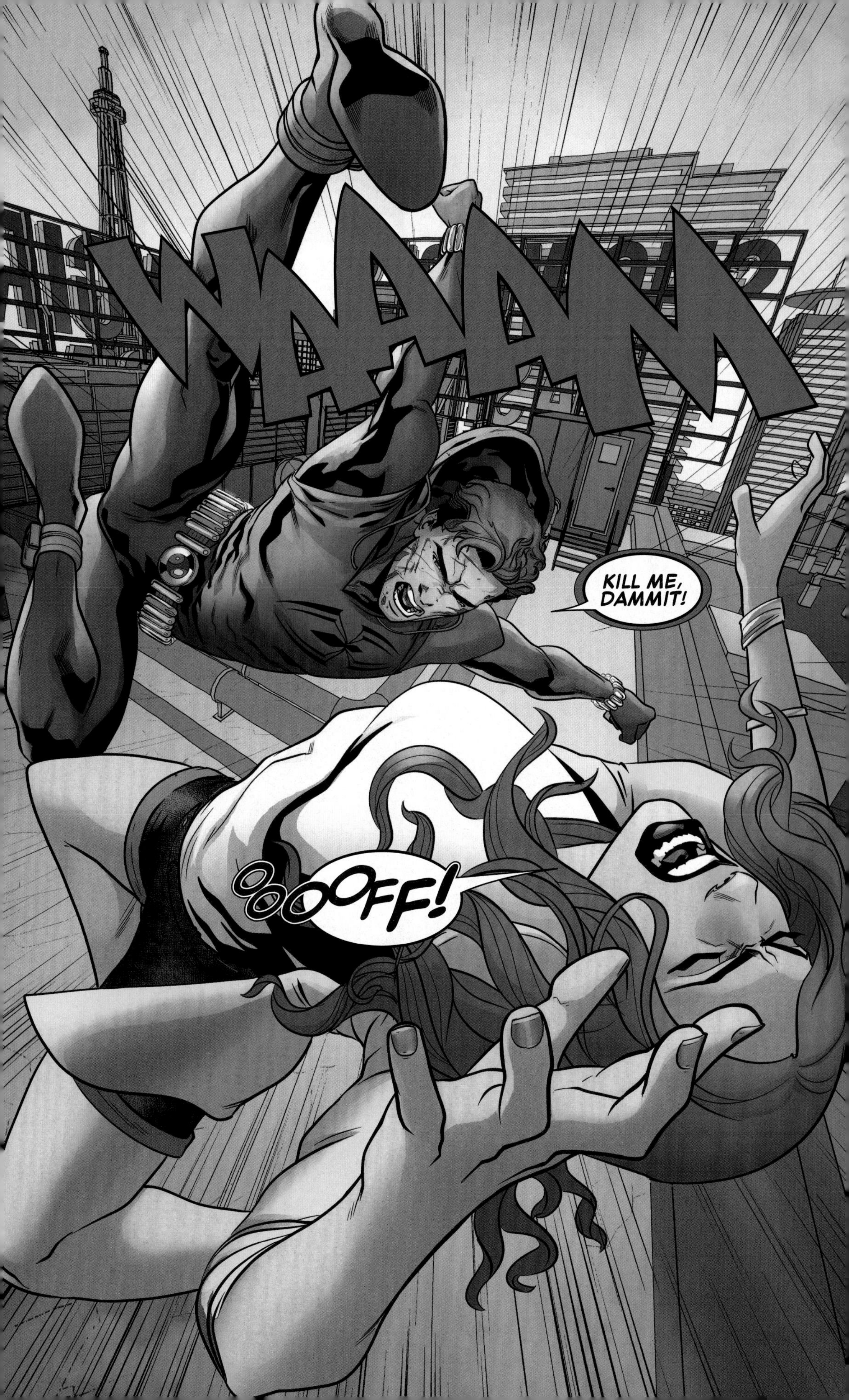
WAAAM
KILL ME, DAMMIT!
OOOOFF!

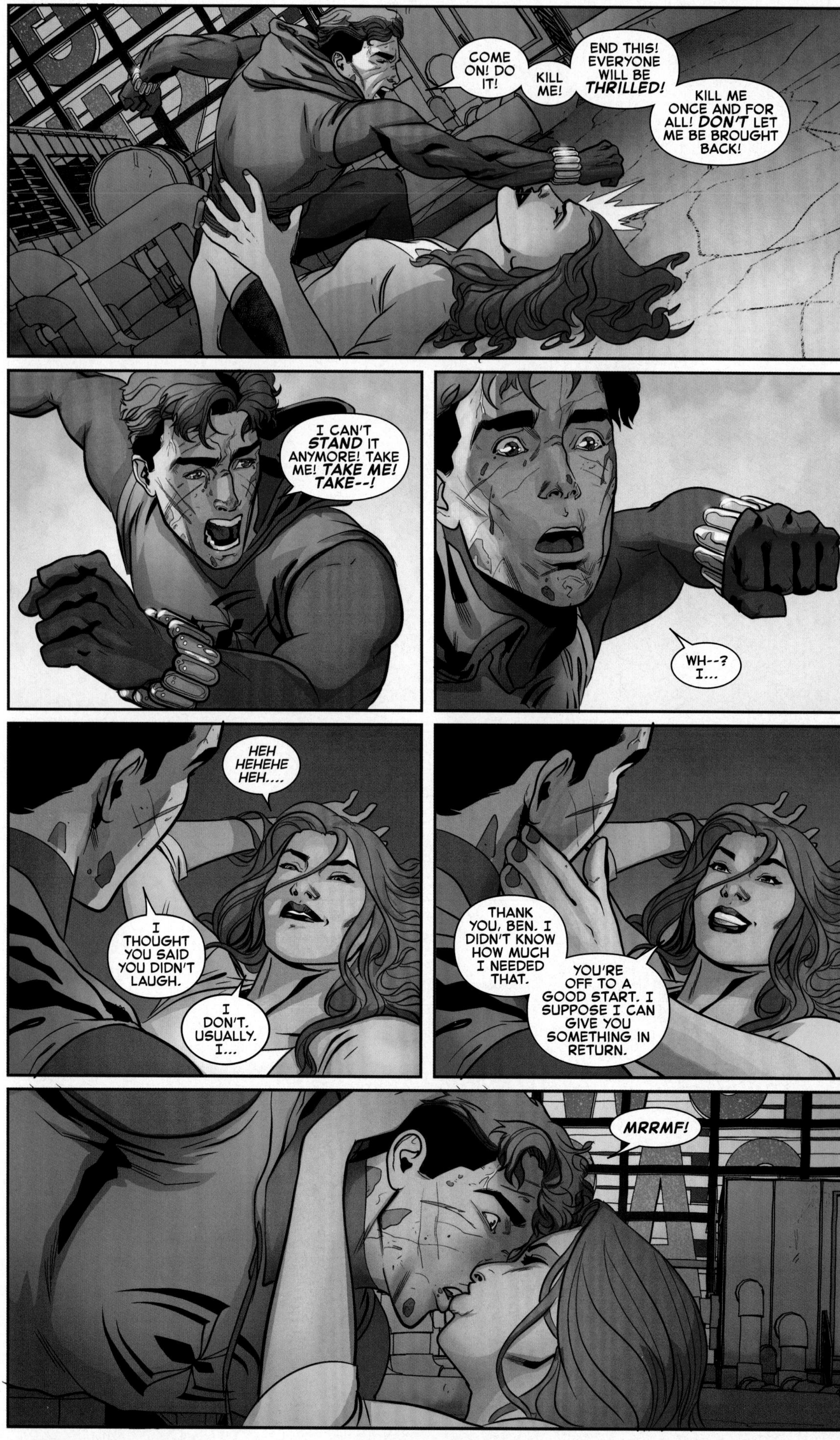
COME ON! DO IT!
KILL ME!
END THIS! EVERYONE WILL BE THRILLED!
KILL ME ONCE AND FOR ALL! DON'T LET ME BE BROUGHT BACK!
I CAN'T STAND IT ANYMORE! TAKE ME! TAKE ME! TAKE--!
WH--? I...
HEH HEHEHE HEH....
I THOUGHT YOU SAID YOU DIDN'T LAUGH.
I DON'T. USUALLY. I...
THANK YOU, BEN. I DIDN'T KNOW HOW MUCH I NEEDED THAT.
YOU'RE OFF TO A GOOD START. I SUPPOSE I CAN GIVE YOU SOMETHING IN RETURN.
MRRMF!

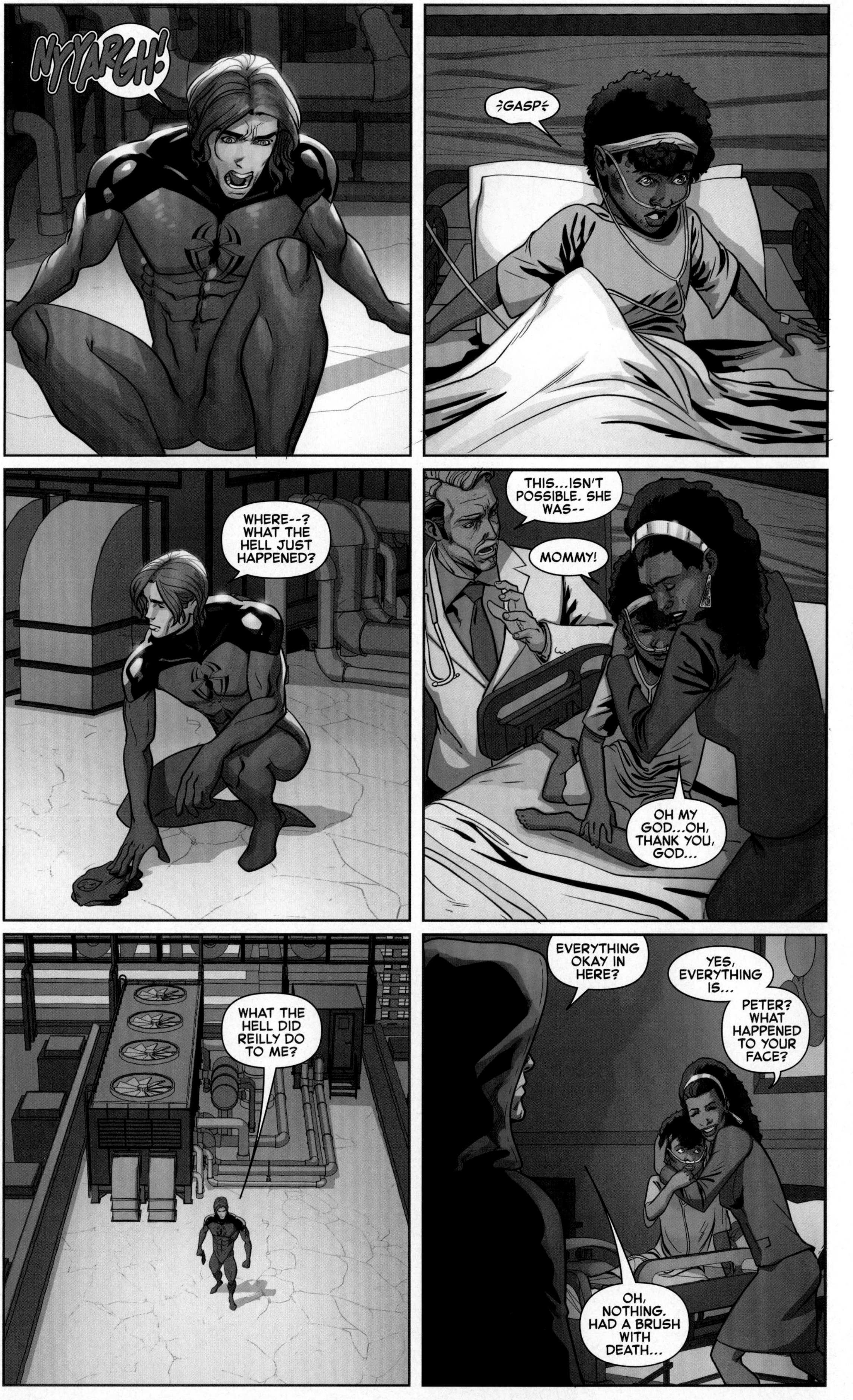
NYYARGH!
GASP
WHERE--? WHAT THE HELL JUST HAPPENED?
THIS...ISN'T POSSIBLE. SHE WAS--
MOMMY!
OH MY GOD...OH, THANK YOU, GOD...
WHAT THE HELL DID REILLY DO TO ME?
EVERYTHING OKAY IN HERE?
YES, EVERYTHING IS...
PETER? WHAT HAPPENED TO YOUR FACE?
OH, NOTHING. HAD A BRUSH WITH DEATH...

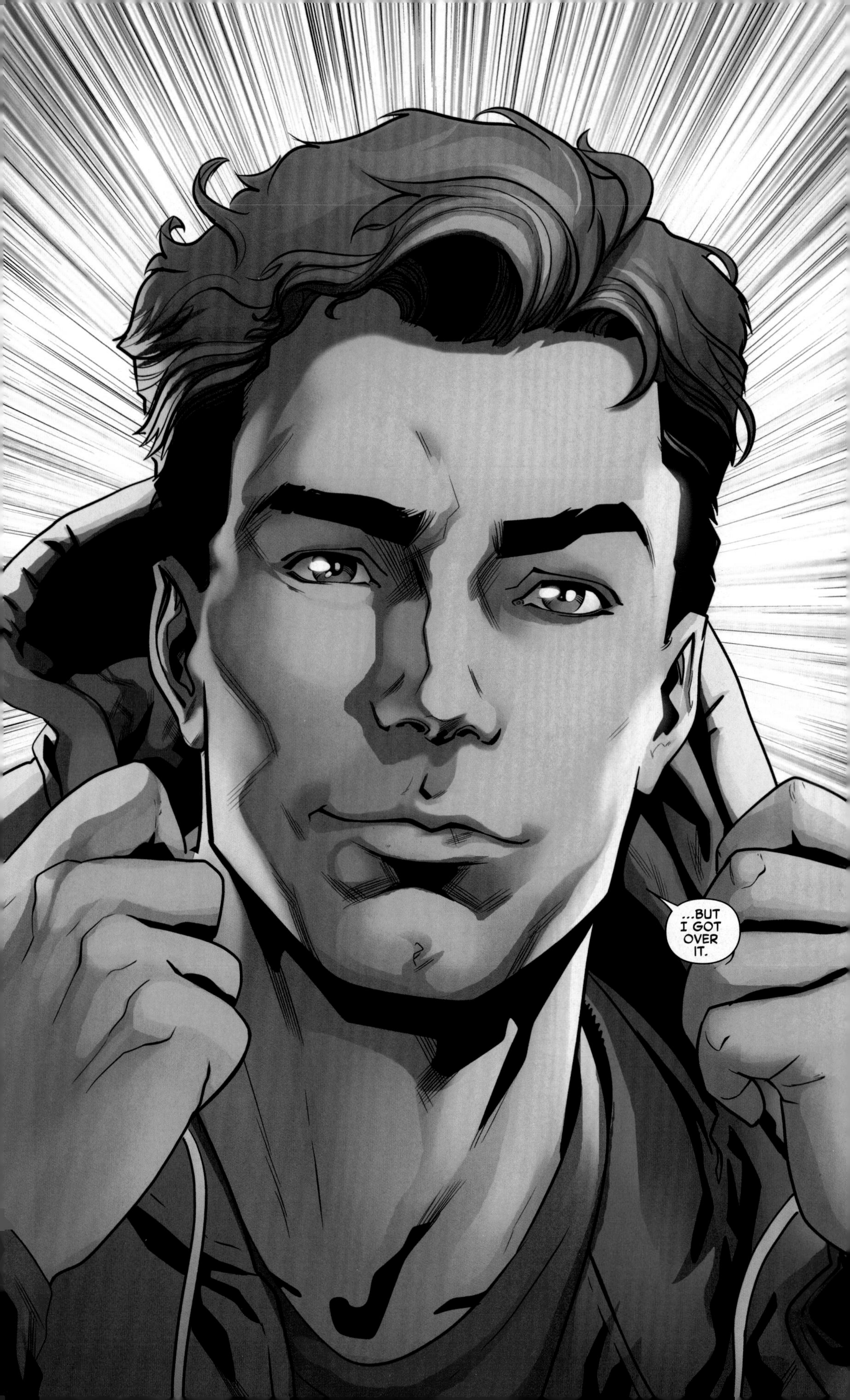
...BUT I GOT OVER IT.

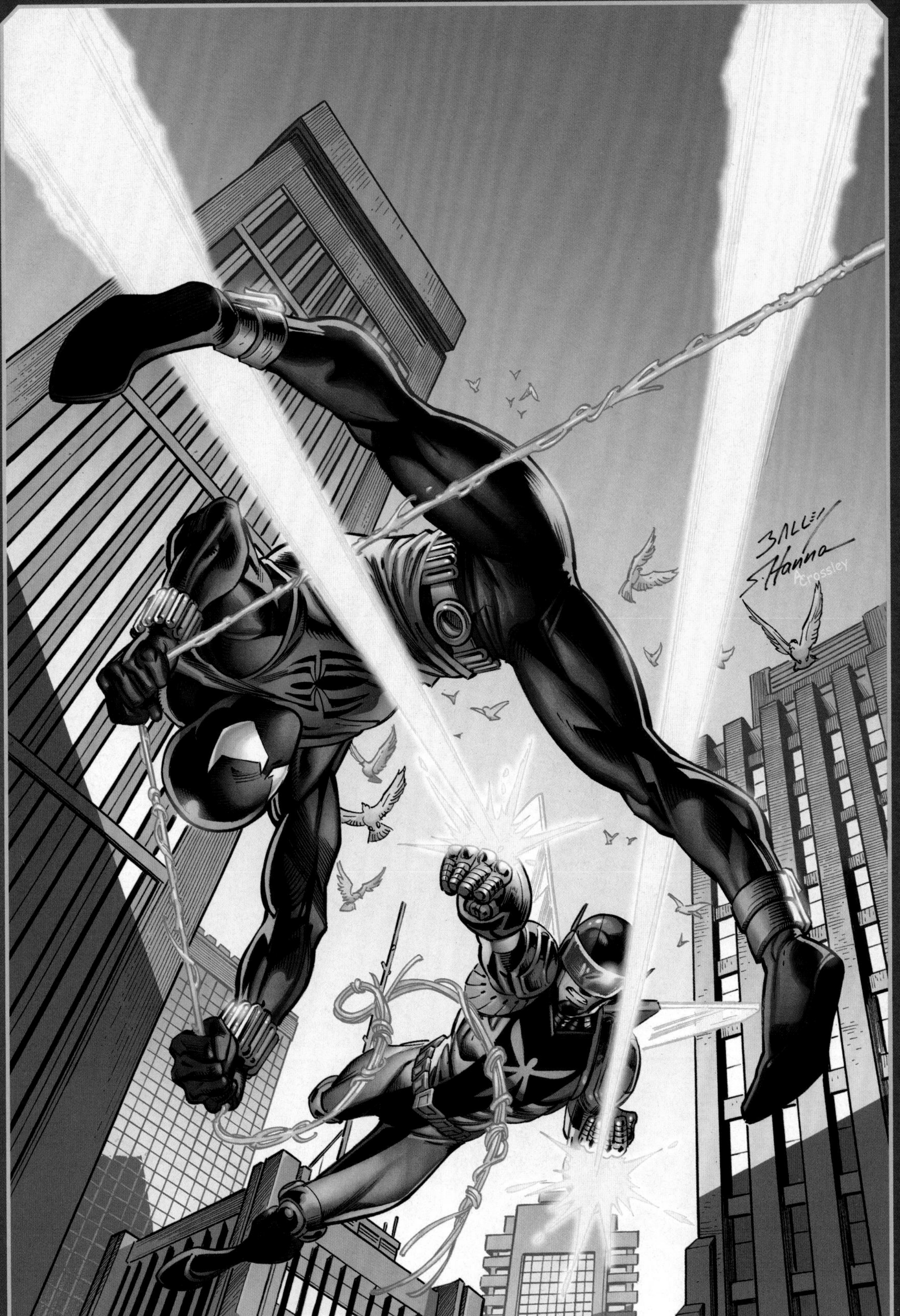

8

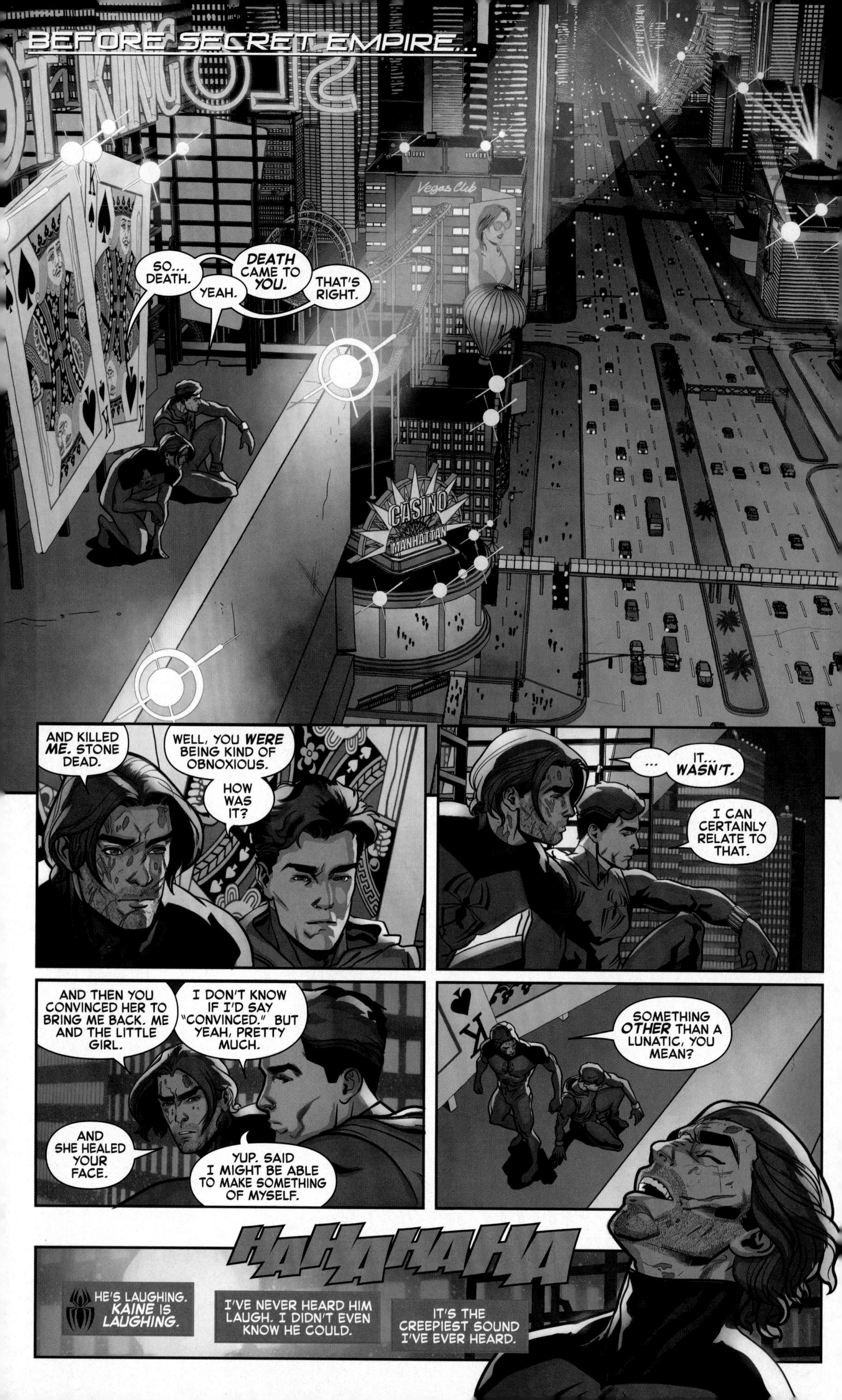

BEFORE SECRET EMPIRE...
SO... DEATH.
YEAH.
DEATH CAME TO YOU.
THAT'S RIGHT.
Vegas Club
CASINO
MANHATTAN
AND KILLED ME. STONE DEAD.
WELL, YOU WERE BEING KIND OF OBNOXIOUS.
HOW WAS IT?
...
IT... WASN'T.
I CAN CERTAINLY RELATE TO THAT.
AND THEN YOU CONVINCED HER TO BRING ME BACK. ME AND THE LITTLE GIRL.
I DON'T KNOW IF I'D SAY "CONVINCED." BUT YEAH, PRETTY MUCH.
AND SHE HEALED YOUR FACE.
YUP. SAID I MIGHT BE ABLE TO MAKE SOMETHING OF MYSELF.
SOMETHING OTHER THAN A LUNATIC, YOU MEAN?
HAHAHAHAHA
HE'S LAUGHING. KAINE IS LAUGHING.
I'VE NEVER HEARD HIM LAUGH. I DIDN'T EVEN KNOW HE COULD.
IT'S THE CREEPIEST SOUND I'VE EVER HEARD.

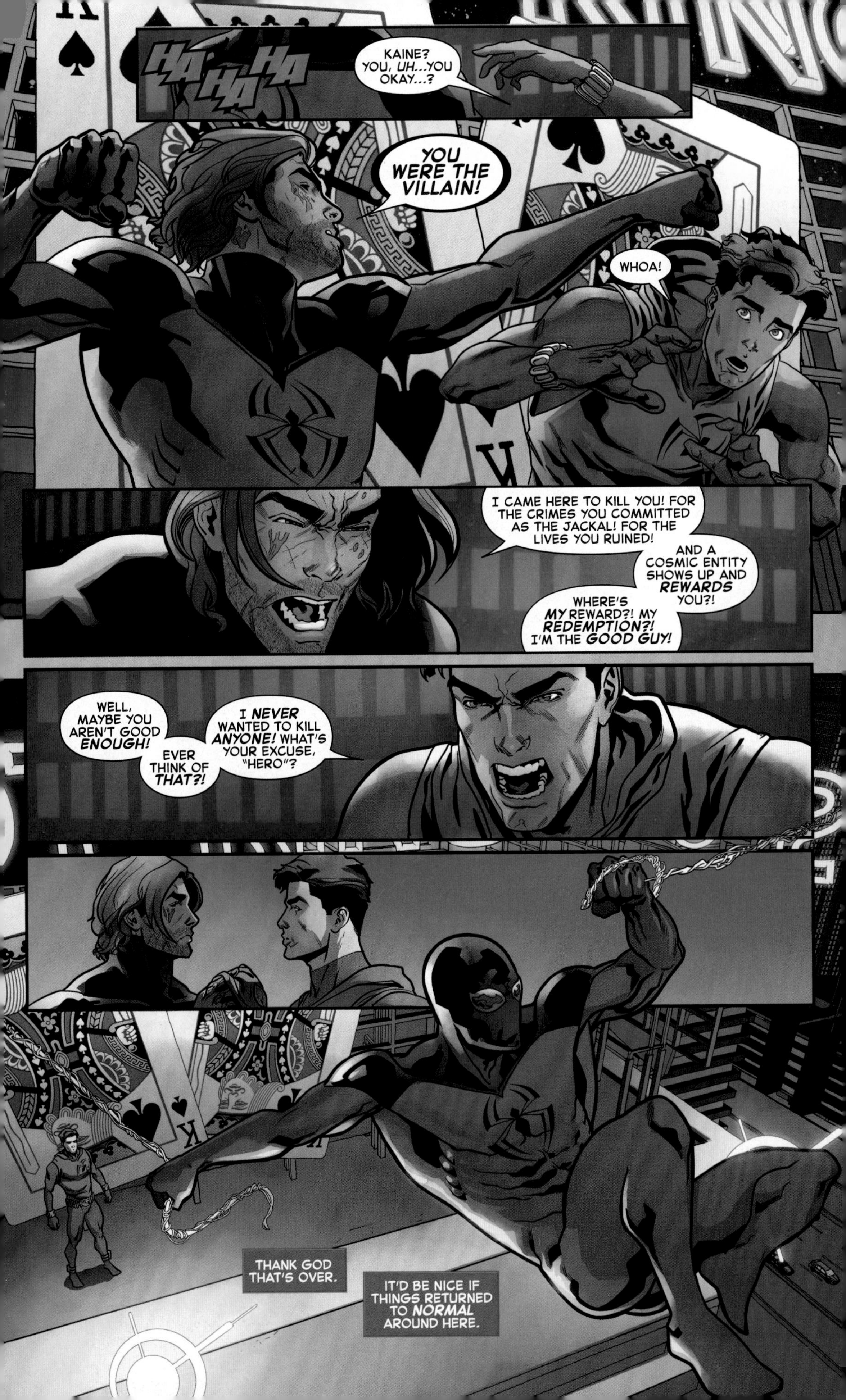
HA HA HA HA
KAINE? YOU, *UH*...YOU OKAY...?
YOU WERE THE VILLAIN!
WHOA!
I CAME HERE TO KILL YOU! FOR THE CRIMES YOU COMMITTED AS THE JACKAL! FOR THE LIVES YOU RUINED!
AND A COSMIC ENTITY SHOWS UP AND *REWARDS* YOU?!
WHERE'S *MY* REWARD?! MY *REDEMPTION?!* I'M THE *GOOD GUY!*
WELL, MAYBE YOU AREN'T GOOD *ENOUGH!*
EVER THINK OF *THAT?!*
I *NEVER* WANTED TO KILL *ANYONE!* WHAT'S YOUR EXCUSE, "HERO"?
THANK GOD THAT'S OVER.
IT'D BE NICE IF THINGS RETURNED TO *NORMAL* AROUND HERE.

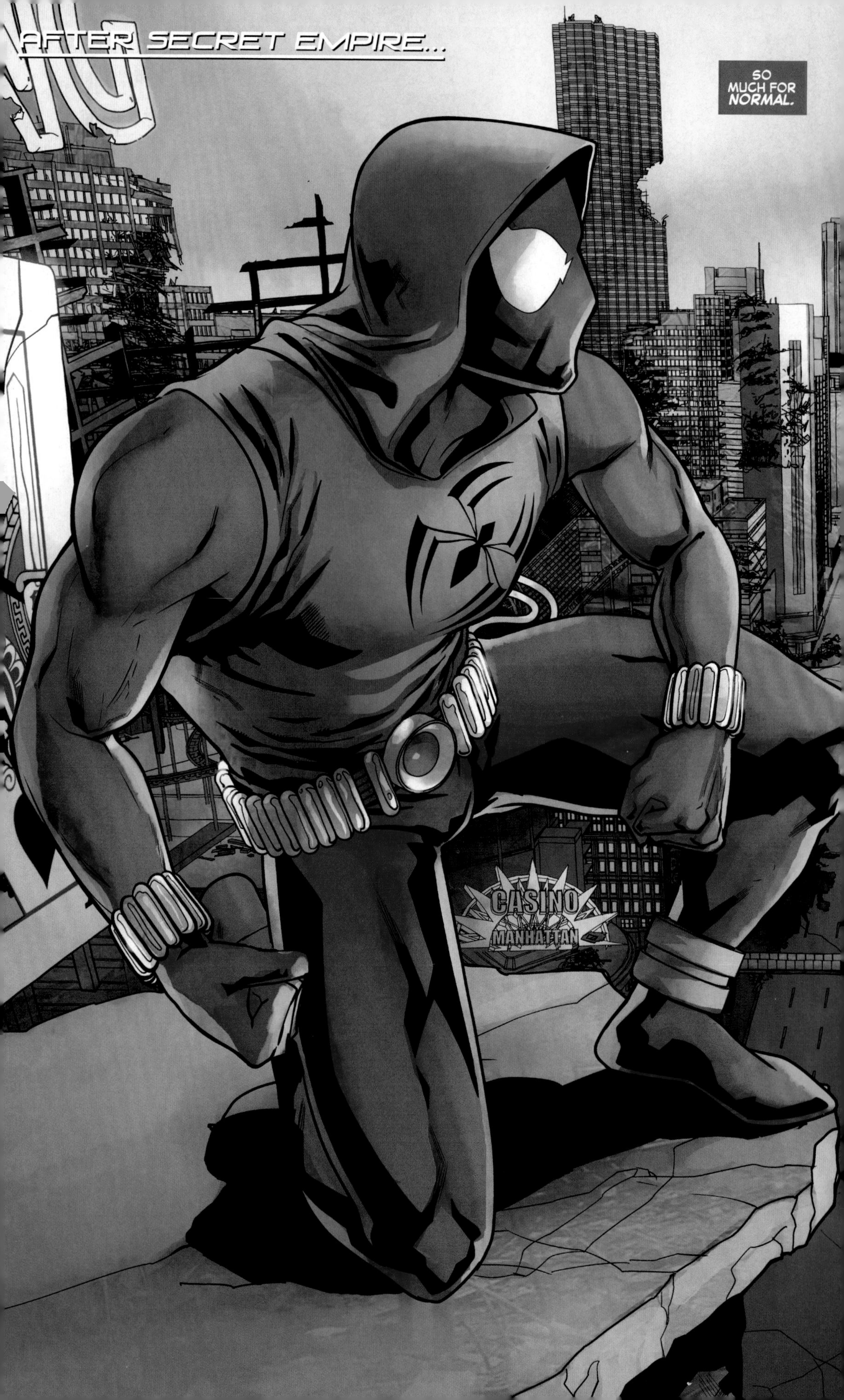

AFTER SECRET EMPIRE...
SO MUCH FOR NORMAL.
CASINO
MANHATTAN

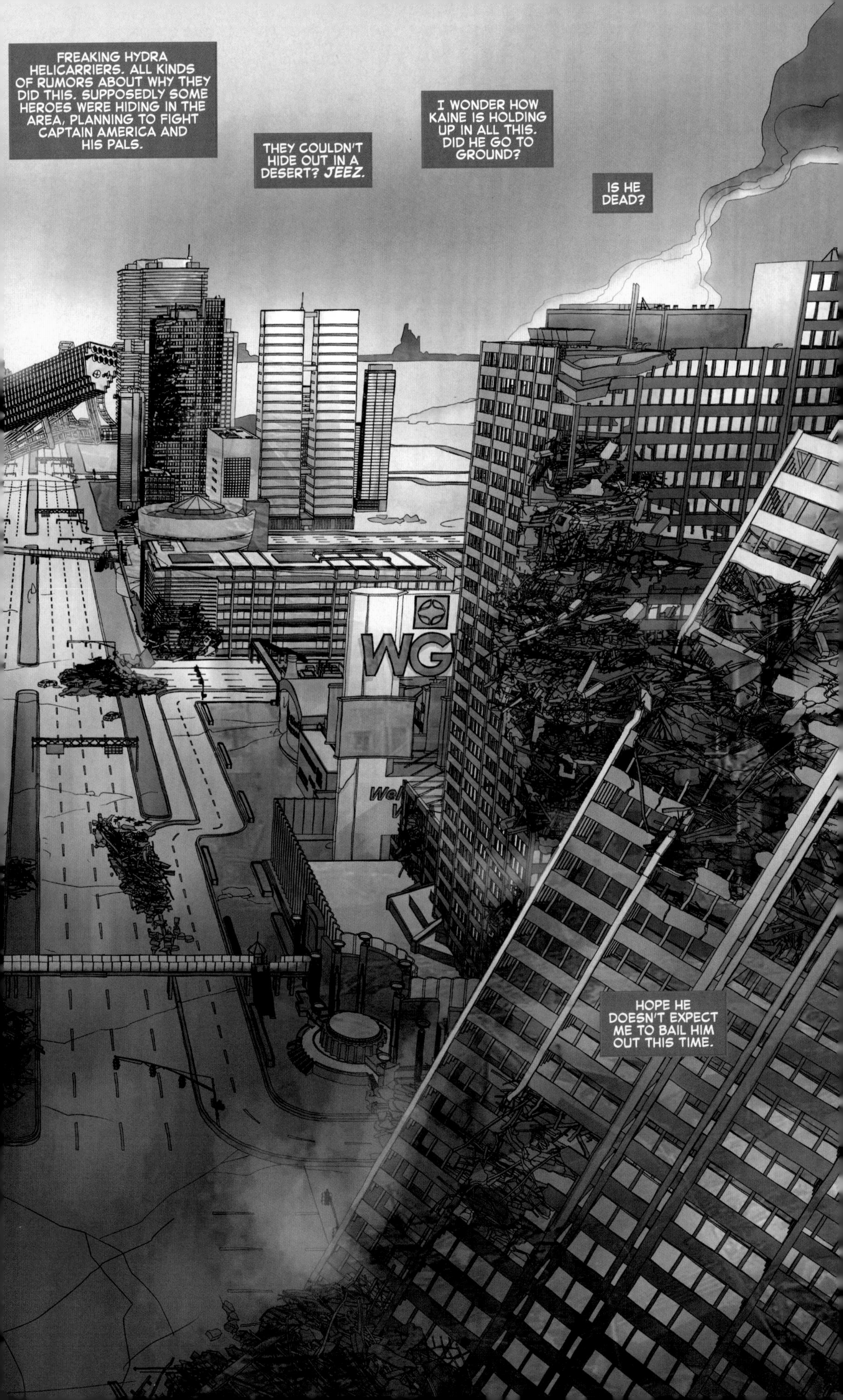
FREAKING HYDRA HELICARRIERS. ALL KINDS OF RUMORS ABOUT WHY THEY DID THIS. SUPPOSEDLY SOME HEROES WERE HIDING IN THE AREA, PLANNING TO FIGHT CAPTAIN AMERICA AND HIS PALS.
THEY COULDN'T HIDE OUT IN A DESERT? *JEEZ.*
I WONDER HOW KAINE IS HOLDING UP IN ALL THIS. DID HE GO TO GROUND?
IS HE DEAD?
WG
HOPE HE DOESN'T EXPECT ME TO BAIL HIM OUT THIS TIME.

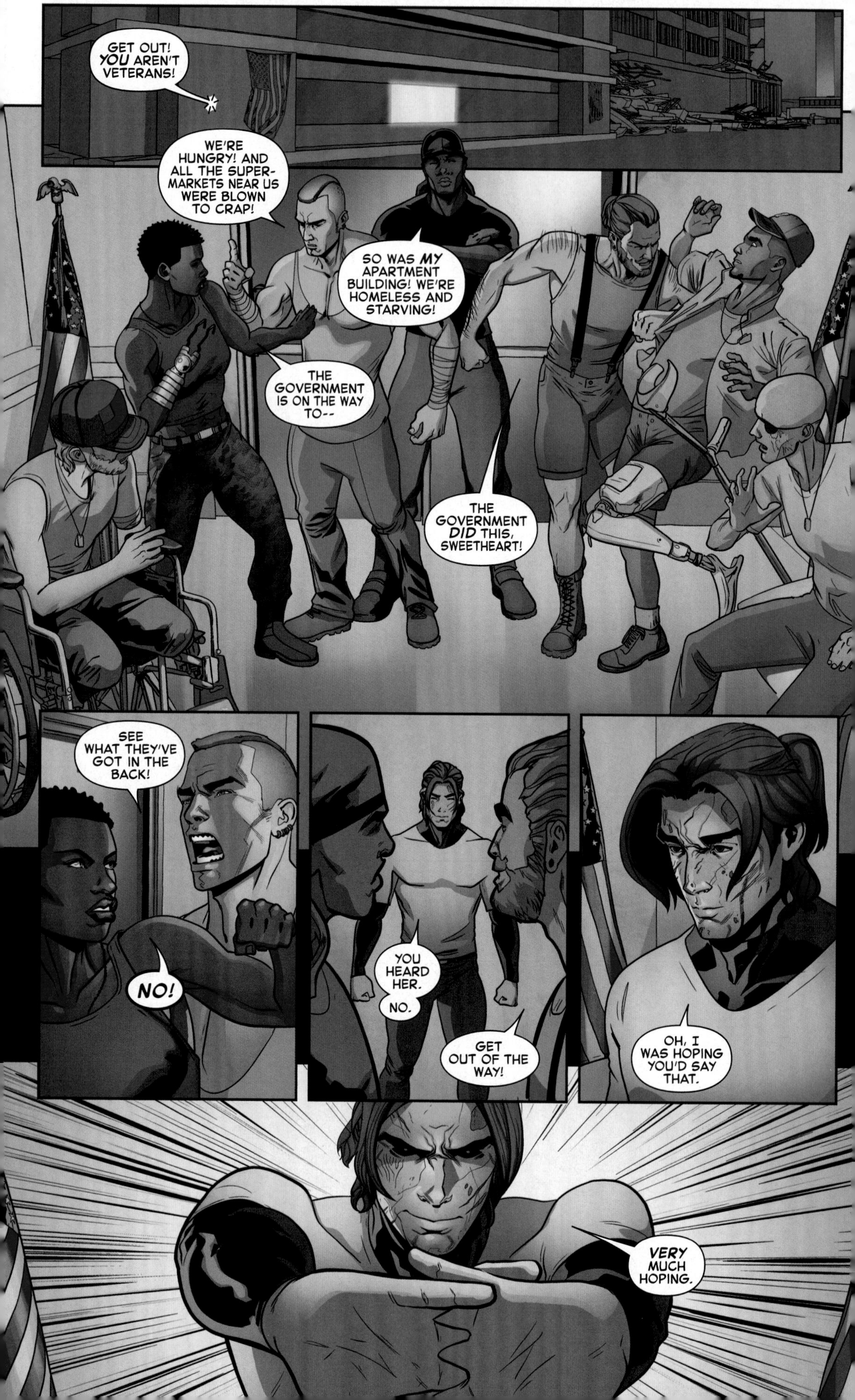

GET OUT! YOU AREN'T VETERANS!
WE'RE HUNGRY! AND ALL THE SUPER-MARKETS NEAR US WERE BLOWN TO CRAP!
SO WAS MY APARTMENT BUILDING! WE'RE HOMELESS AND STARVING!
THE GOVERNMENT IS ON THE WAY TO--
THE GOVERNMENT DID THIS, SWEETHEART!
SEE WHAT THEY'VE GOT IN THE BACK!
NO!
YOU HEARD HER.
NO.
GET OUT OF THE WAY!
OH, I WAS HOPING YOU'D SAY THAT.
VERY MUCH HOPING.

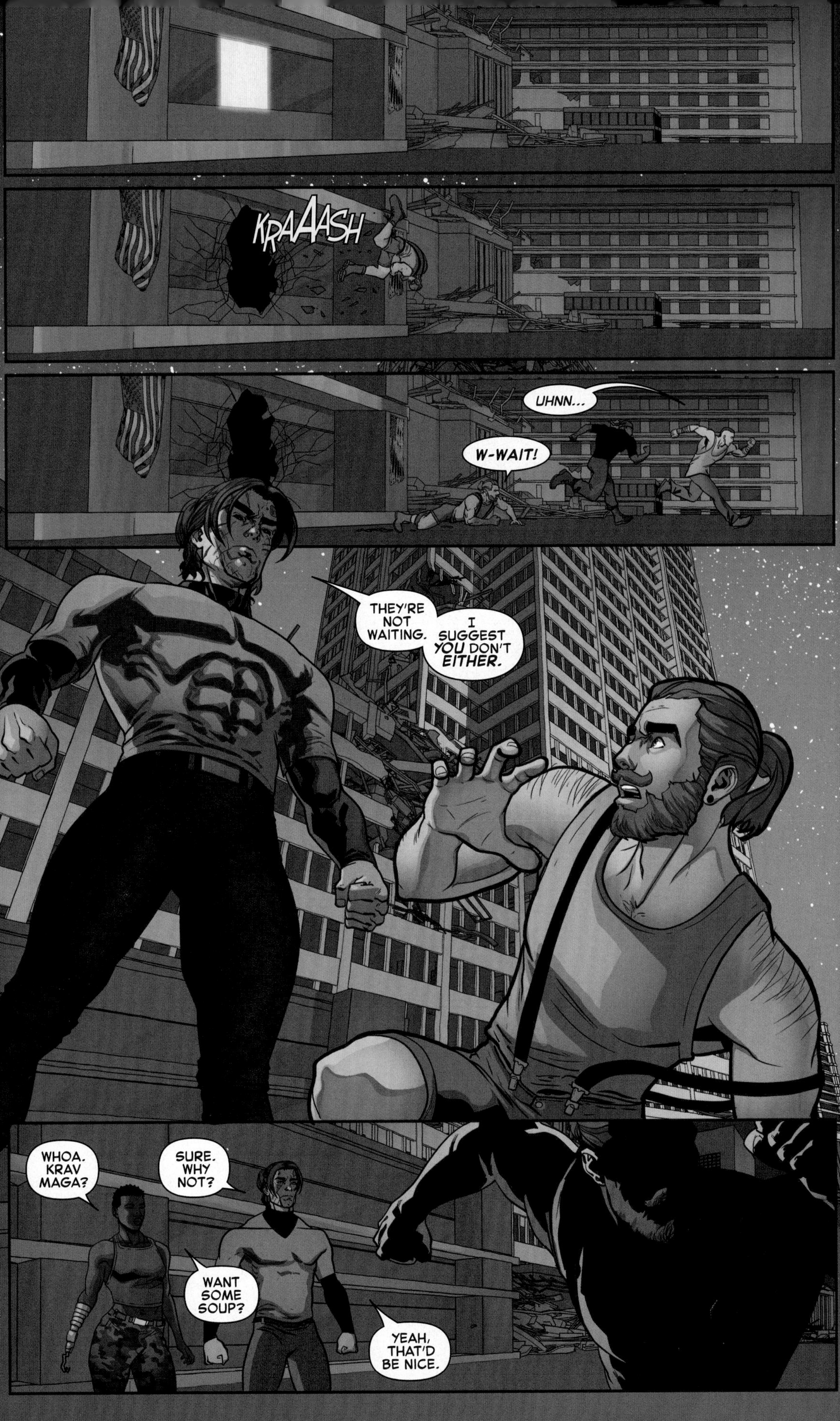
KRAAASH
UHNN...
W-WAIT!
THEY'RE NOT WAITING.
I SUGGEST YOU DON'T EITHER.
WHOA. KRAV MAGA?
SURE. WHY NOT?
WANT SOME SOUP?
YEAH, THAT'D BE NICE.

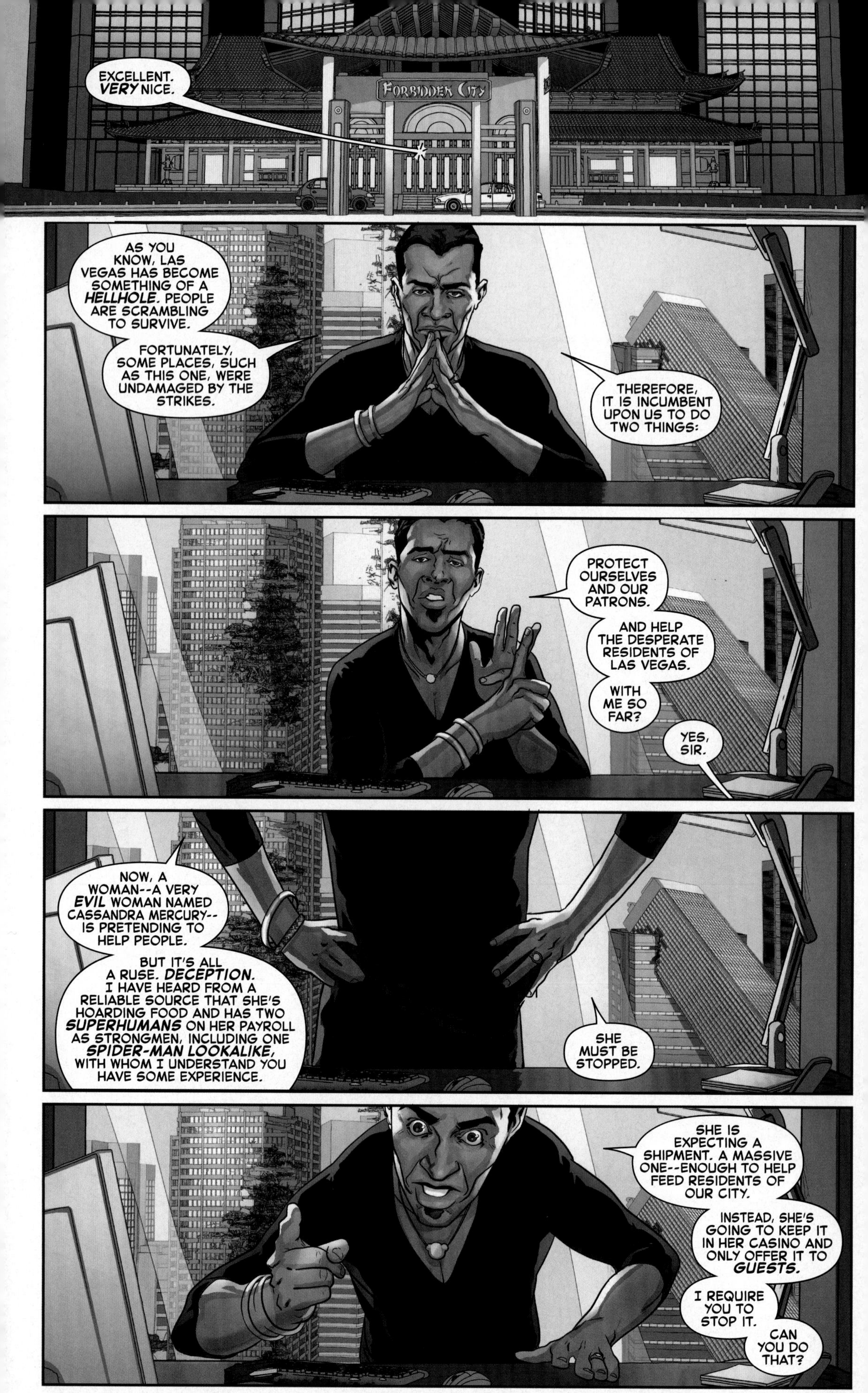
FORBIDDEN CITY
EXCELLENT. VERY NICE.
AS YOU KNOW, LAS VEGAS HAS BECOME SOMETHING OF A HELLHOLE. PEOPLE ARE SCRAMBLING TO SURVIVE.
FORTUNATELY, SOME PLACES, SUCH AS THIS ONE, WERE UNDAMAGED BY THE STRIKES.
THEREFORE, IT IS INCUMBENT UPON US TO DO TWO THINGS:
PROTECT OURSELVES AND OUR PATRONS.
AND HELP THE DESPERATE RESIDENTS OF LAS VEGAS.
WITH ME SO FAR?
YES, SIR.
NOW, A WOMAN--A VERY EVIL WOMAN NAMED CASSANDRA MERCURY--IS PRETENDING TO HELP PEOPLE.
BUT IT'S ALL A RUSE. DECEPTION. I HAVE HEARD FROM A RELIABLE SOURCE THAT SHE'S HOARDING FOOD AND HAS TWO SUPERHUMANS ON HER PAYROLL AS STRONGMEN, INCLUDING ONE SPIDER-MAN LOOKALIKE, WITH WHOM I UNDERSTAND YOU HAVE SOME EXPERIENCE.
SHE MUST BE STOPPED.
SHE IS EXPECTING A SHIPMENT. A MASSIVE ONE--ENOUGH TO HELP FEED RESIDENTS OF OUR CITY.
INSTEAD, SHE'S GOING TO KEEP IT IN HER CASINO AND ONLY OFFER IT TO GUESTS.
I REQUIRE YOU TO STOP IT.
CAN YOU DO THAT?

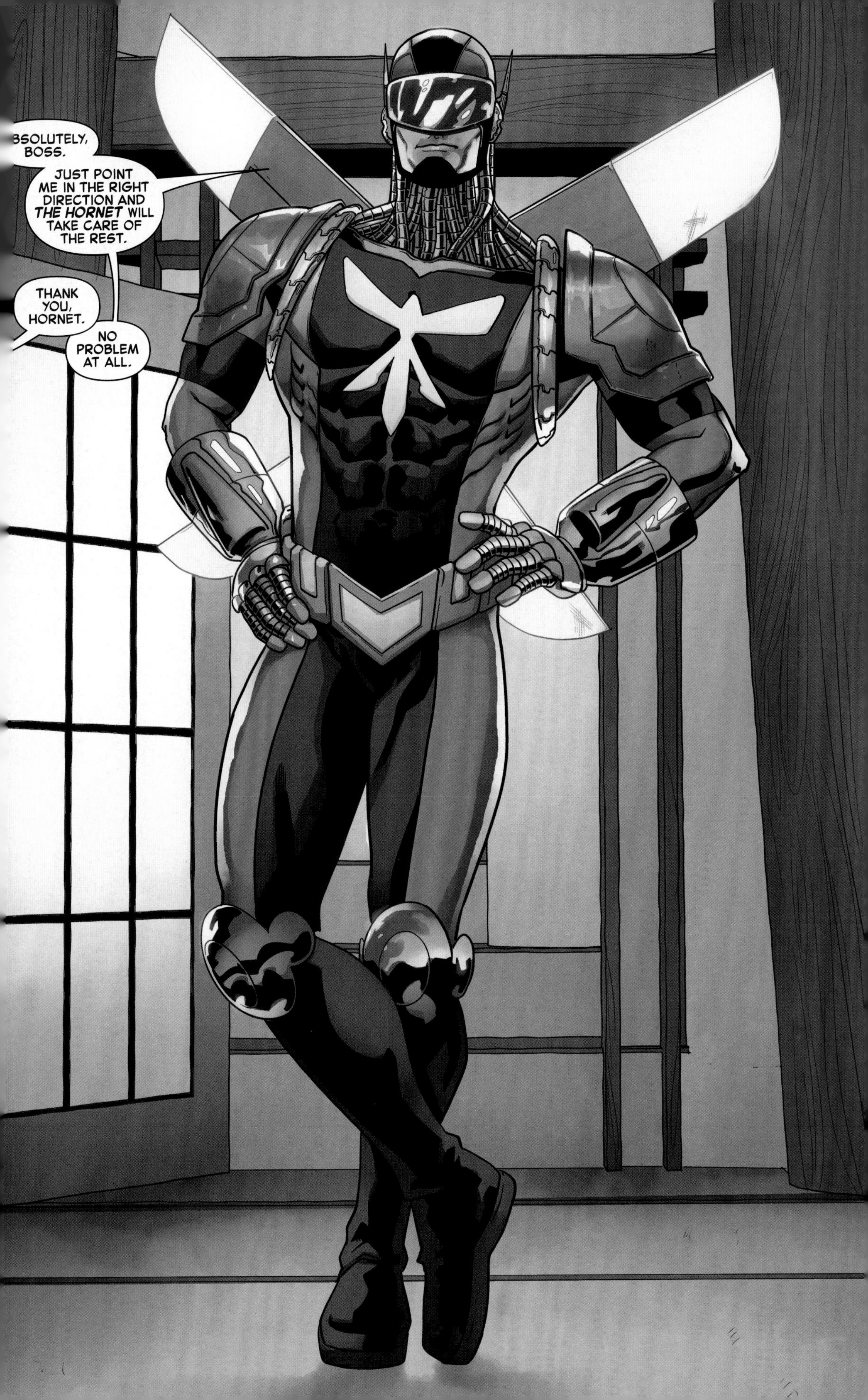
BSOLUTELY, BOSS.
JUST POINT ME IN THE RIGHT DIRECTION AND *THE HORNET* WILL TAKE CARE OF THE REST.
THANK YOU, HORNET.
NO PROBLEM AT ALL.

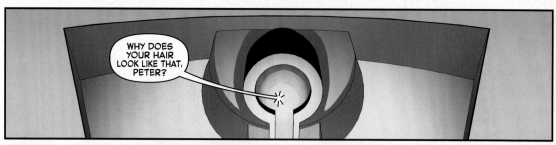

WHY DOES YOUR HAIR LOOK LIKE THAT, PETER?

BECAUSE SINCE MY FACE HEALED, I DON'T WANT PEOPLE MISTAKING ME FOR PETER PARKER.

I JUST FELT LIKE MAKING A CHANGE.

I'VE WANTED TO DO SOMETHING LIKE THAT.

WHY DON'T YOU?

BECAUSE MY HAIR MIGHT START FALLING OUT BECAUSE OF THE MEDICINE I'M TAKING, SO IT'D BE A WASTE.

RIGHT, DOCTOR, RYDER?

WE DON'T REALLY KNOW, ABBY. THERE'S MUCH ABOUT YOUR...

...UH, SITUATION...

YOU CAN SAY "DISEASE." I WON'T CRY.

I'M NOT A BABY.

ALL RIGHT. ABOUT YOUR DISEASE THAT WE'RE STILL FINDING OUT. BUT, DON'T WORRY, WE'LL CRACK IT SOON. I PROMISE.

PETER, CAN WE SPEAK OUTSIDE?

ABSOLUTELY.

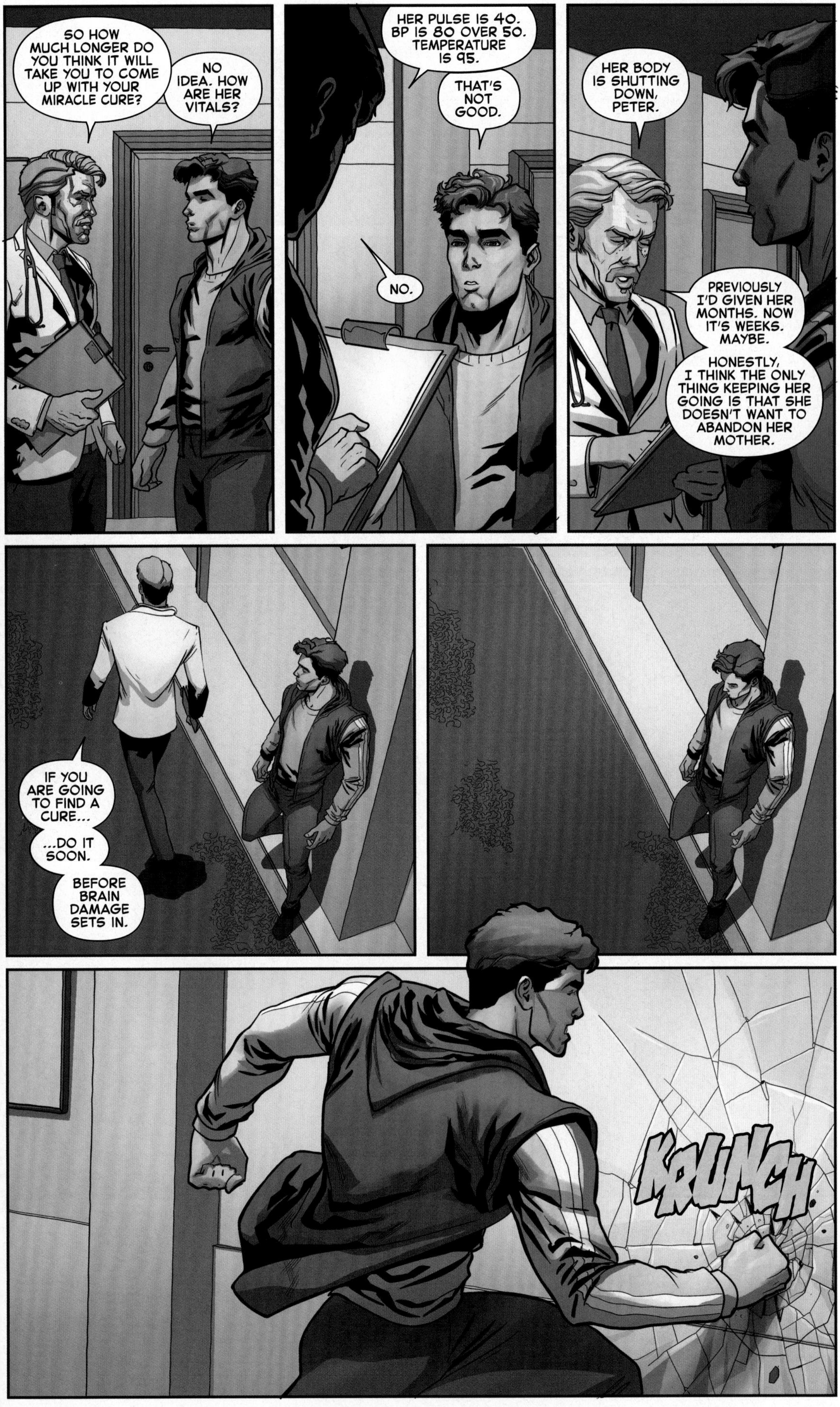
SO HOW MUCH LONGER DO YOU THINK IT WILL TAKE YOU TO COME UP WITH YOUR MIRACLE CURE?
NO IDEA. HOW ARE HER VITALS?
HER PULSE IS 40. BP IS 80 OVER 50. TEMPERATURE IS 95.
THAT'S NOT GOOD.
NO.
HER BODY IS SHUTTING DOWN, PETER.
PREVIOUSLY I'D GIVEN HER MONTHS. NOW IT'S WEEKS. MAYBE.
HONESTLY, I THINK THE ONLY THING KEEPING HER GOING IS THAT SHE DOESN'T WANT TO ABANDON HER MOTHER.
IF YOU ARE GOING TO FIND A CURE...
...DO IT SOON.
BEFORE BRAIN DAMAGE SETS IN.
KRUNCH

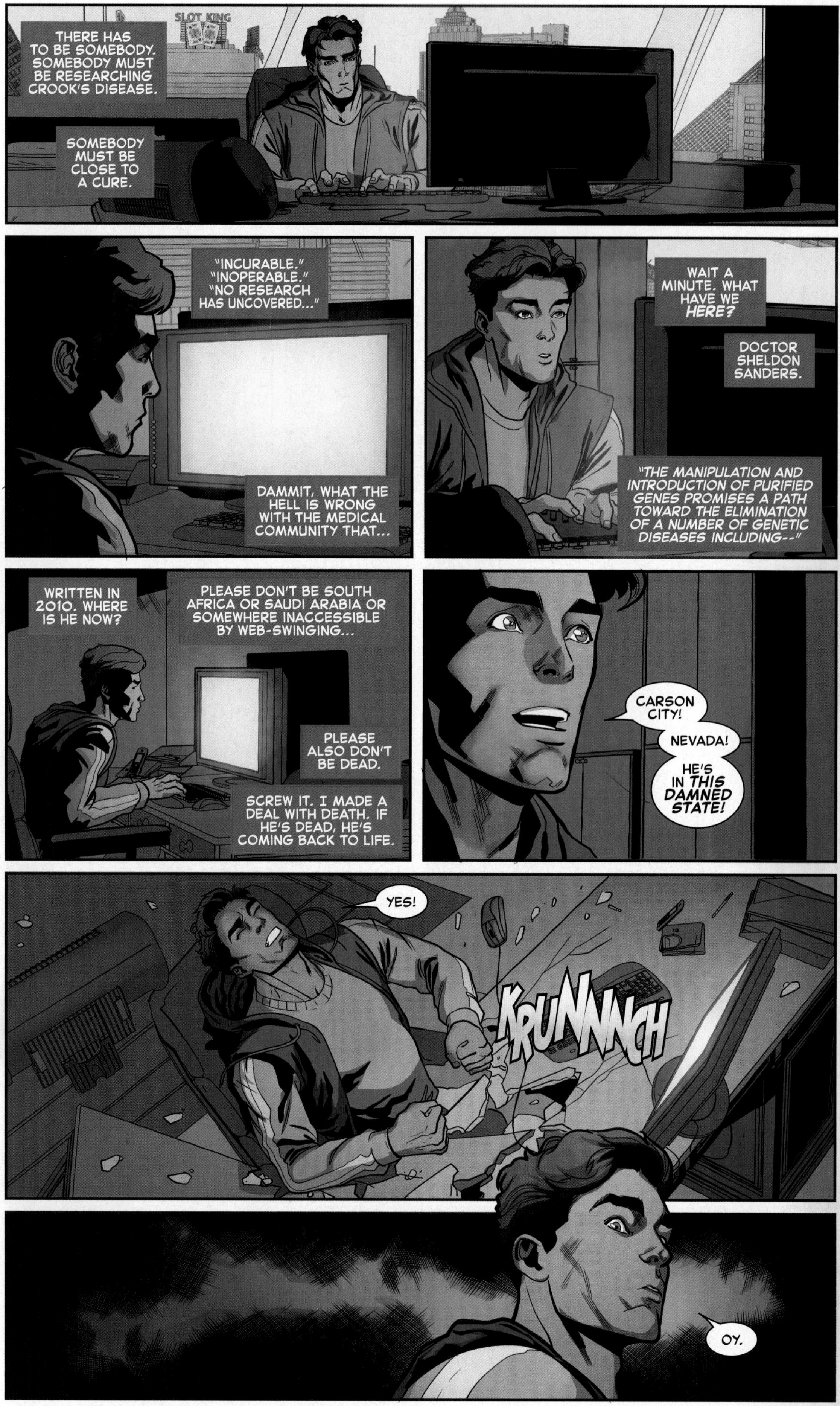
SLOT KING
THERE HAS TO BE SOMEBODY. SOMEBODY MUST BE RESEARCHING CROOK'S DISEASE.
SOMEBODY MUST BE CLOSE TO A CURE.
"INCURABLE." "INOPERABLE." "NO RESEARCH HAS UNCOVERED..."
DAMMIT, WHAT THE HELL IS WRONG WITH THE MEDICAL COMMUNITY THAT...
WAIT A MINUTE. WHAT HAVE WE *HERE?*
DOCTOR SHELDON SANDERS.
"THE MANIPULATION AND INTRODUCTION OF PURIFIED GENES PROMISES A PATH TOWARD THE ELIMINATION OF A NUMBER OF GENETIC DISEASES INCLUDING--"
WRITTEN IN 2010. WHERE IS HE NOW?
PLEASE DON'T BE SOUTH AFRICA OR SAUDI ARABIA OR SOMEWHERE INACCESSIBLE BY WEB-SWINGING...
PLEASE ALSO DON'T BE DEAD.
SCREW IT. I MADE A DEAL WITH DEATH. IF HE'S DEAD, HE'S COMING BACK TO LIFE.
CARSON CITY!
NEVADA!
HE'S IN *THIS DAMNED STATE!*
YES!
KRUNNNCH
OY.

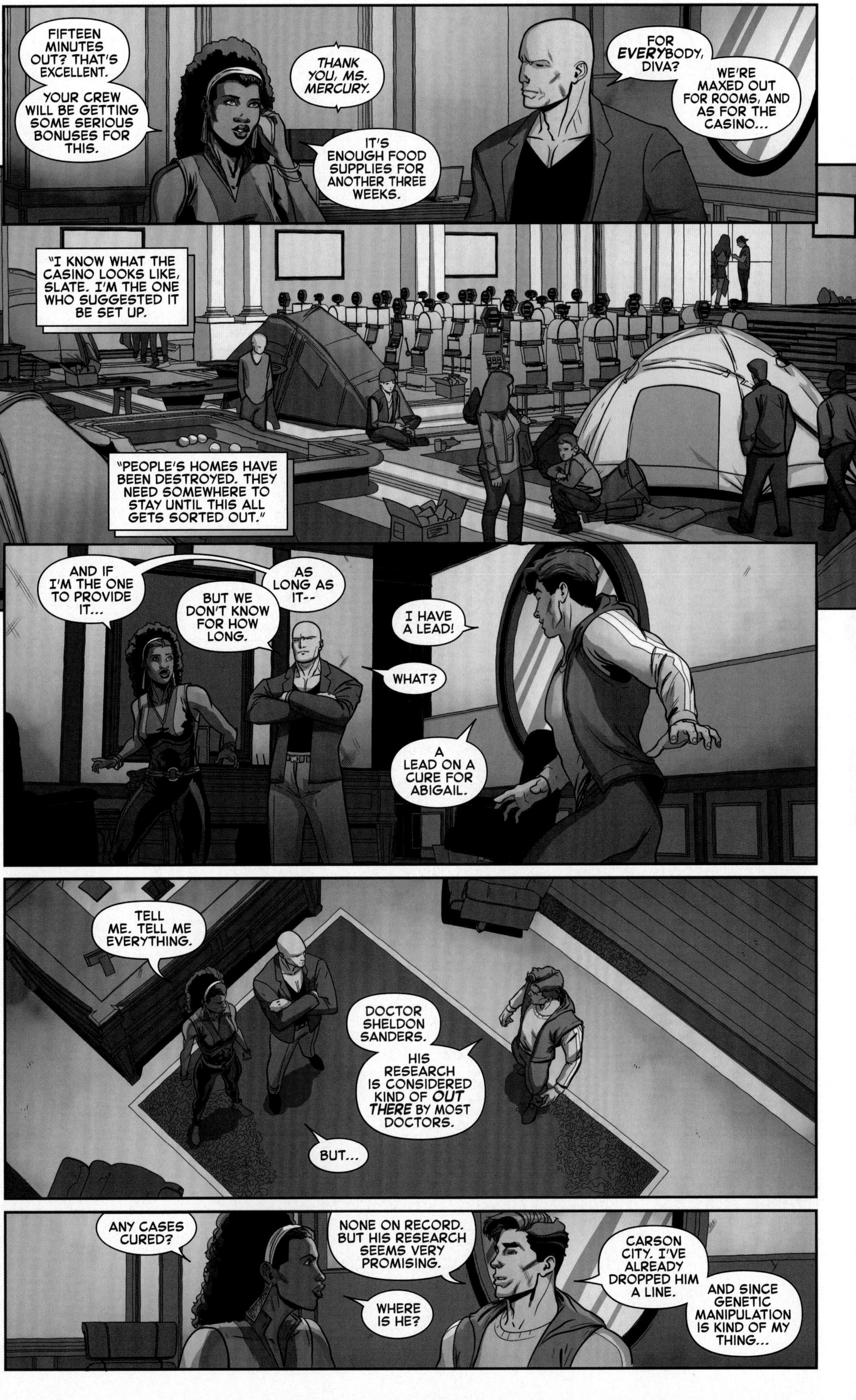
FIFTEEN MINUTES OUT? THAT'S EXCELLENT.
YOUR CREW WILL BE GETTING SOME SERIOUS BONUSES FOR THIS.
THANK YOU, MS. MERCURY.
IT'S ENOUGH FOOD SUPPLIES FOR ANOTHER THREE WEEKS.
FOR EVERYBODY, DIVA?
WE'RE MAXED OUT FOR ROOMS, AND AS FOR THE CASINO...
"I KNOW WHAT THE CASINO LOOKS LIKE, SLATE. I'M THE ONE WHO SUGGESTED IT BE SET UP.
"PEOPLE'S HOMES HAVE BEEN DESTROYED. THEY NEED SOMEWHERE TO STAY UNTIL THIS ALL GETS SORTED OUT."
AND IF I'M THE ONE TO PROVIDE IT...
BUT WE DON'T KNOW FOR HOW LONG.
AS LONG AS IT--
I HAVE A LEAD!
WHAT?
A LEAD ON A CURE FOR ABIGAIL.
TELL ME. TELL ME EVERYTHING.
DOCTOR SHELDON SANDERS.
HIS RESEARCH IS CONSIDERED KIND OF OUT THERE BY MOST DOCTORS.
BUT...
ANY CASES CURED?
NONE ON RECORD. BUT HIS RESEARCH SEEMS VERY PROMISING.
WHERE IS HE?
CARSON CITY. I'VE ALREADY DROPPED HIM A LINE.
AND SINCE GENETIC MANIPULATION IS KIND OF MY THING...

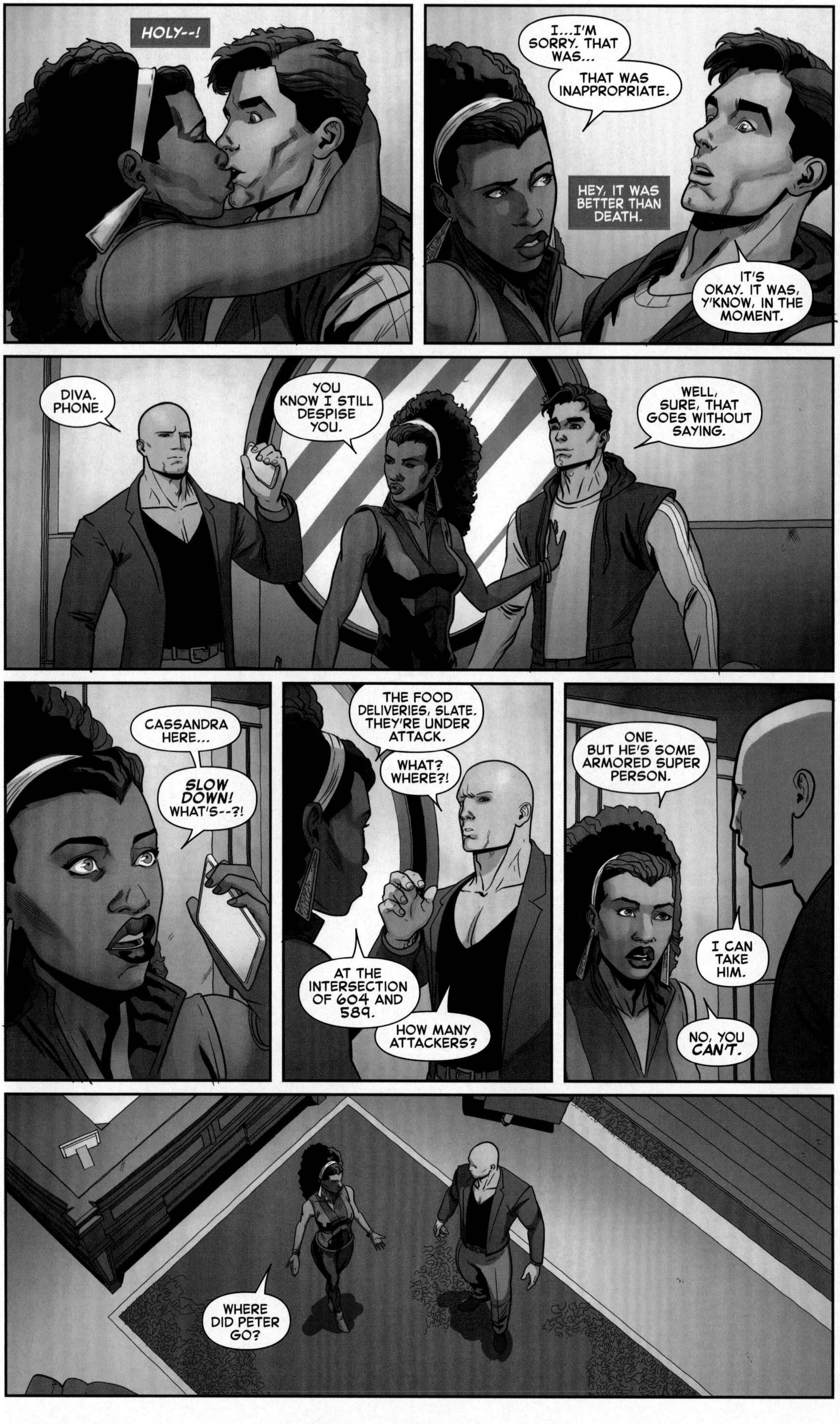
HOLY--!
I...I'M SORRY. THAT WAS...
THAT WAS INAPPROPRIATE.
HEY, IT WAS BETTER THAN DEATH.
IT'S OKAY. IT WAS, Y'KNOW, IN THE MOMENT.
DIVA. PHONE.
YOU KNOW I STILL DESPISE YOU.
WELL, SURE, THAT GOES WITHOUT SAYING.
CASSANDRA HERE...
SLOW DOWN! WHAT'S--?!
THE FOOD DELIVERIES, SLATE. THEY'RE UNDER ATTACK.
WHAT? WHERE?!
AT THE INTERSECTION OF 604 AND 589.
HOW MANY ATTACKERS?
ONE. BUT HE'S SOME ARMORED SUPER PERSON.
I CAN TAKE HIM.
NO, YOU CAN'T.
WHERE DID PETER GO?

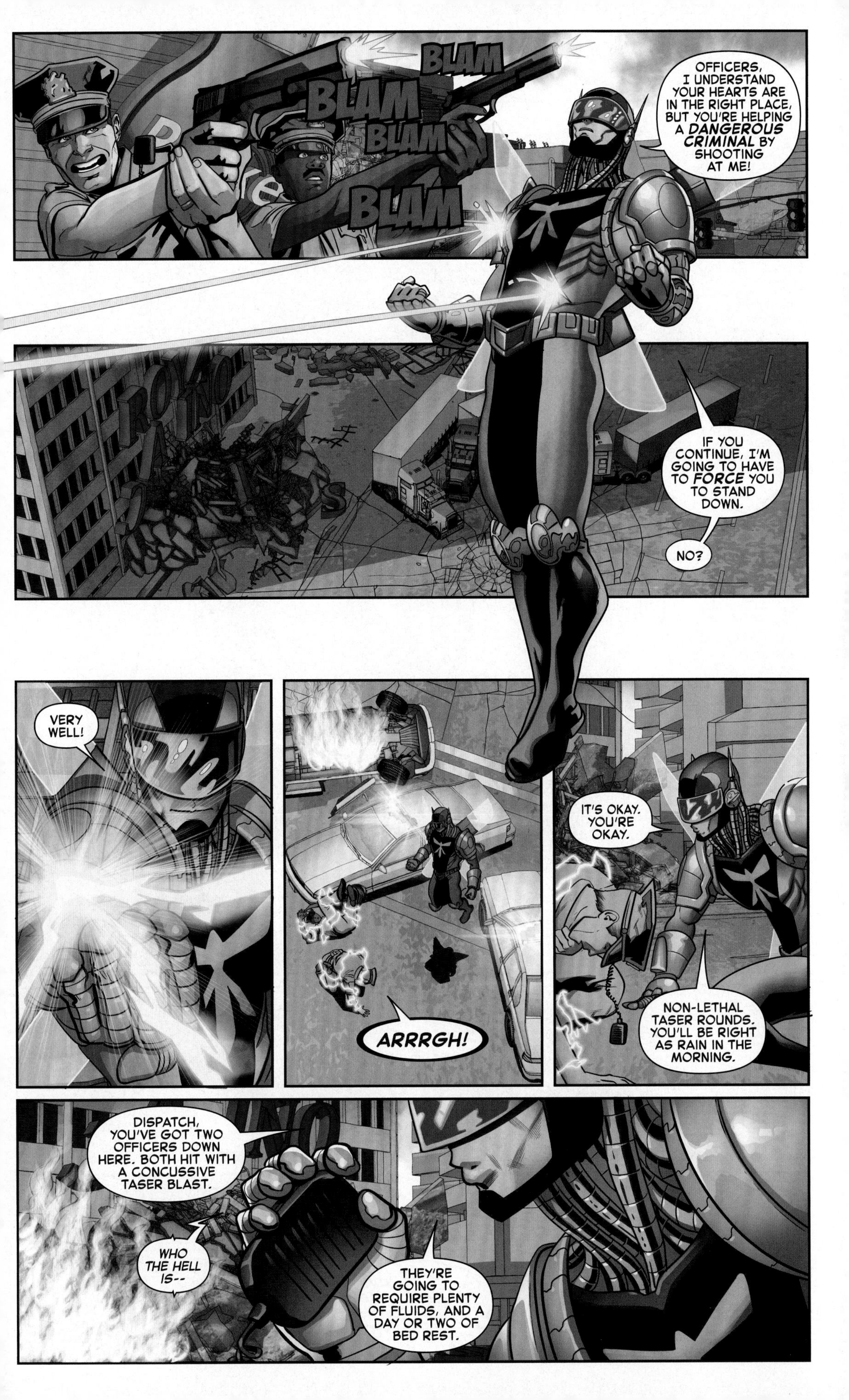
BLAM
BLAM
BLAM
BLAM
OFFICERS, I UNDERSTAND YOUR HEARTS ARE IN THE RIGHT PLACE, BUT YOU'RE HELPING A DANGEROUS CRIMINAL BY SHOOTING AT ME!
IF YOU CONTINUE, I'M GOING TO HAVE TO FORCE YOU TO STAND DOWN.
NO?
VERY WELL!
ARRRGH!
IT'S OKAY. YOU'RE OKAY.
NON-LETHAL TASER ROUNDS. YOU'LL BE RIGHT AS RAIN IN THE MORNING.
DISPATCH, YOU'VE GOT TWO OFFICERS DOWN HERE. BOTH HIT WITH A CONCUSSIVE TASER BLAST.
WHO THE HELL IS--
THEY'RE GOING TO REQUIRE PLENTY OF FLUIDS, AND A DAY OR TWO OF BED REST.

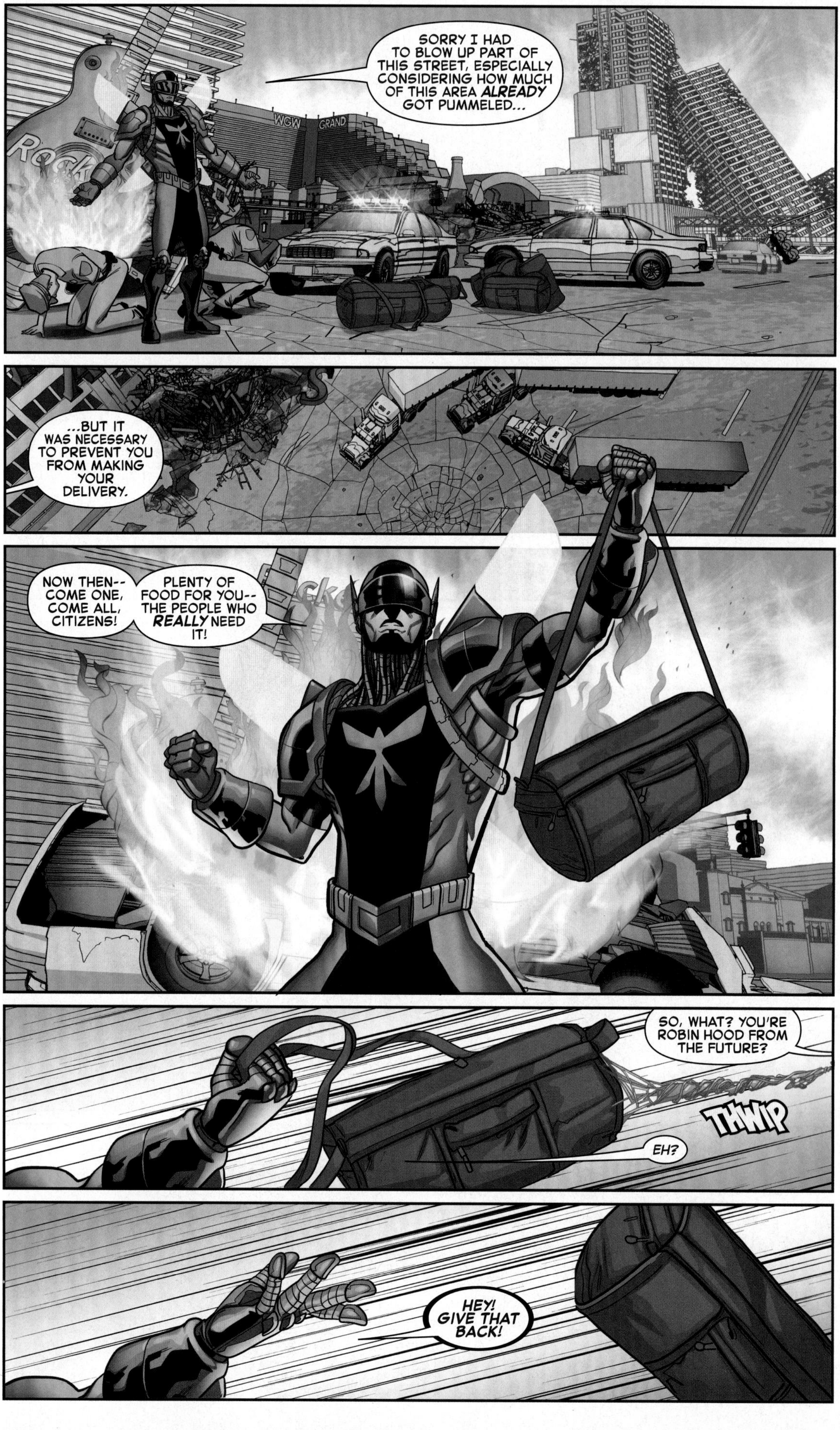
SORRY I HAD TO BLOW UP PART OF THIS STREET, ESPECIALLY CONSIDERING HOW MUCH OF THIS AREA *ALREADY* GOT PUMMELED...
WGW GRAND
...BUT IT WAS NECESSARY TO PREVENT YOU FROM MAKING YOUR DELIVERY.
NOW THEN-- COME ONE, COME ALL, CITIZENS!
PLENTY OF FOOD FOR YOU-- THE PEOPLE WHO *REALLY* NEED IT!
SO, WHAT? YOU'RE ROBIN HOOD FROM THE FUTURE?
THWIP
EH?
HEY! GIVE THAT BACK!

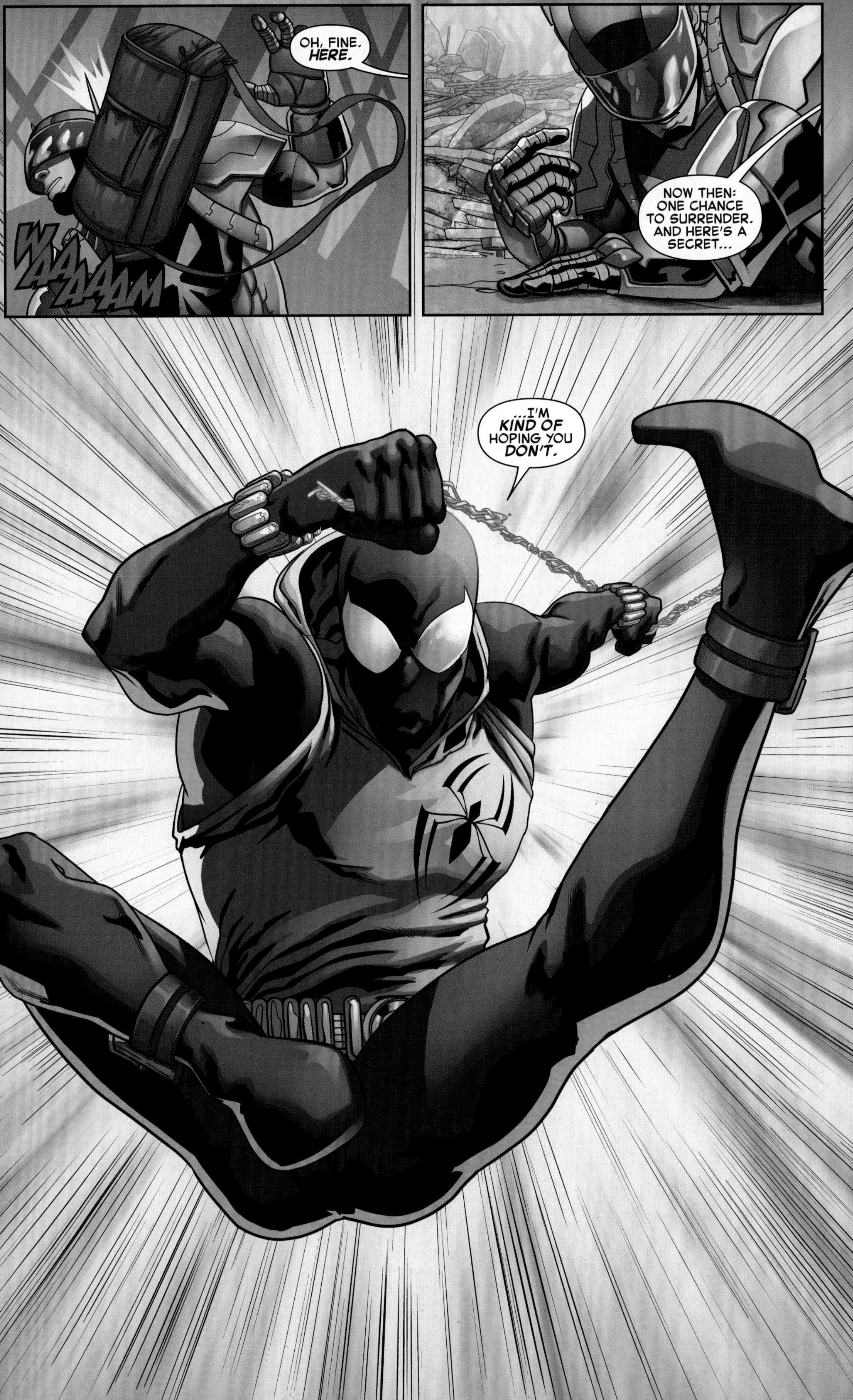
OH, FINE. HERE.
WAAAAAAM
NOW THEN: ONE CHANCE TO SURRENDER. AND HERE'S A SECRET...
...I'M KIND OF HOPING YOU DON'T.

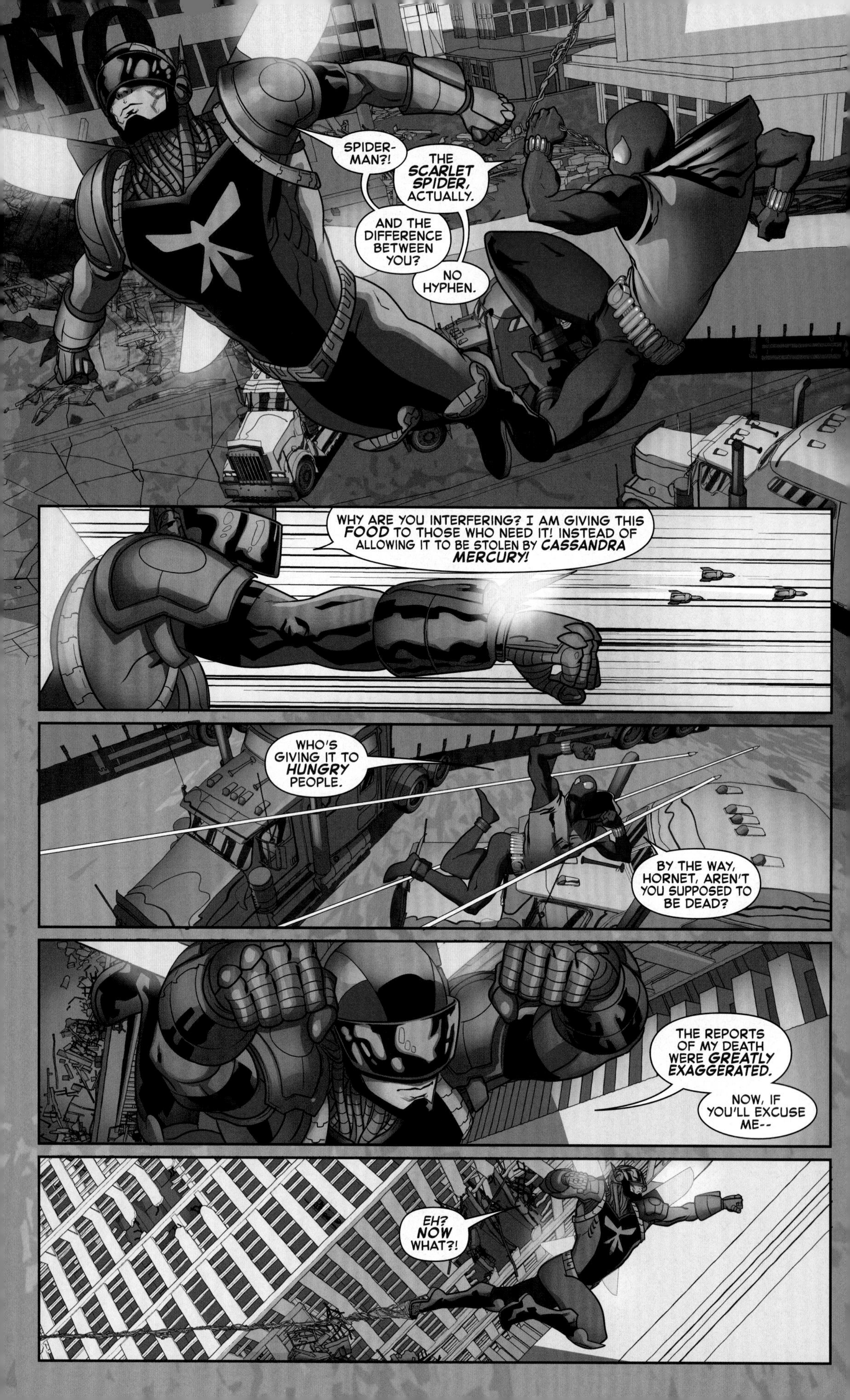
SPIDER-MAN?!
THE SCARLET SPIDER, ACTUALLY.
AND THE DIFFERENCE BETWEEN YOU?
NO HYPHEN.
WHY ARE YOU INTERFERING? I AM GIVING THIS FOOD TO THOSE WHO NEED IT! INSTEAD OF ALLOWING IT TO BE STOLEN BY CASSANDRA MERCURY!
WHO'S GIVING IT TO HUNGRY PEOPLE.
BY THE WAY, HORNET, AREN'T YOU SUPPOSED TO BE DEAD?
THE REPORTS OF MY DEATH WERE GREATLY EXAGGERATED.
NOW, IF YOU'LL EXCUSE ME--
EH? NOW WHAT?!

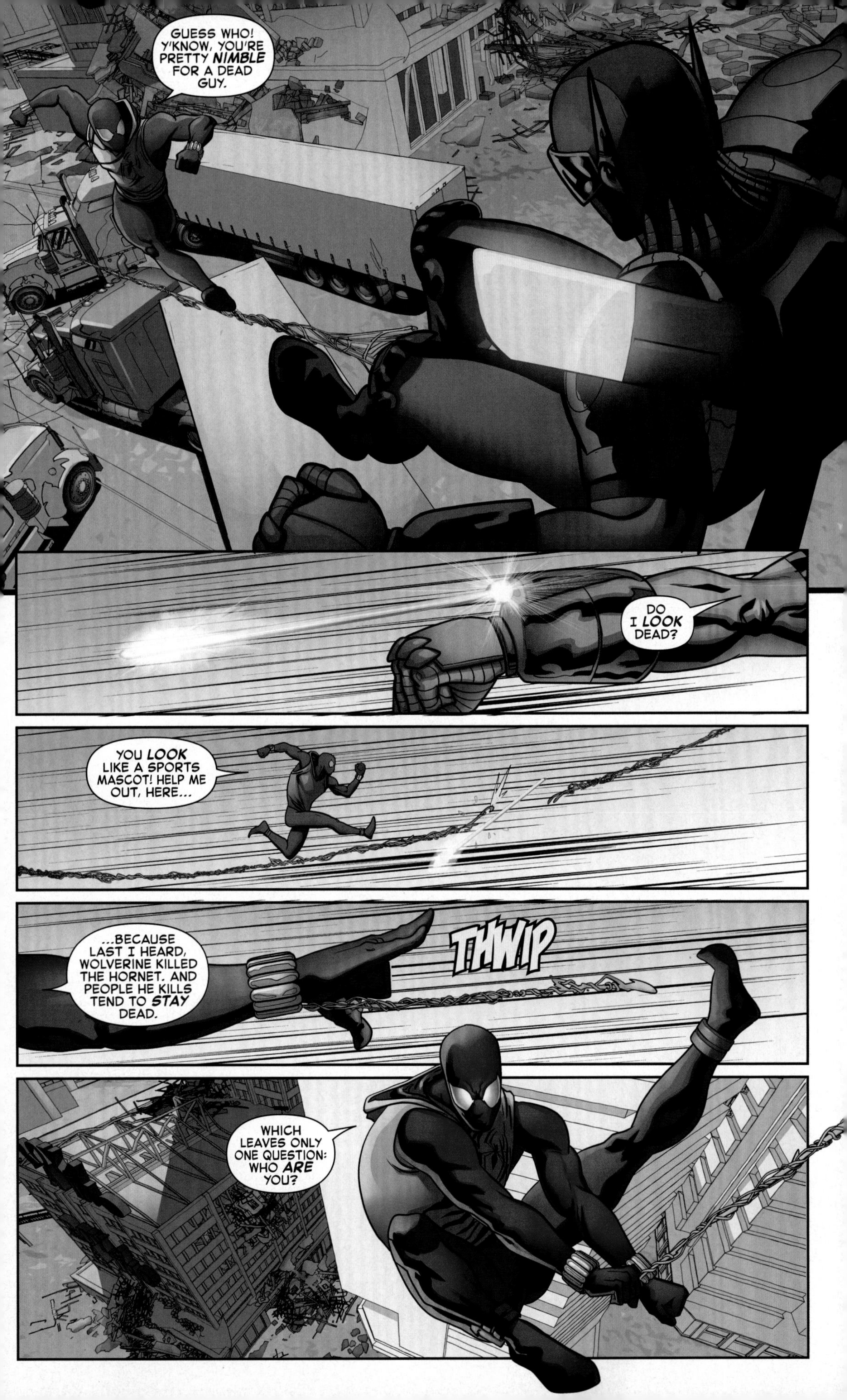
GUESS WHO! Y'KNOW, YOU'RE PRETTY NIMBLE FOR A DEAD GUY.
DO I LOOK DEAD?
YOU LOOK LIKE A SPORTS MASCOT! HELP ME OUT, HERE...
...BECAUSE LAST I HEARD, WOLVERINE KILLED THE HORNET. AND PEOPLE HE KILLS TEND TO STAY DEAD.
THWIP
WHICH LEAVES ONLY ONE QUESTION: WHO ARE YOU?

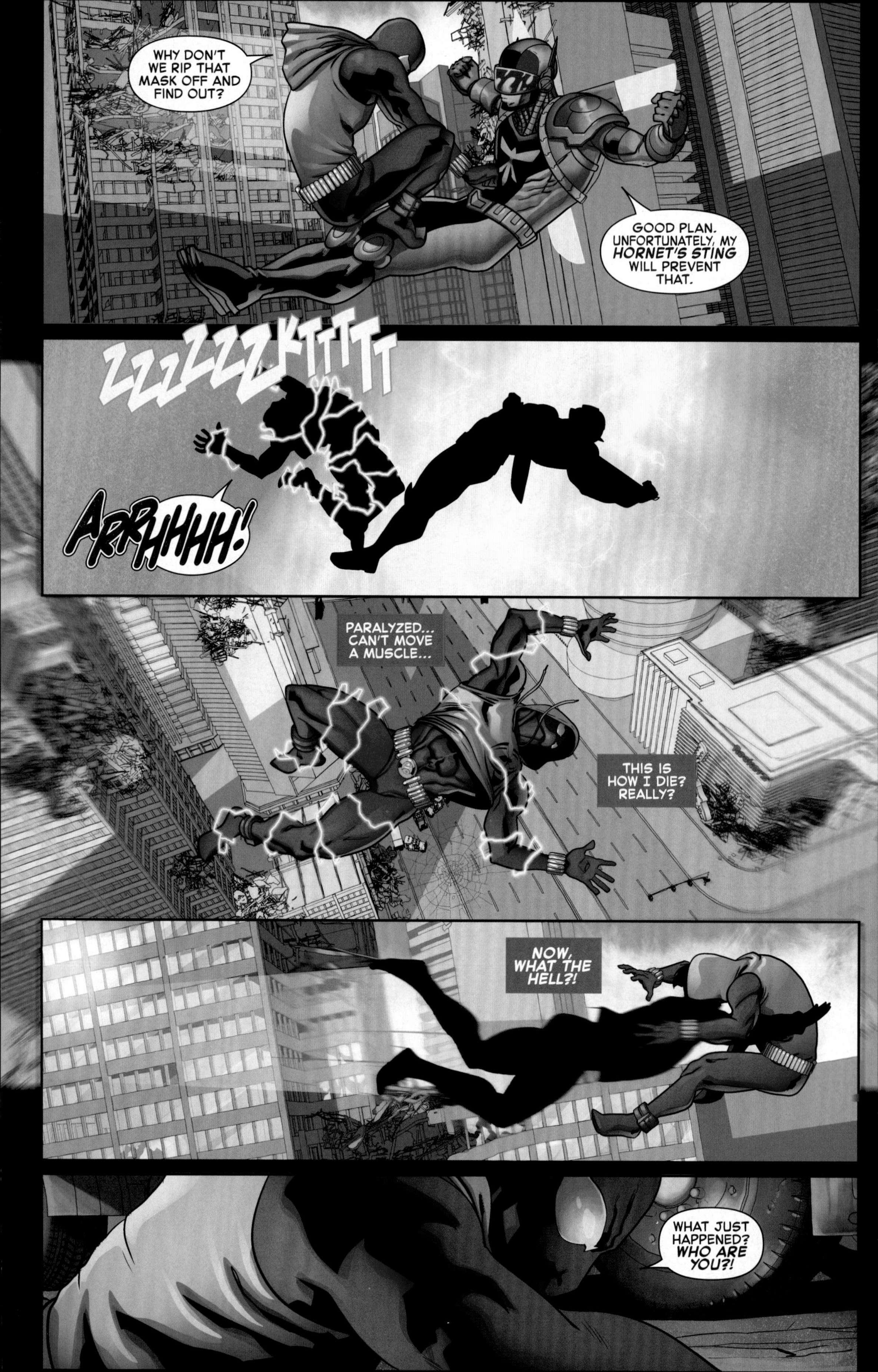
WHY DON'T WE RIP THAT MASK OFF AND FIND OUT?
GOOD PLAN. UNFORTUNATELY, MY *HORNET'S STING* WILL PREVENT THAT.
ZZZZZZKTTTTTT
ARRHHHH!
PARALYZED... CAN'T MOVE A MUSCLE...
THIS IS HOW I DIE? REALLY?
NOW, WHAT THE HELL?!
WHAT JUST HAPPENED? *WHO ARE YOU?!*

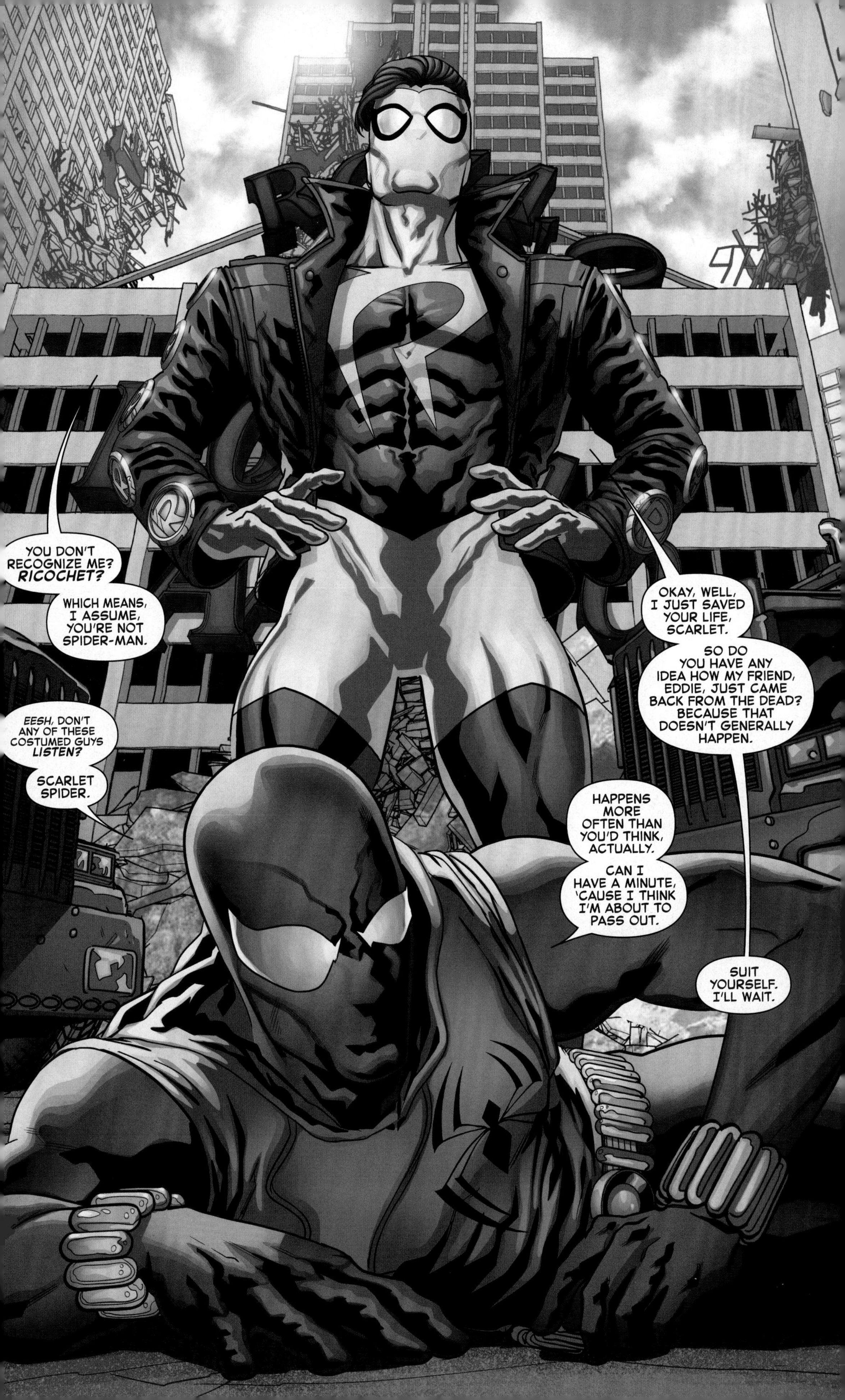

YOU DON'T RECOGNIZE ME? ***RICOCHET?***
WHICH MEANS, I ASSUME, YOU'RE NOT SPIDER-MAN.
EESH, DON'T ANY OF THESE COSTUMED GUYS ***LISTEN?***
SCARLET SPIDER.
OKAY, WELL, I JUST SAVED YOUR LIFE, SCARLET.
SO DO YOU HAVE ANY IDEA HOW MY FRIEND, EDDIE, JUST CAME BACK FROM THE DEAD? BECAUSE THAT DOESN'T GENERALLY HAPPEN.
HAPPENS MORE OFTEN THAN YOU'D THINK, ACTUALLY.
CAN I HAVE A MINUTE, 'CAUSE I THINK I'M ABOUT TO PASS OUT.
SUIT YOURSELF. I'LL WAIT.

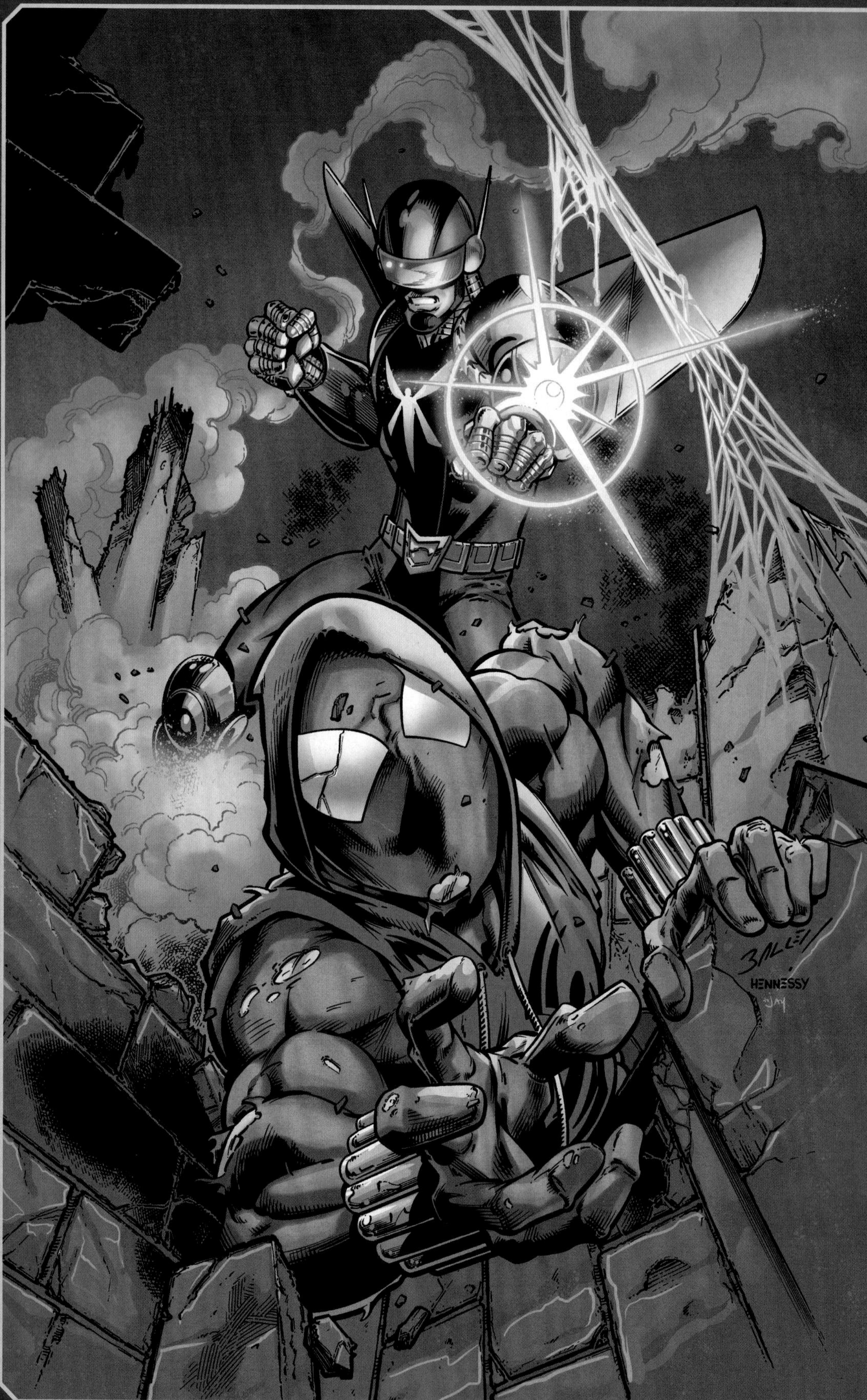
BAGLEY
HENNESSY
JAY

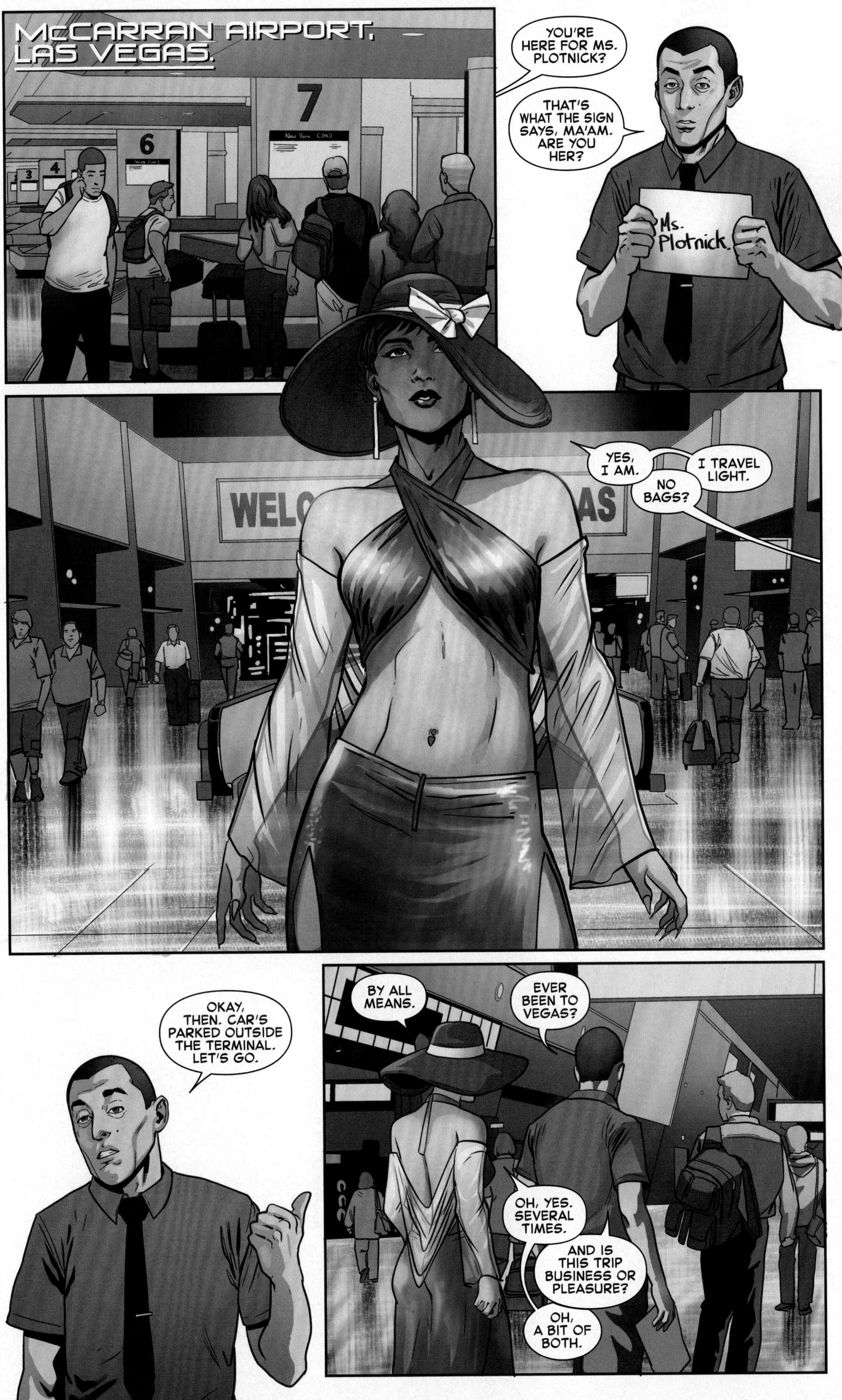
McCARRAN AIRPORT, LAS VEGAS.
YOU'RE HERE FOR MS. PLOTNICK?
THAT'S WHAT THE SIGN SAYS, MA'AM. ARE YOU HER?
Ms. Plotnick
YES, I AM.
NO BAGS?
I TRAVEL LIGHT.
OKAY, THEN. CAR'S PARKED OUTSIDE THE TERMINAL. LET'S GO.
BY ALL MEANS.
EVER BEEN TO VEGAS?
OH, YES. SEVERAL TIMES.
AND IS THIS TRIP BUSINESS OR PLEASURE?
OH, A BIT OF BOTH.

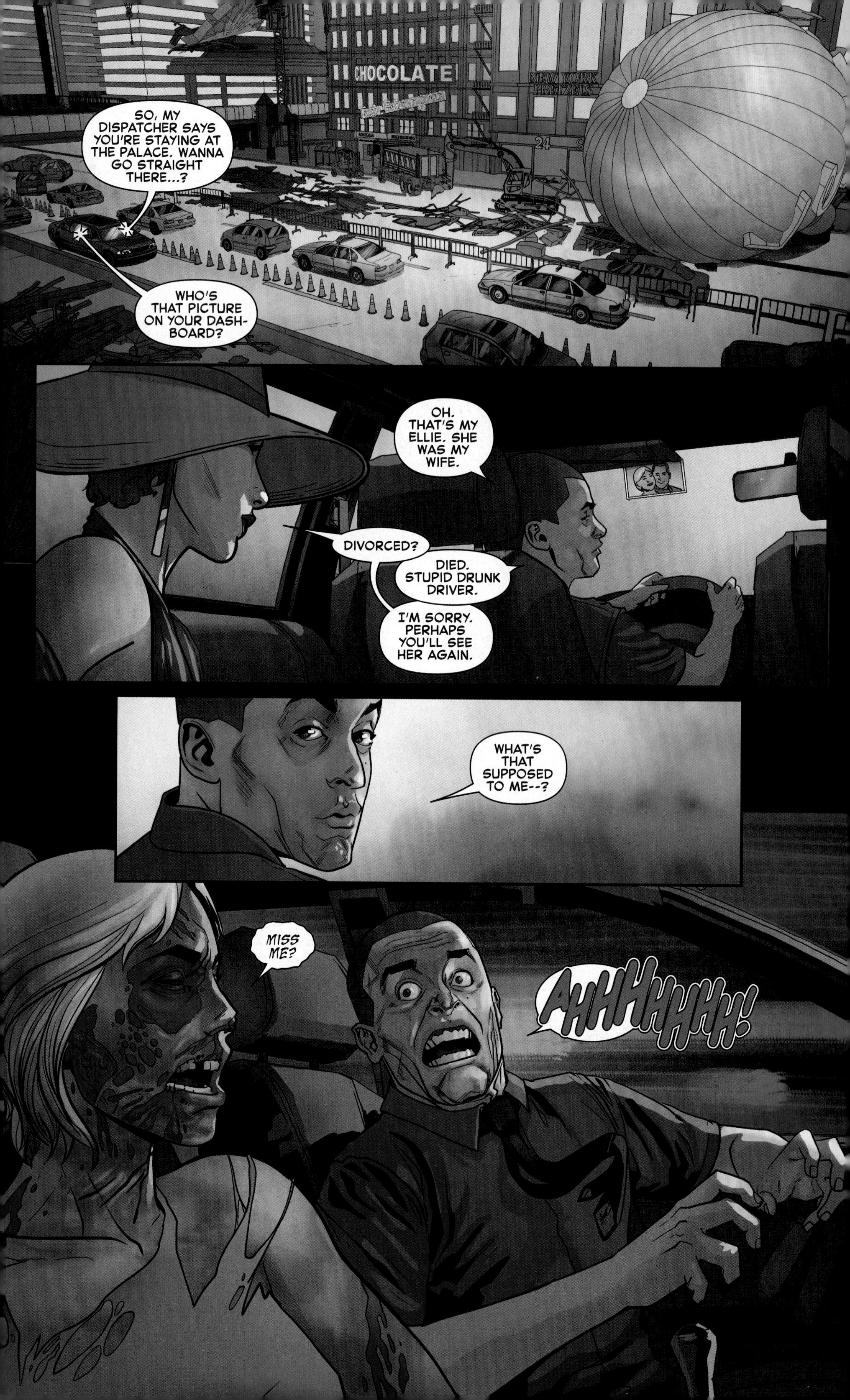
CHOCOLATE
NEW YORK PRETZELS
SO, MY DISPATCHER SAYS YOU'RE STAYING AT THE PALACE. WANNA GO STRAIGHT THERE...?
WHO'S THAT PICTURE ON YOUR DASH-BOARD?
OH. THAT'S MY ELLIE. SHE WAS MY WIFE.
DIVORCED?
DIED. STUPID DRUNK DRIVER.
I'M SORRY. PERHAPS YOU'LL SEE HER AGAIN.
WHAT'S THAT SUPPOSED TO ME--?
MISS ME?
AHHHHHHH!

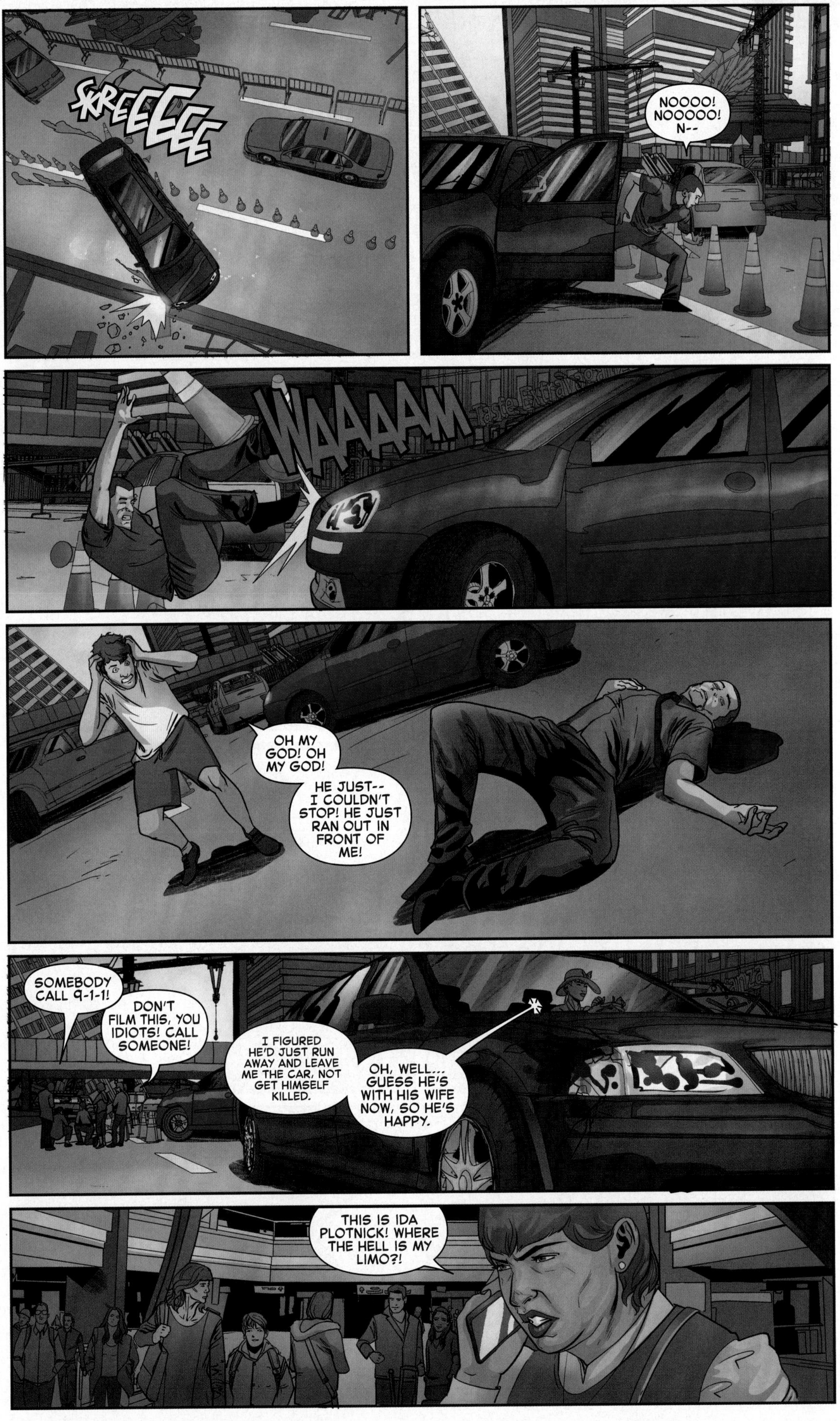
SKREEEEEE
NOOOO! NOOOOO! N--
WAAAAM
OH MY GOD! OH MY GOD!
HE JUST-- I COULDN'T STOP! HE JUST RAN OUT IN FRONT OF ME!
SOMEBODY CALL 9-1-1!
DON'T FILM THIS, YOU IDIOTS! CALL SOMEONE!
I FIGURED HE'D JUST RUN AWAY AND LEAVE ME THE CAR, NOT GET HIMSELF KILLED.
OH, WELL... GUESS HE'S WITH HIS WIFE NOW, SO HE'S HAPPY.
THIS IS IDA PLOTNICK! WHERE THE HELL IS MY LIMO?!

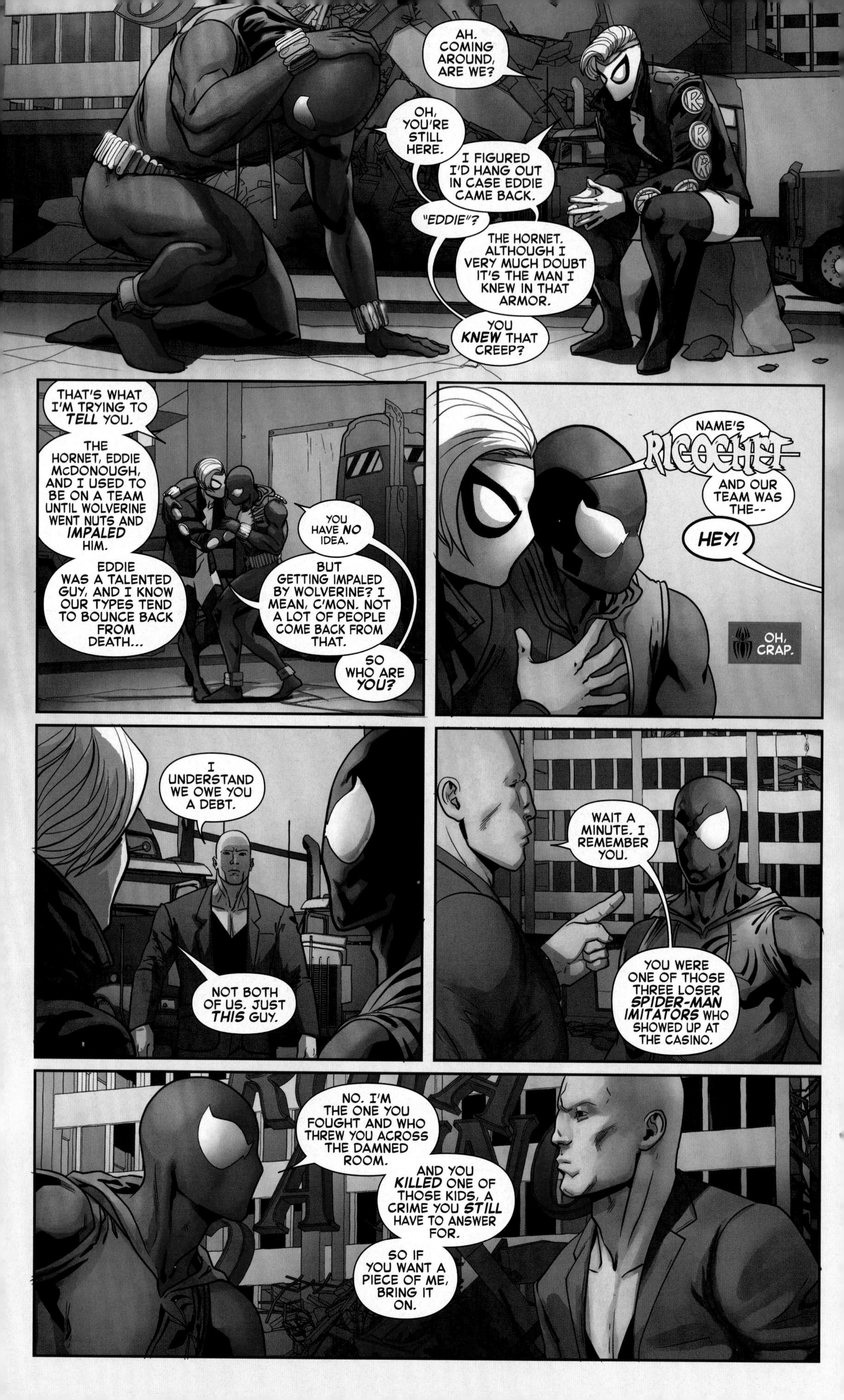

AH. COMING AROUND, ARE WE?
OH, YOU'RE STILL HERE.
I FIGURED I'D HANG OUT IN CASE EDDIE CAME BACK.
"EDDIE"?
THE HORNET. ALTHOUGH I VERY MUCH DOUBT IT'S THE MAN I KNEW IN THAT ARMOR.
YOU KNEW THAT CREEP?
THAT'S WHAT I'M TRYING TO TELL YOU.
THE HORNET, EDDIE McDONOUGH, AND I USED TO BE ON A TEAM UNTIL WOLVERINE WENT NUTS AND IMPALED HIM.
EDDIE WAS A TALENTED GUY, AND I KNOW OUR TYPES TEND TO BOUNCE BACK FROM DEATH...
YOU HAVE NO IDEA.
BUT GETTING IMPALED BY WOLVERINE? I MEAN, C'MON. NOT A LOT OF PEOPLE COME BACK FROM THAT.
SO WHO ARE YOU?
NAME'S RICOCHET
AND OUR TEAM WAS THE--
HEY!
OH, CRAP.
I UNDERSTAND WE OWE YOU A DEBT.
NOT BOTH OF US. JUST THIS GUY.
WAIT A MINUTE. I REMEMBER YOU.
YOU WERE ONE OF THOSE THREE LOSER SPIDER-MAN IMITATORS WHO SHOWED UP AT THE CASINO.
NO. I'M THE ONE YOU FOUGHT AND WHO THREW YOU ACROSS THE DAMNED ROOM.
AND YOU KILLED ONE OF THOSE KIDS, A CRIME YOU STILL HAVE TO ANSWER FOR.
SO IF YOU WANT A PIECE OF ME, BRING IT ON.

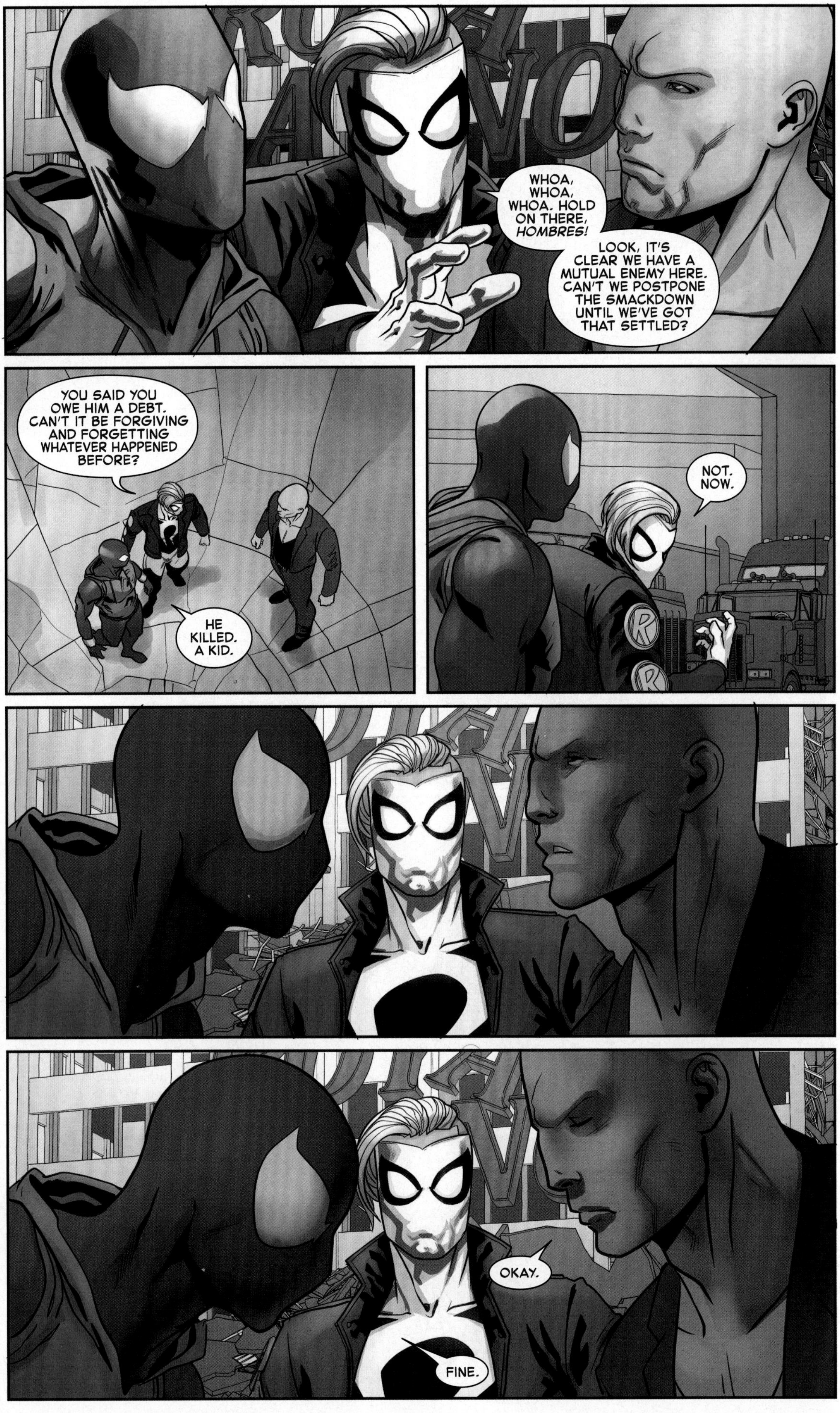
WHOA, WHOA, WHOA. HOLD ON THERE, *HOMBRES!*
LOOK, IT'S CLEAR WE HAVE A MUTUAL ENEMY HERE. CAN'T WE POSTPONE THE SMACKDOWN UNTIL WE'VE GOT THAT SETTLED?
YOU SAID YOU OWE HIM A DEBT. CAN'T IT BE FORGIVING AND FORGETTING WHATEVER HAPPENED BEFORE?
HE KILLED. A KID.
NOT. NOW.
OKAY.
FINE.

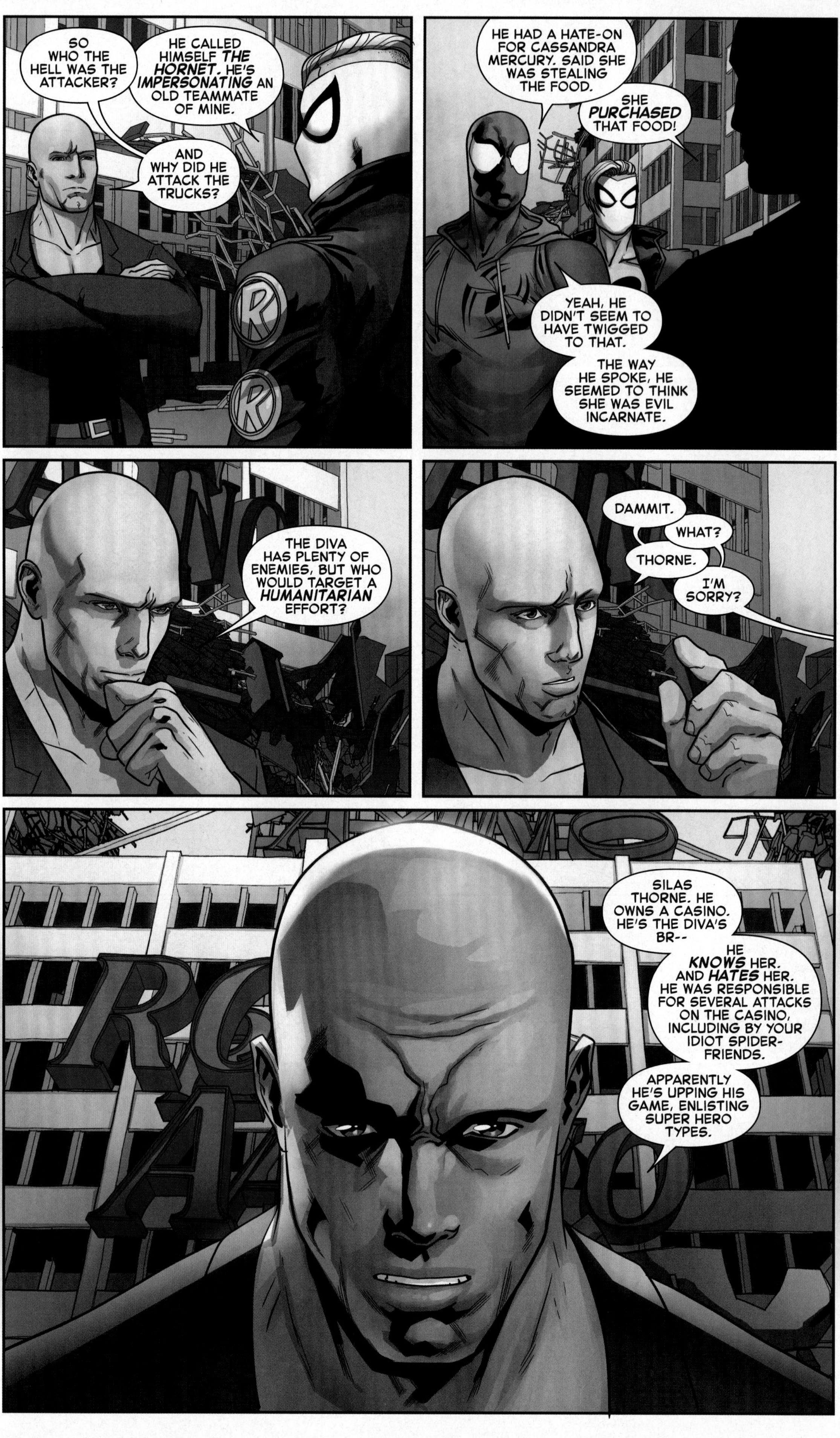

SO WHO THE HELL WAS THE ATTACKER?
HE CALLED HIMSELF **THE HORNET.** HE'S ***IMPERSONATING*** AN OLD TEAMMATE OF MINE.
AND WHY DID HE ATTACK THE TRUCKS?
HE HAD A HATE-ON FOR CASSANDRA MERCURY. SAID SHE WAS STEALING THE FOOD.
SHE ***PURCHASED*** THAT FOOD!
YEAH, HE DIDN'T SEEM TO HAVE TWIGGED TO THAT.
THE WAY HE SPOKE, HE SEEMED TO THINK SHE WAS EVIL INCARNATE.
THE DIVA HAS PLENTY OF ENEMIES, BUT WHO WOULD TARGET A ***HUMANITARIAN*** EFFORT?
DAMMIT.
WHAT?
THORNE.
I'M SORRY?
SILAS THORNE. HE OWNS A CASINO. HE'S THE DIVA'S BR--
HE ***KNOWS*** HER. AND ***HATES*** HER. HE WAS RESPONSIBLE FOR SEVERAL ATTACKS ON THE CASINO, INCLUDING BY YOUR IDIOT SPIDER-FRIENDS.
APPARENTLY HE'S UPPING HIS GAME, ENLISTING SUPER HERO TYPES.

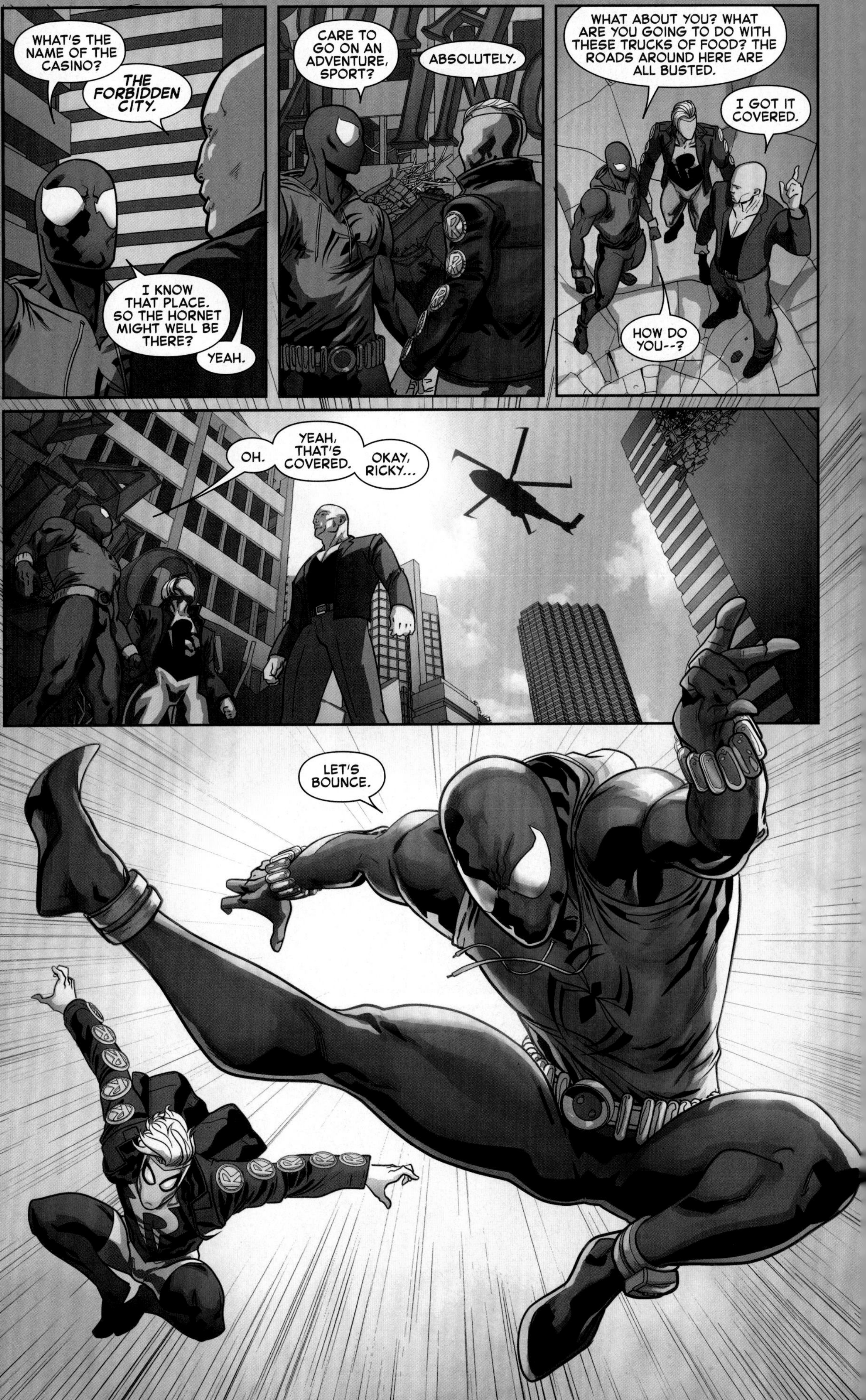

WHAT'S THE NAME OF THE CASINO?
THE FORBIDDEN CITY.
I KNOW THAT PLACE. SO THE HORNET MIGHT WELL BE THERE?
YEAH.
CARE TO GO ON AN ADVENTURE, SPORT?
ABSOLUTELY.
WHAT ABOUT YOU? WHAT ARE YOU GOING TO DO WITH THESE TRUCKS OF FOOD? THE ROADS AROUND HERE ARE ALL BUSTED.
I GOT IT COVERED.
HOW DO YOU--?
OH.
YEAH, THAT'S COVERED.
OKAY, RICKY...
LET'S BOUNCE.

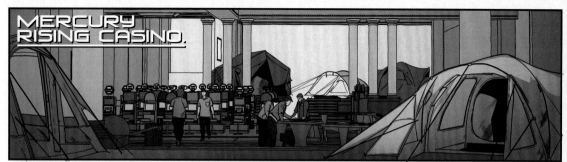

CAN I TRY?

NO. GO TO YOUR MOTHER.

SHE'S DEAD. MY DADDY, TOO. WHEN THE BAD MEN BOMBED EVERYONE.

PULL THAT CHAIR OVER.

UH, MA'AM, A CHILD CAN'T PLAY ANY OF THE GAMES IN THE CAS--

DROP DEAD!

RIGHT, OKAY.

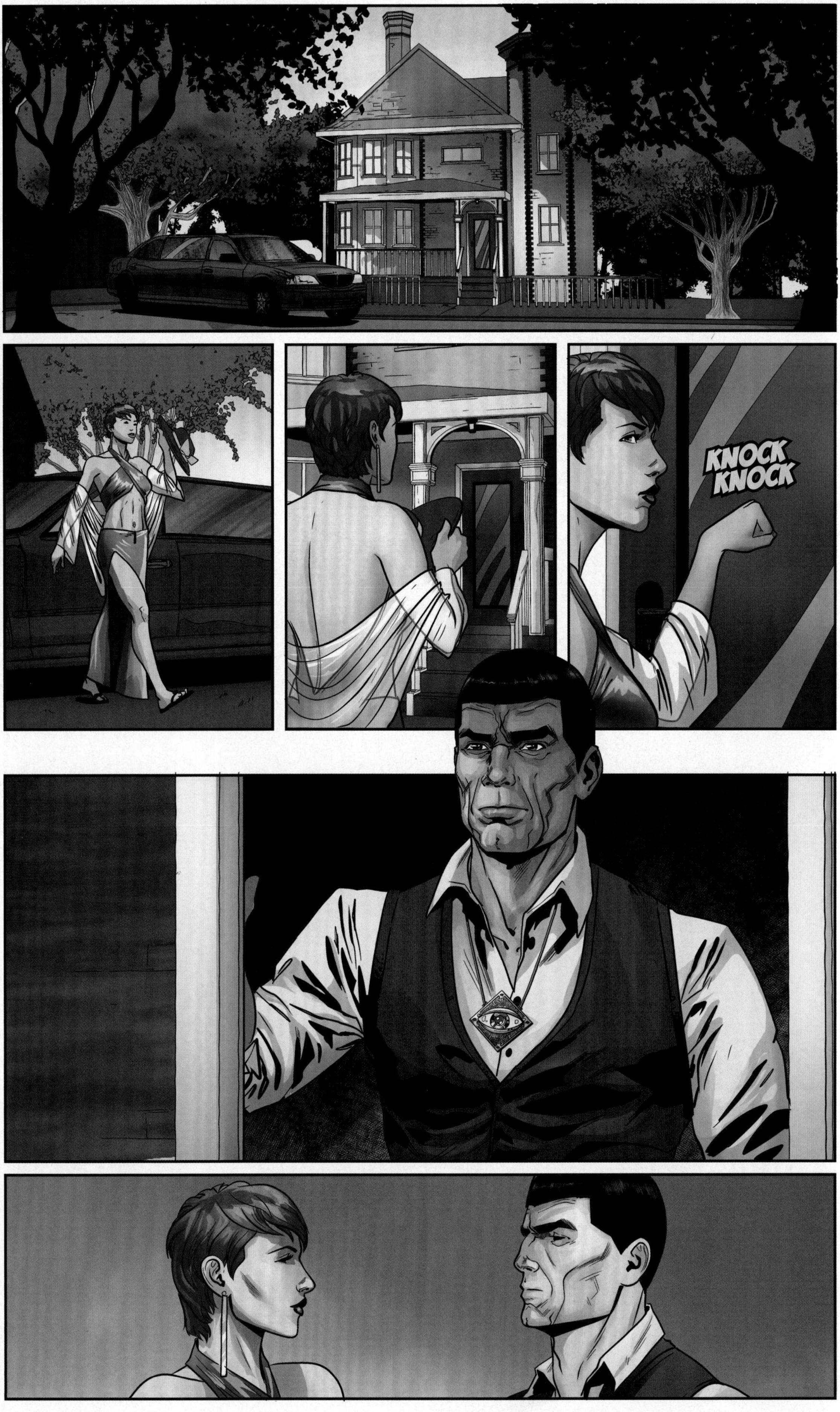
KNOCK KNOCK

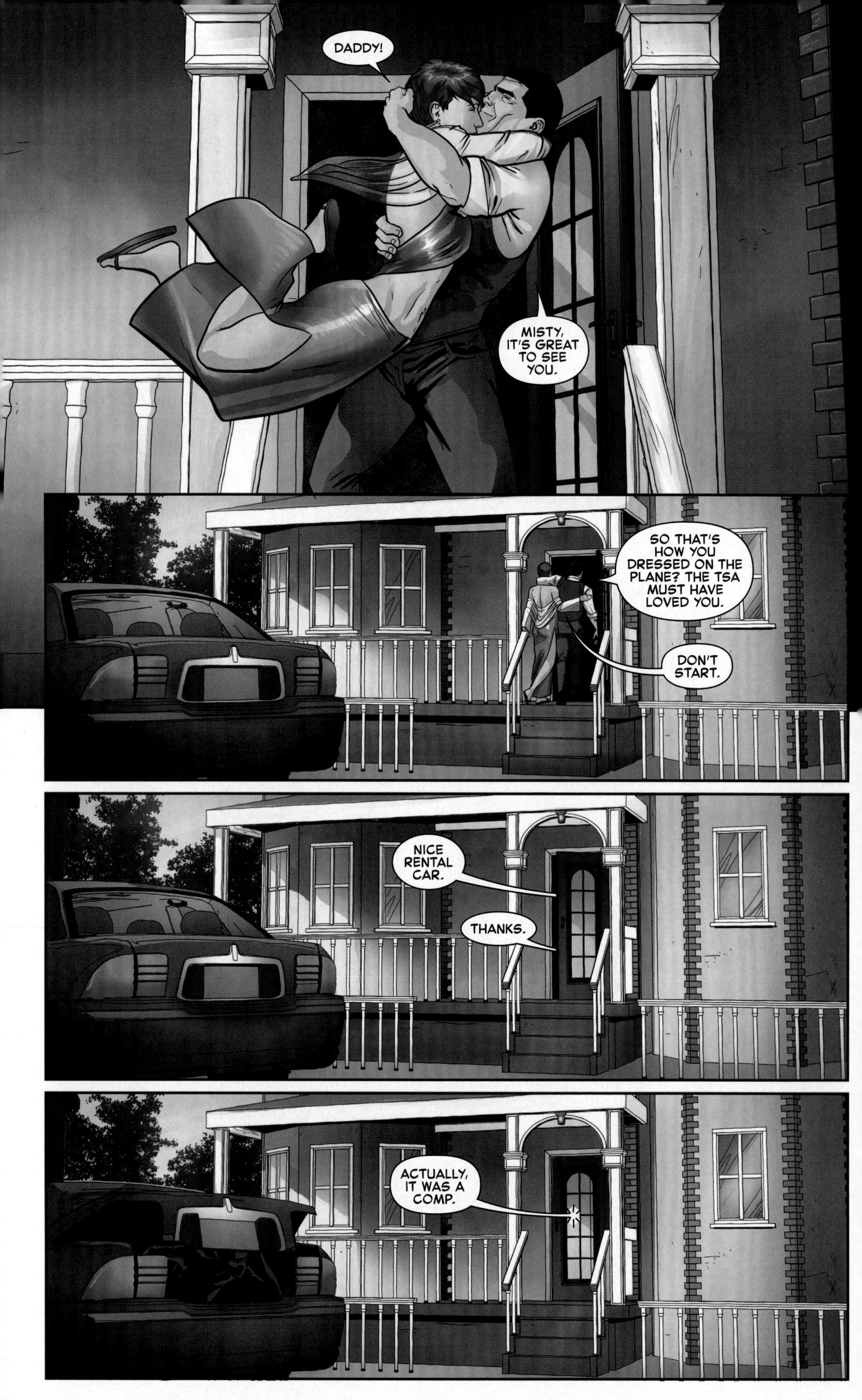
DADDY!
MISTY, IT'S GREAT TO SEE YOU.
SO THAT'S HOW YOU DRESSED ON THE PLANE? THE TSA MUST HAVE LOVED YOU.
DON'T START.
NICE RENTAL CAR.
THANKS.
ACTUALLY, IT WAS A COMP.

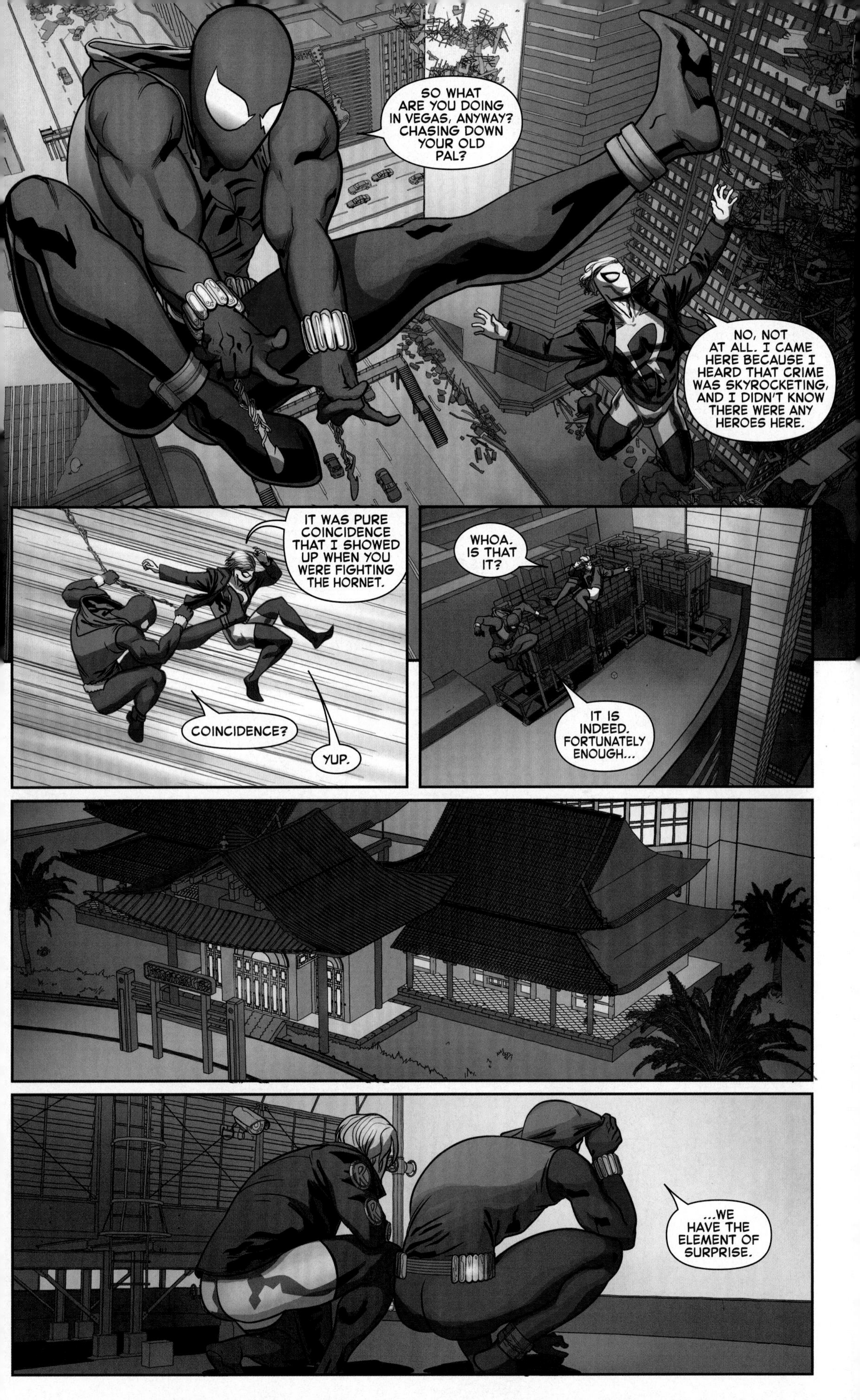
SO WHAT ARE YOU DOING IN VEGAS, ANYWAY? CHASING DOWN YOUR OLD PAL?
NO, NOT AT ALL. I CAME HERE BECAUSE I HEARD THAT CRIME WAS SKYROCKETING, AND I DIDN'T KNOW THERE WERE ANY HEROES HERE.
IT WAS PURE COINCIDENCE THAT I SHOWED UP WHEN YOU WERE FIGHTING THE HORNET.
COINCIDENCE?
YUP.
WHOA. IS THAT IT?
IT IS INDEED. FORTUNATELY ENOUGH...
...WE HAVE THE ELEMENT OF SURPRISE.

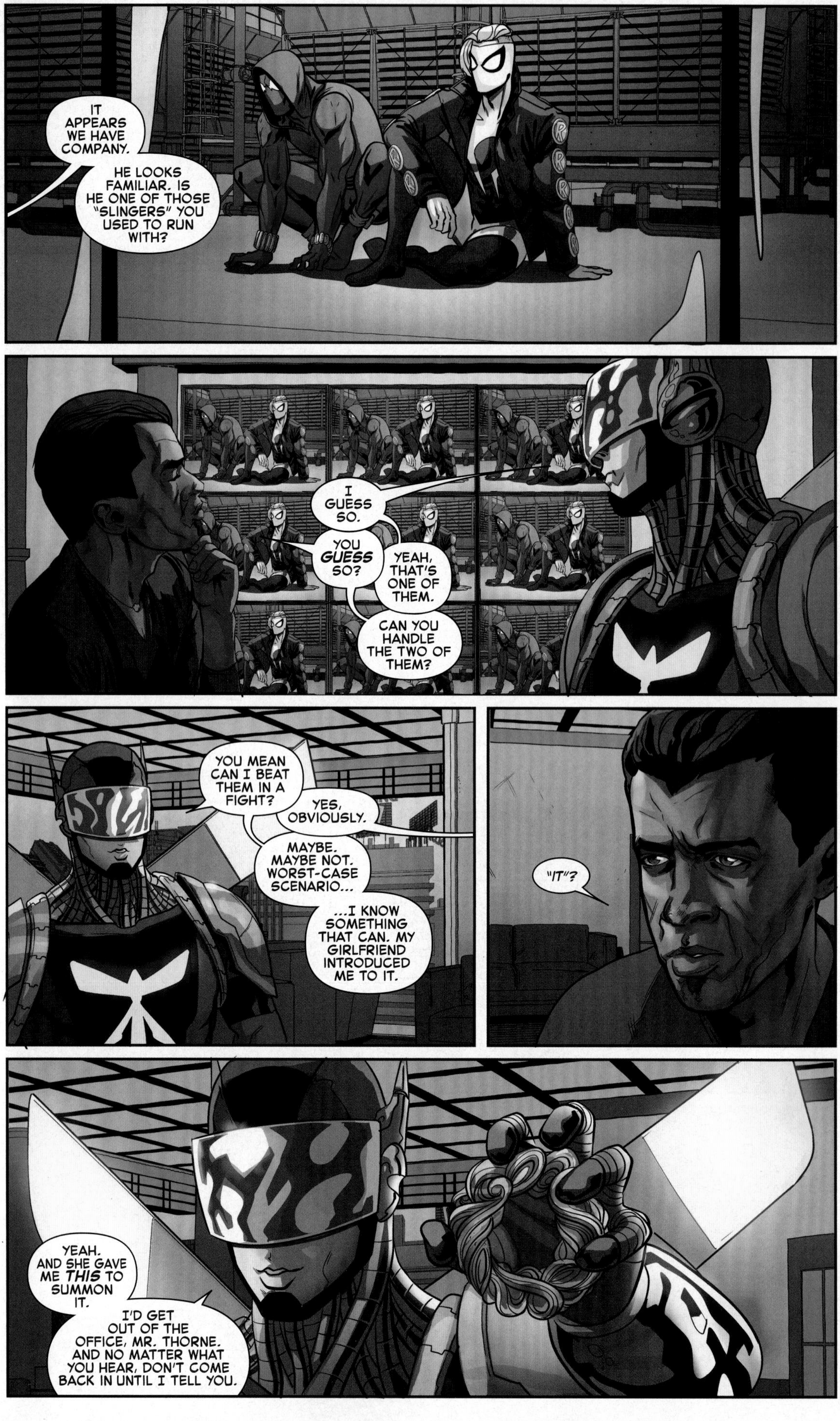
IT APPEARS WE HAVE COMPANY.
HE LOOKS FAMILIAR. IS HE ONE OF THOSE "SLINGERS" YOU USED TO RUN WITH?
I GUESS SO.
YOU *GUESS* SO?
YEAH, THAT'S ONE OF THEM.
CAN YOU HANDLE THE TWO OF THEM?
YOU MEAN CAN I BEAT THEM IN A FIGHT?
YES, OBVIOUSLY.
MAYBE. MAYBE NOT. WORST-CASE SCENARIO...
...I KNOW SOMETHING THAT CAN. MY GIRLFRIEND INTRODUCED ME TO IT.
"IT"?
YEAH. AND SHE GAVE ME *THIS* TO SUMMON IT.
I'D GET OUT OF THE OFFICE, MR. THORNE. AND NO MATTER WHAT YOU HEAR, DON'T COME BACK IN UNTIL I TELL YOU.

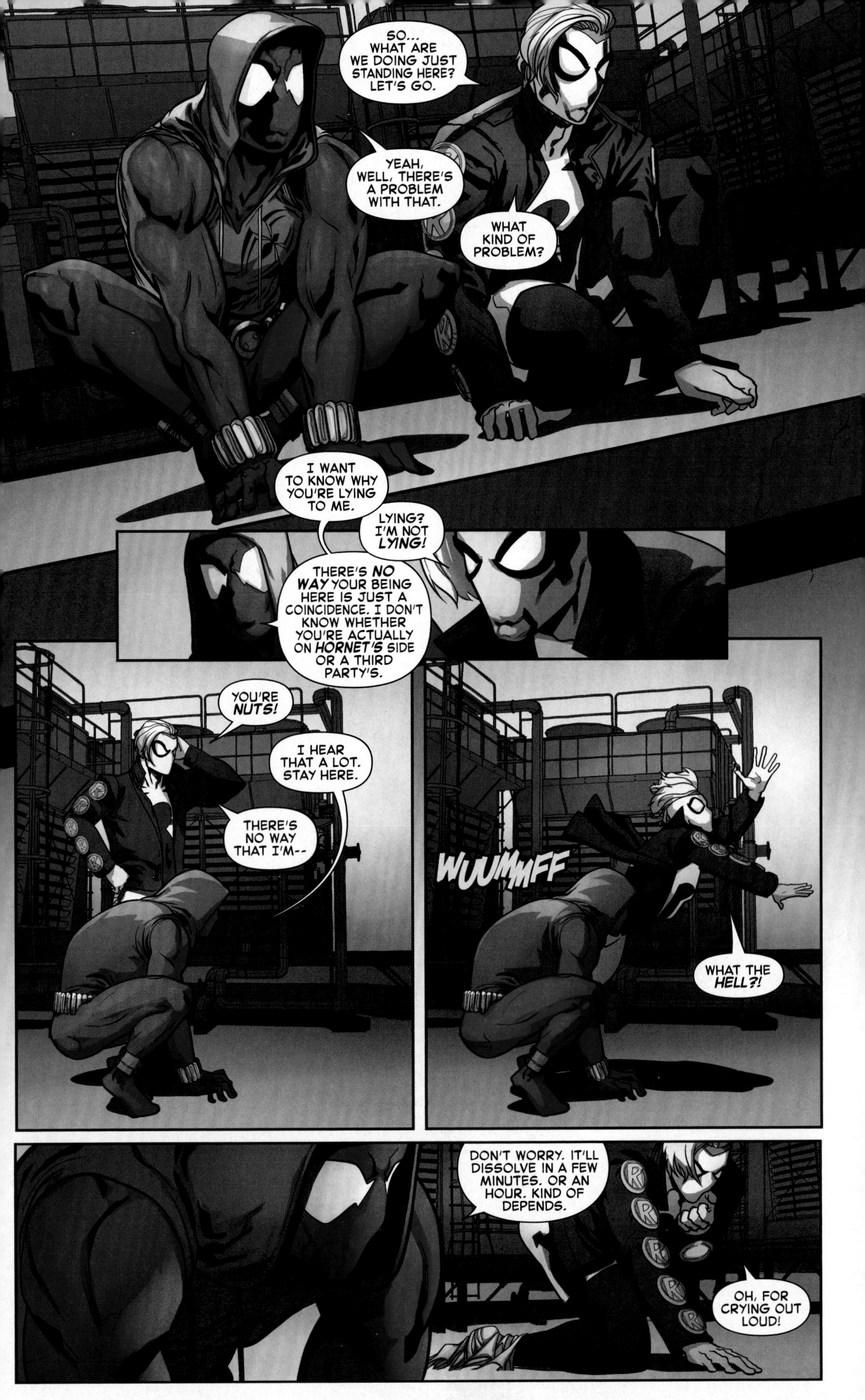

SO... WHAT ARE WE DOING JUST STANDING HERE? LET'S GO.
YEAH, WELL, THERE'S A PROBLEM WITH THAT.
WHAT KIND OF PROBLEM?
I WANT TO KNOW WHY YOU'RE LYING TO ME.
LYING? I'M NOT LYING!
THERE'S NO WAY YOUR BEING HERE IS JUST A COINCIDENCE. I DON'T KNOW WHETHER YOU'RE ACTUALLY ON HORNET'S SIDE OR A THIRD PARTY'S.
YOU'RE NUTS!
I HEAR THAT A LOT. STAY HERE.
THERE'S NO WAY THAT I'M--
WUUMMFF
WHAT THE HELL?!
DON'T WORRY. IT'LL DISSOLVE IN A FEW MINUTES. OR AN HOUR. KIND OF DEPENDS.
OH, FOR CRYING OUT LOUD!

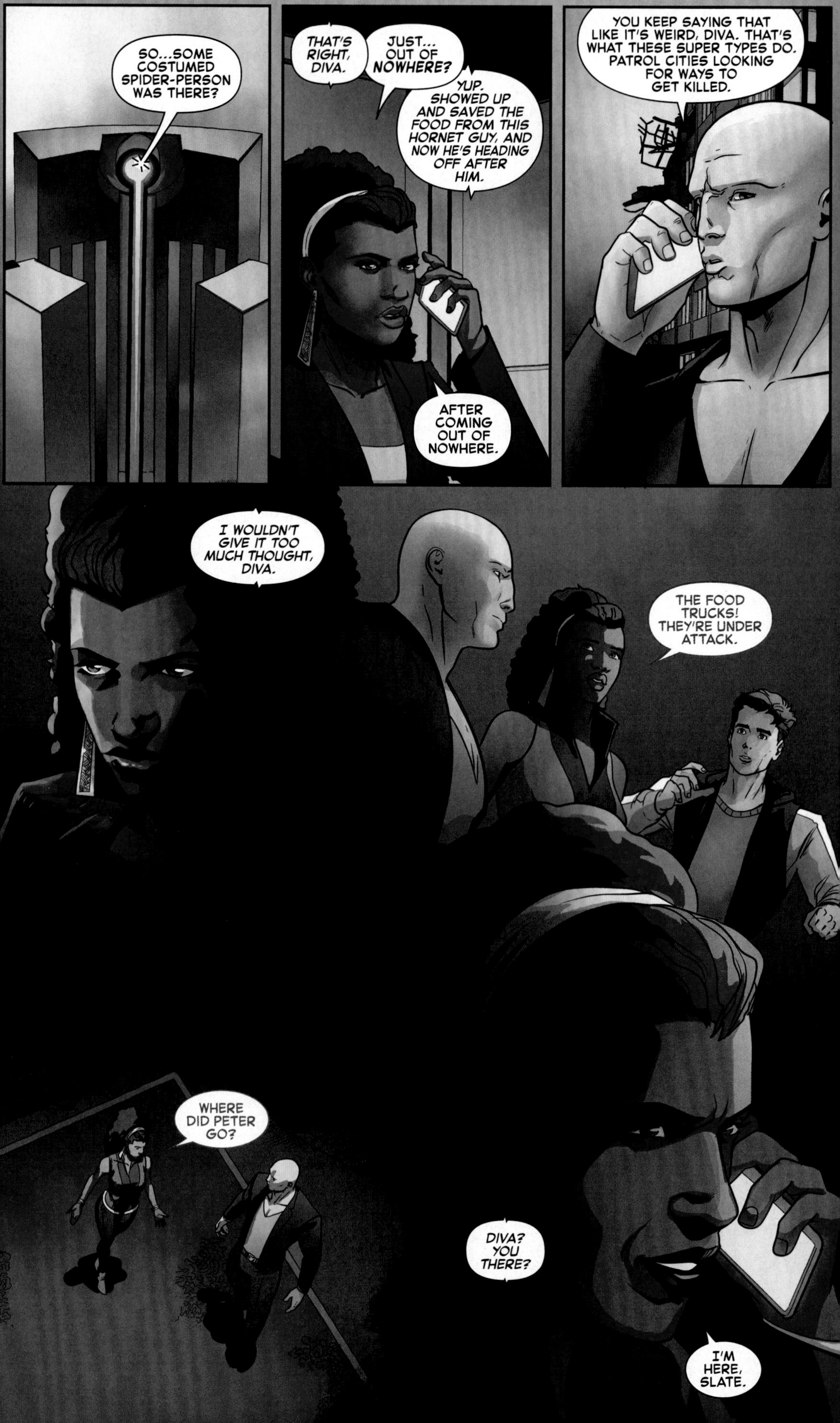
SO...SOME COSTUMED SPIDER-PERSON WAS THERE?
THAT'S RIGHT, DIVA.
JUST... OUT OF NOWHERE?
YUP. SHOWED UP AND SAVED THE FOOD FROM THIS HORNET GUY, AND NOW HE'S HEADING OFF AFTER HIM.
AFTER COMING OUT OF NOWHERE.
YOU KEEP SAYING THAT LIKE IT'S WEIRD, DIVA. THAT'S WHAT THESE SUPER TYPES DO. PATROL CITIES LOOKING FOR WAYS TO GET KILLED.
I WOULDN'T GIVE IT TOO MUCH THOUGHT, DIVA.
THE FOOD TRUCKS! THEY'RE UNDER ATTACK.
WHERE DID PETER GO?
DIVA? YOU THERE?
I'M HERE, SLATE.

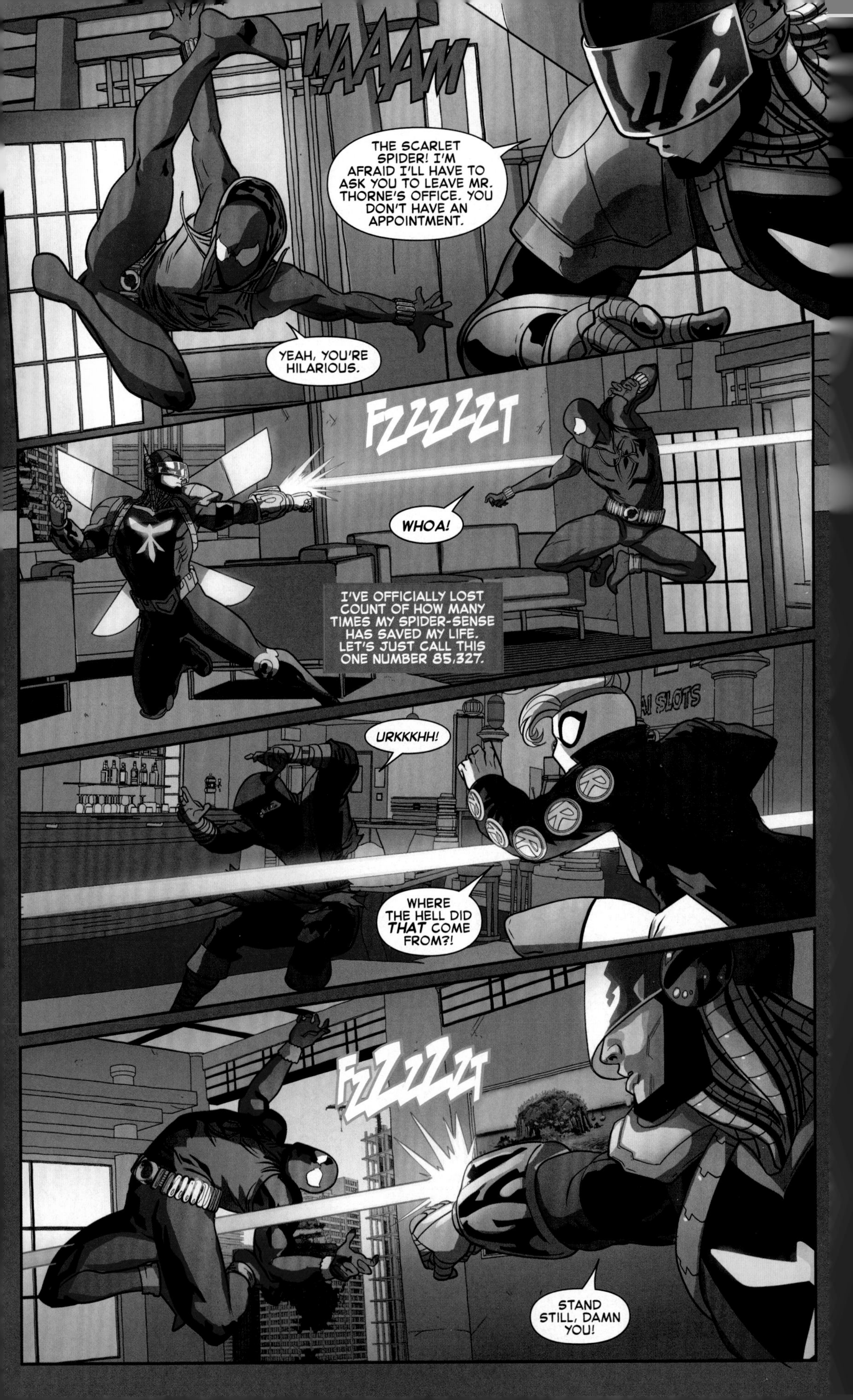
WAAAM
THE SCARLET SPIDER! I'M AFRAID I'LL HAVE TO ASK YOU TO LEAVE MR. THORNE'S OFFICE. YOU DON'T HAVE AN APPOINTMENT.
YEAH, YOU'RE HILARIOUS.
FZZZZZT
WHOA!
I'VE OFFICIALLY LOST COUNT OF HOW MANY TIMES MY SPIDER-SENSE HAS SAVED MY LIFE. LET'S JUST CALL THIS ONE NUMBER 85,327.
URKKKHH!
WHERE THE HELL DID THAT COME FROM?!
FZZZZZT
STAND STILL, DAMN YOU!

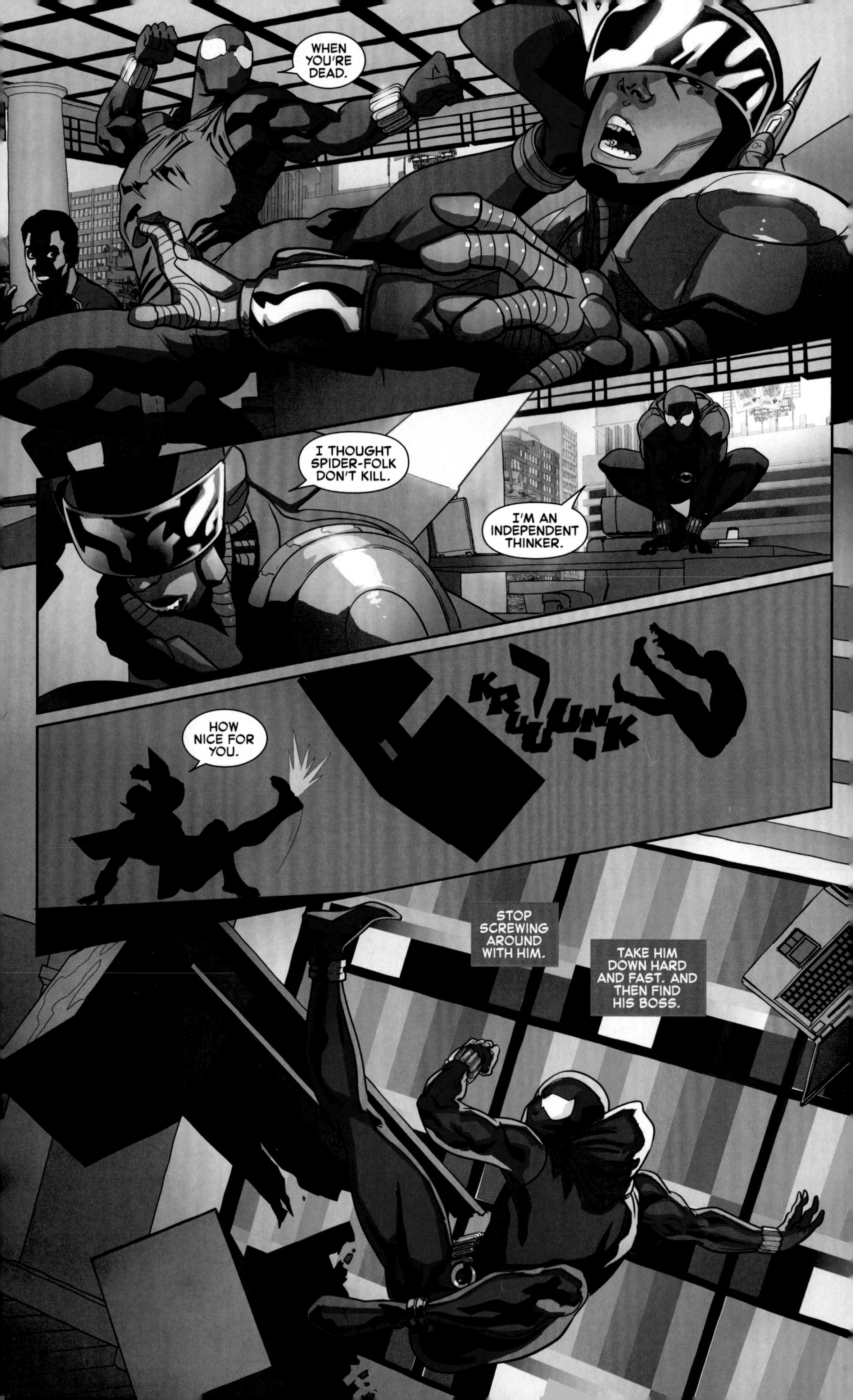
WHEN YOU'RE DEAD.
I THOUGHT SPIDER-FOLK DON'T KILL.
I'M AN INDEPENDENT THINKER.
HOW NICE FOR YOU.
KRUUUNK
STOP SCREWING AROUND WITH HIM.
TAKE HIM DOWN HARD AND FAST. AND THEN FIND HIS BOSS.

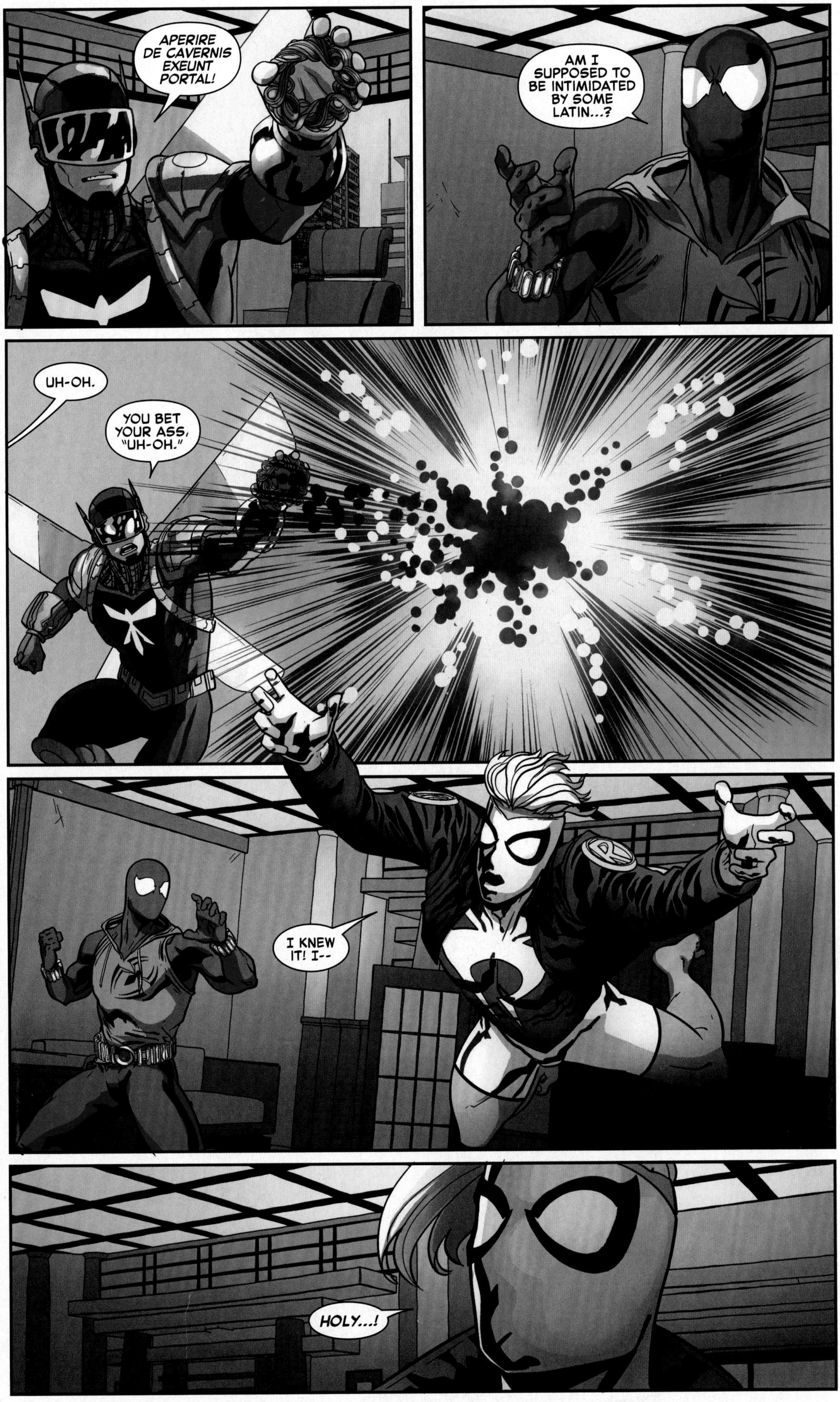
APERIRE DE CAVERNIS EXEUNT PORTAL!
AM I SUPPOSED TO BE INTIMIDATED BY SOME LATIN...?
UH-OH.
YOU BET YOUR ASS, "UH-OH."
I KNEW IT! I--
HOLY...!

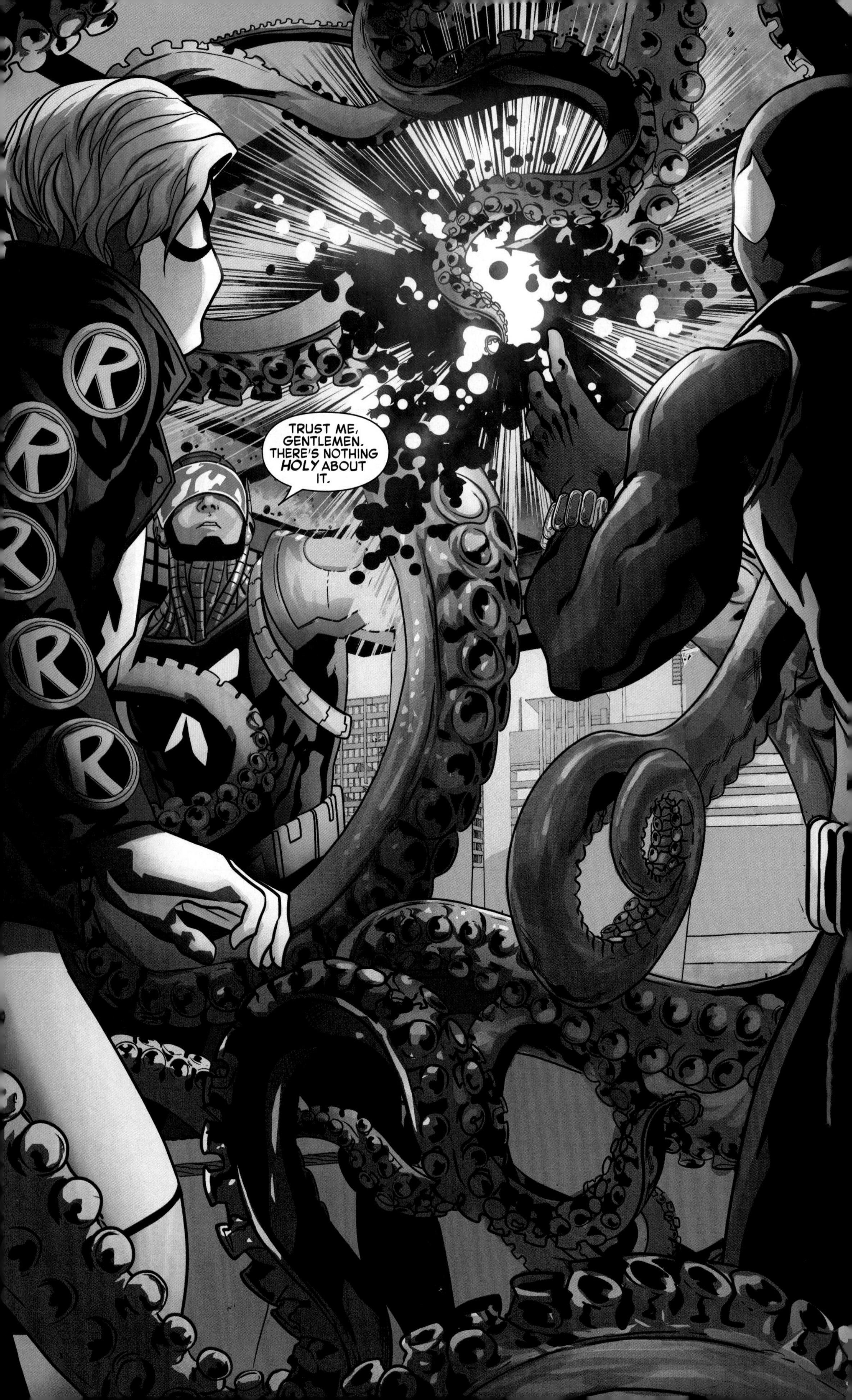
TRUST ME, GENTLEMEN. THERE'S NOTHING *HOLY* ABOUT IT.

SLINGERS #0, released in October 1998 as a *Wizard Magazine* supplement, introduced a team of teenage heroes, each of whom had taken up a heroic identity briefly used by Spider-Man. It was soon followed by an ongoing series.

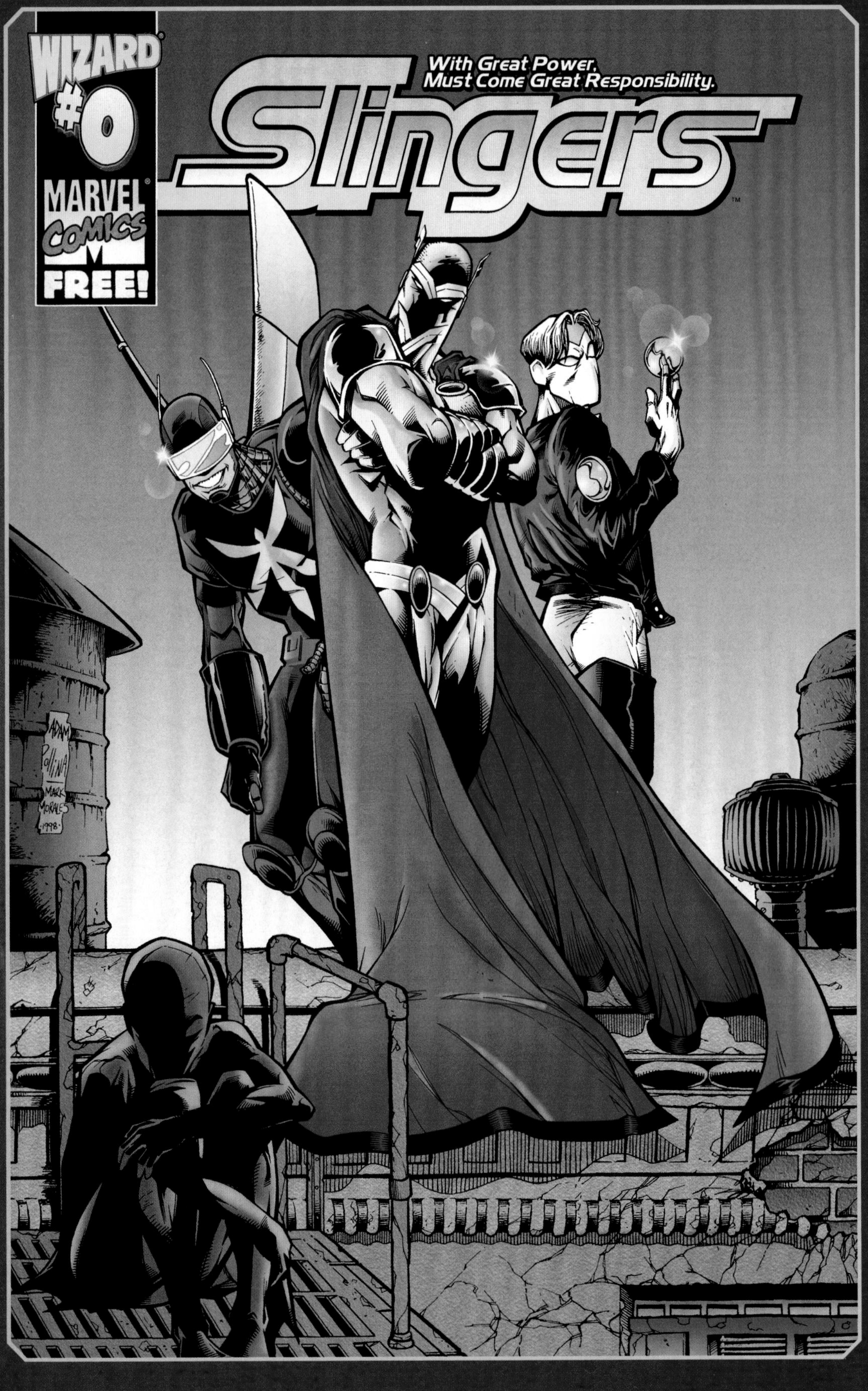
WIZARD
#0
MARVEL COMICS
FREE!
With Great Power,
Must Come Great Responsibility.
Slingers
ADAM POLLINA MARK MORALES 1998

With Great Power. Must Come Great Responsibility.

Slingers ™

Stan Lee presents

SLINGERS #0

MARVEL COMICS

Writer
JOSEPH HARRIS

Penciller
ADAM POLLINA

Inker
JIMMY PALMIOTTI

Colorist
KEVIN "STICK" TINSLEY

Lettering
RS & COMICRAFT'S LIZ AGRAPHIOTIS

Assistant Editor
ZENA TSARFIN

Editor
RUBEN DIAZ

Editor-in-chief
BOB HARRAS

WIZARD ENTERTAINMENT

President/Publisher
GAREB S. SHAMUS

Executive VP
FRED PIERCE

Editor-in-Chief
PATRICK McCALLUM

Promotions Manager
IAN M. FELLER

Design Manager
STEVE BLACKWELL

Production Director
DARREN SANCHEZ

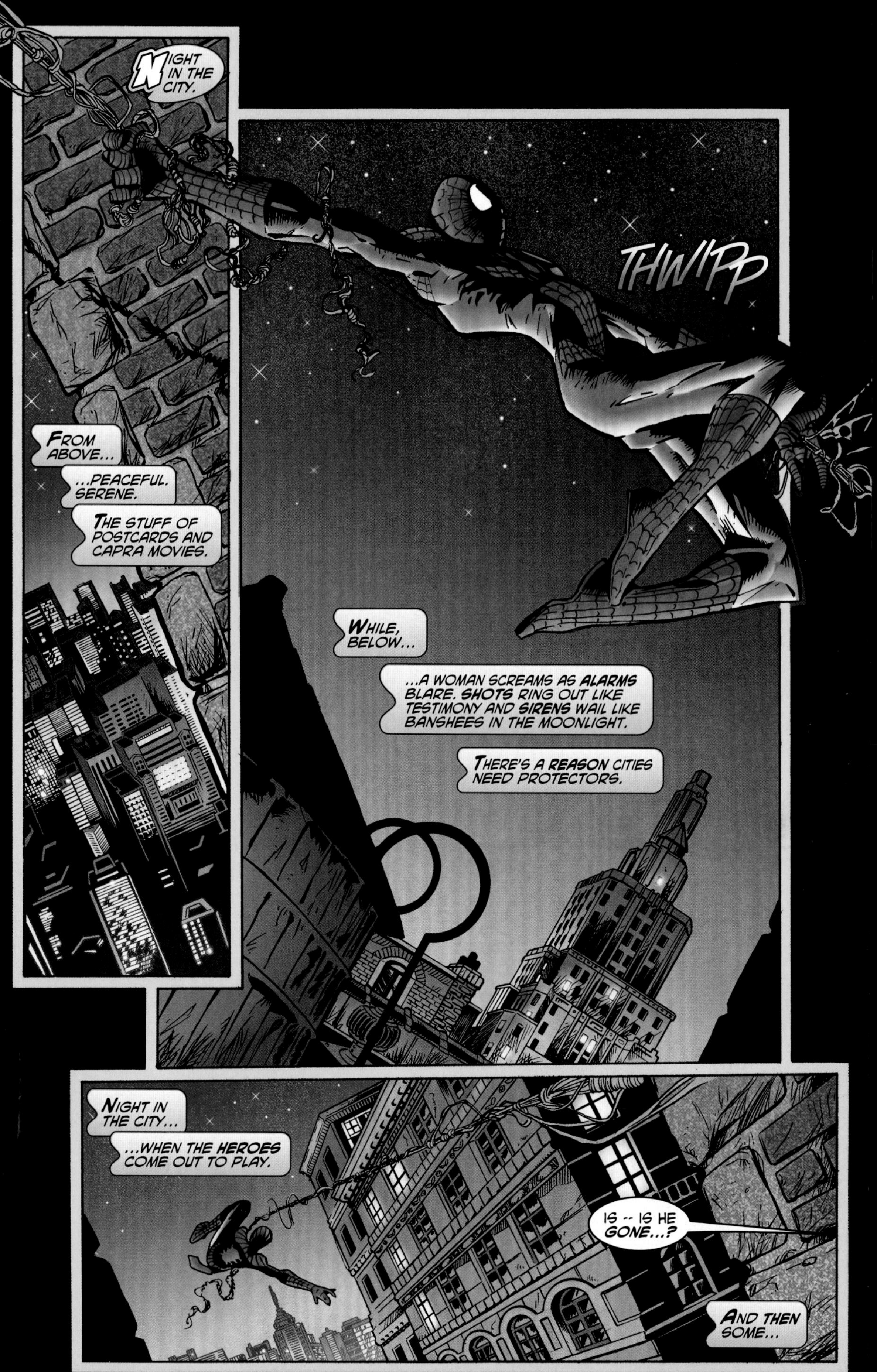
NIGHT IN THE CITY.
FROM ABOVE...
...PEACEFUL. SERENE.
THE STUFF OF POSTCARDS AND CAPRA MOVIES.
THWIPP
WHILE, BELOW...
...A WOMAN SCREAMS AS ALARMS BLARE. SHOTS RING OUT LIKE TESTIMONY AND SIRENS WAIL LIKE BANSHEES IN THE MOONLIGHT.
THERE'S A REASON CITIES NEED PROTECTORS.
NIGHT IN THE CITY...
...WHEN THE HEROES COME OUT TO PLAY.
IS -- IS HE GONE...?
AND THEN SOME...

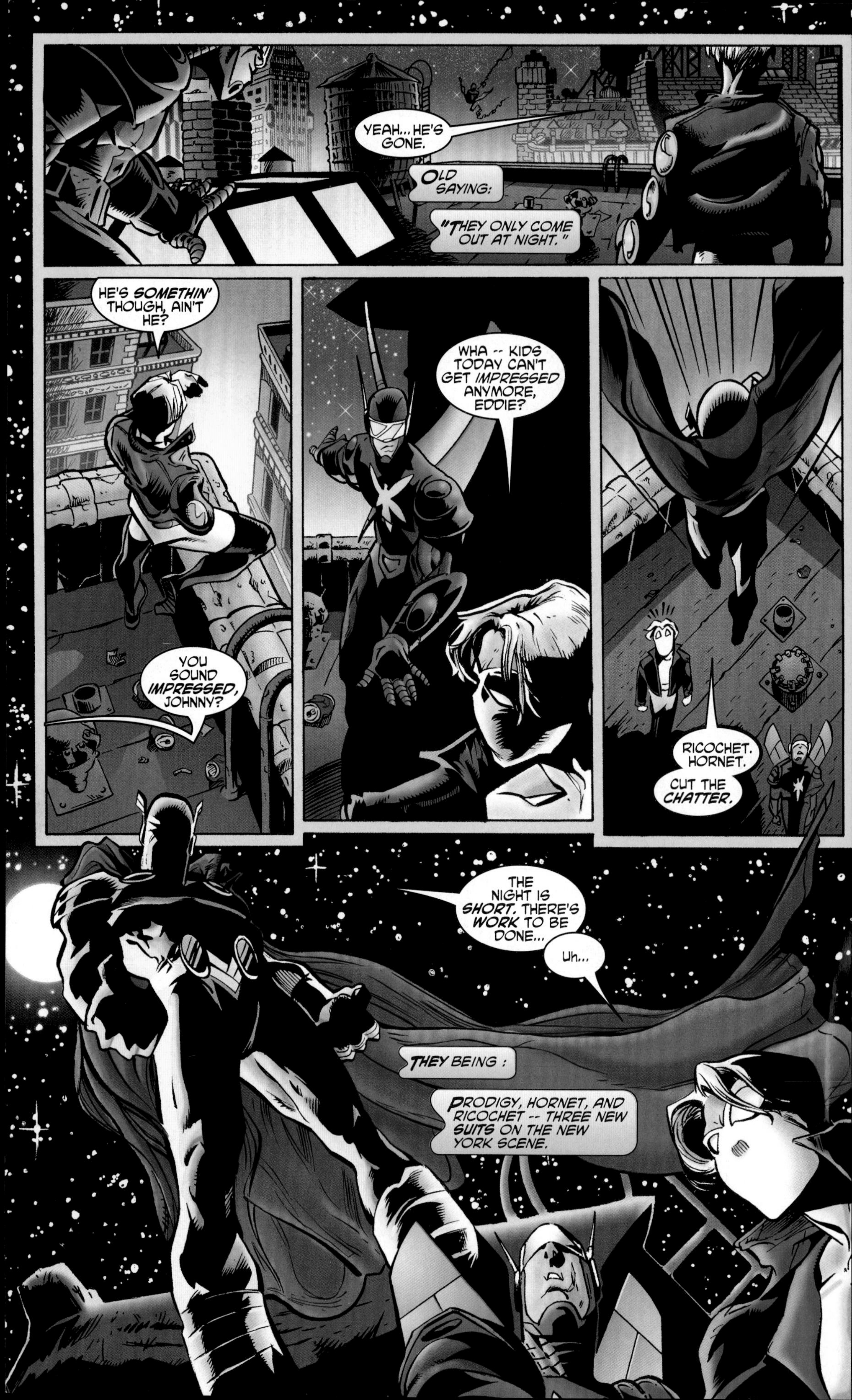
YEAH... HE'S GONE.
OLD SAYING:
"THEY ONLY COME OUT AT NIGHT."
HE'S SOMETHIN' THOUGH, AIN'T HE?
YOU SOUND IMPRESSED, JOHNNY?
WHA -- KIDS TODAY CAN'T GET IMPRESSED ANYMORE, EDDIE?
RICOCHET. HORNET.
CUT THE CHATTER.
THE NIGHT IS SHORT. THERE'S WORK TO BE DONE...
Uh...
THEY BEING :
PRODIGY, HORNET, AND RICOCHET -- THREE NEW SUITS ON THE NEW YORK SCENE.

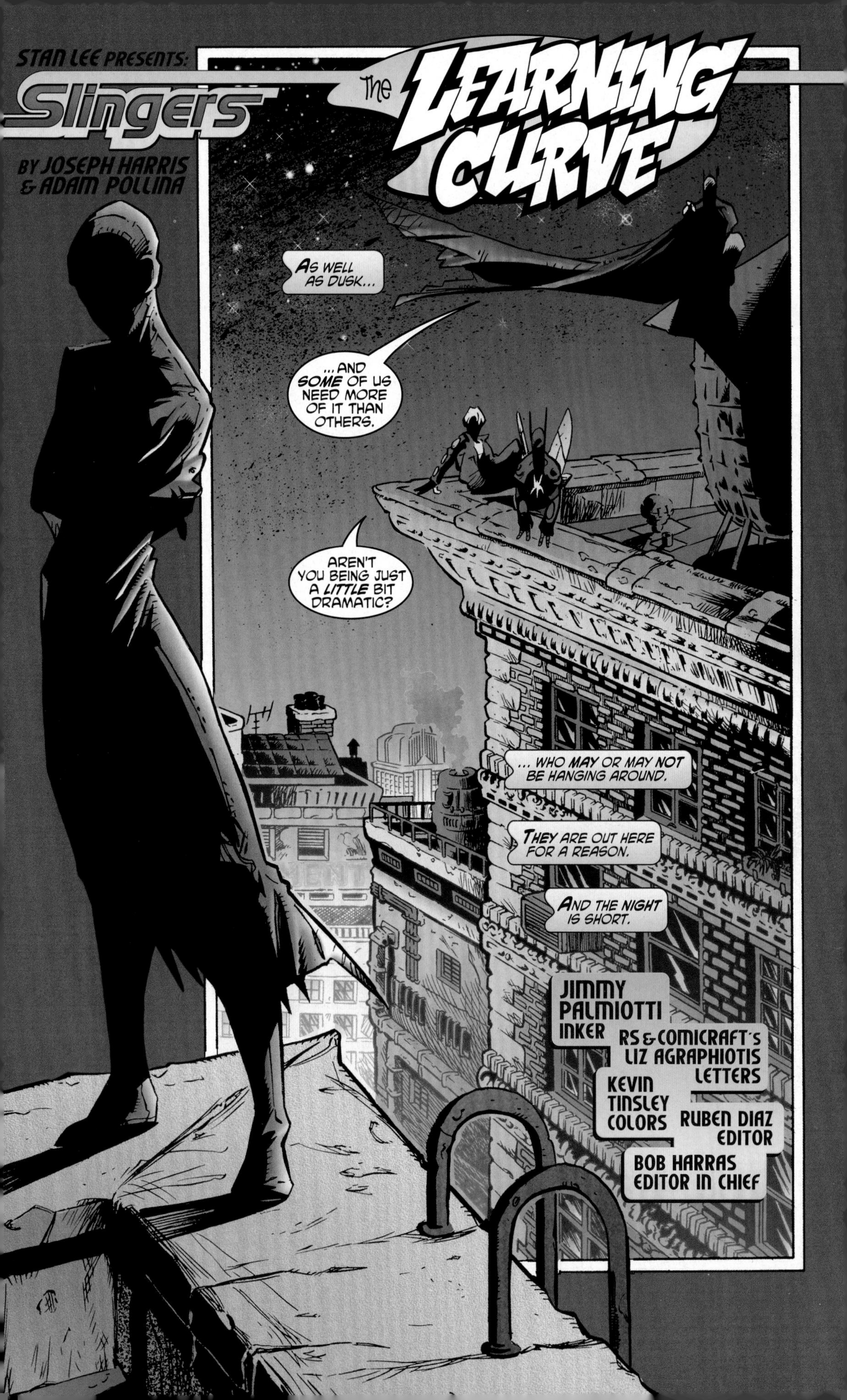
STAN LEE PRESENTS:
SLINGERS
BY JOSEPH HARRIS
& ADAM POLLINA
THE LEARNING CURVE
AS WELL AS DUSK...
...AND SOME OF US NEED MORE OF IT THAN OTHERS.
AREN'T YOU BEING JUST A LITTLE BIT DRAMATIC?
... WHO MAY OR MAY NOT BE HANGING AROUND.
THEY ARE OUT HERE FOR A REASON.
AND THE NIGHT IS SHORT.
JIMMY PALMIOTTI INKER
RS & COMICRAFT'S LIZ AGRAPHIOTIS LETTERS
KEVIN TINSLEY COLORS
RUBEN DIAZ EDITOR
BOB HARRAS EDITOR IN CHIEF

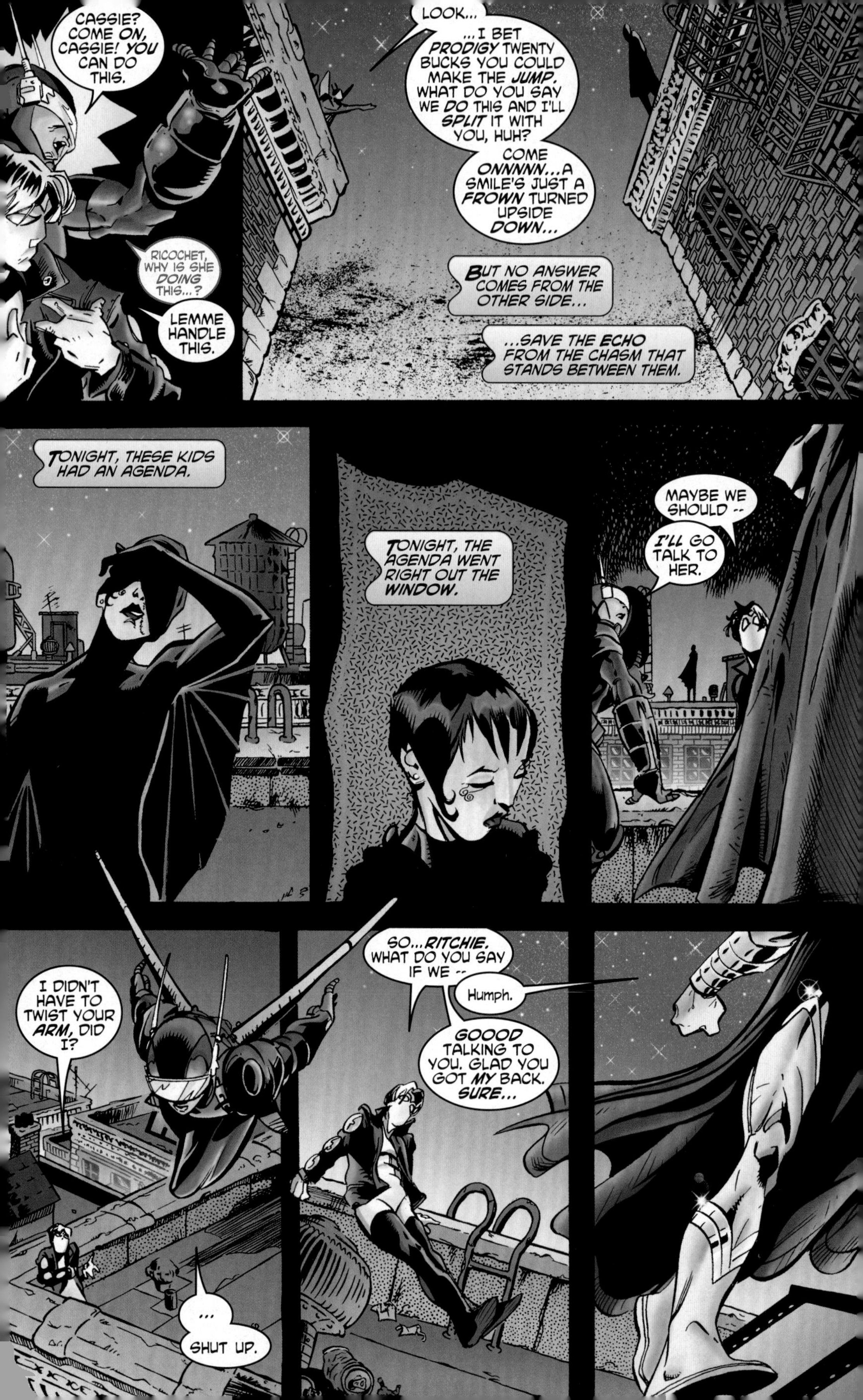
CASSIE? COME ON, CASSIE! YOU CAN DO THIS.
RICOCHET, WHY IS SHE DOING THIS...?
LEMME HANDLE THIS.
LOOK...
...I BET PRODIGY TWENTY BUCKS YOU COULD MAKE THE JUMP. WHAT DO YOU SAY WE DO THIS AND I'LL SPLIT IT WITH YOU, HUH?
COME ONNNNN...A SMILE'S JUST A FROWN TURNED UPSIDE DOWN...
BUT NO ANSWER COMES FROM THE OTHER SIDE...
...SAVE THE ECHO FROM THE CHASM THAT STANDS BETWEEN THEM.
TONIGHT, THESE KIDS HAD AN AGENDA.
TONIGHT, THE AGENDA WENT RIGHT OUT THE WINDOW.
MAYBE WE SHOULD --
I'LL GO TALK TO HER.
I DIDN'T HAVE TO TWIST YOUR ARM, DID I?
...
SHUT UP.
SO...RITCHIE. WHAT DO YOU SAY IF WE --
Humph.
GOOOD TALKING TO YOU. GLAD YOU GOT MY BACK. SURE...

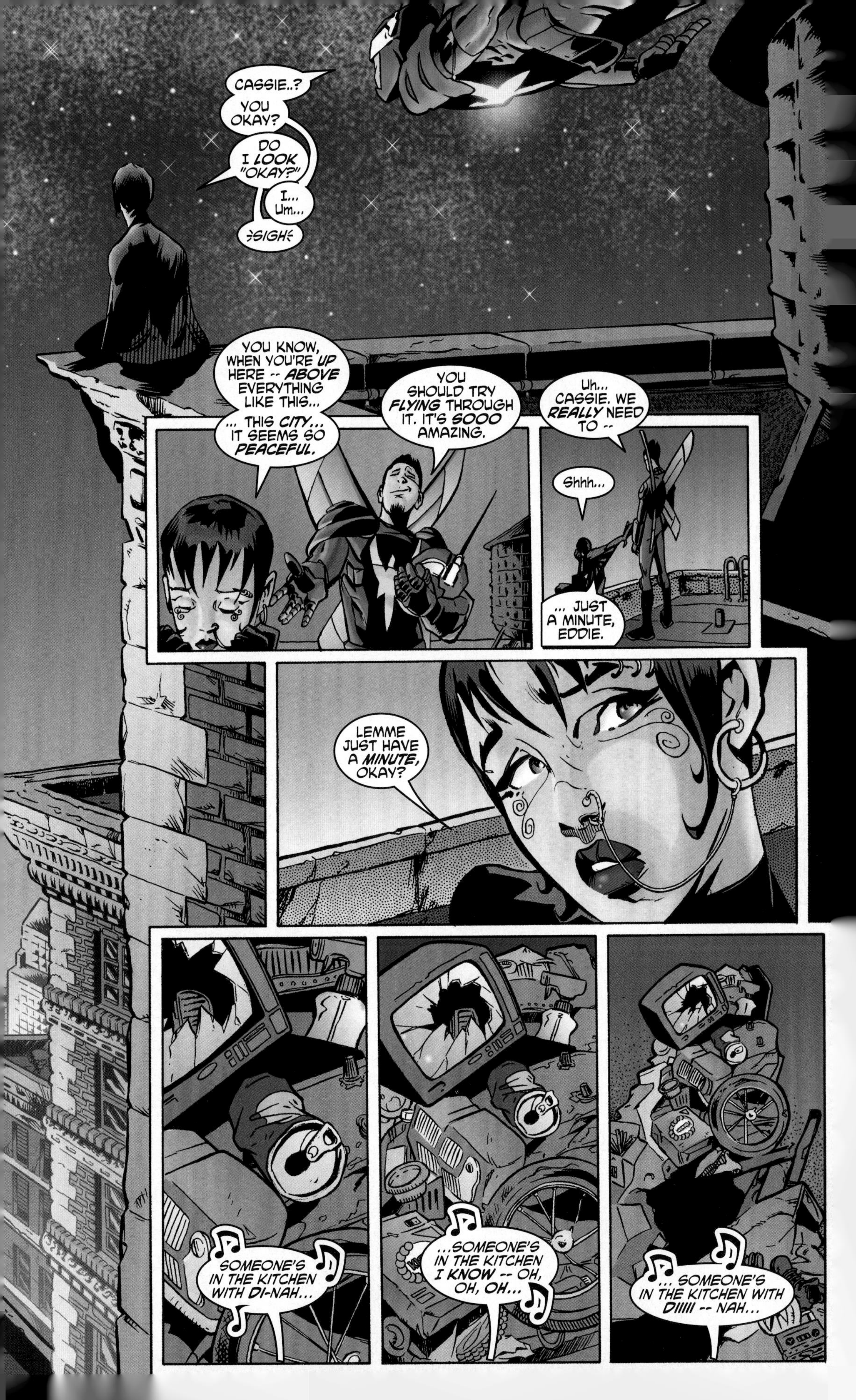
CASSIE..?
YOU OKAY?
DO I LOOK "OKAY?"
I... Um...
SIGH
YOU KNOW, WHEN YOU'RE UP HERE -- ABOVE EVERYTHING LIKE THIS...
... THIS CITY... IT SEEMS SO PEACEFUL.
YOU SHOULD TRY FLYING THROUGH IT. IT'S SOOO AMAZING.
Uh... CASSIE. WE REALLY NEED TO --
Shhh...
... JUST A MINUTE, EDDIE.
LEMME JUST HAVE A MINUTE, OKAY?
SOMEONE'S IN THE KITCHEN WITH DI-NAH...
...SOMEONE'S IN THE KITCHEN I KNOW -- OH, OH, OH...
... SOMEONE'S IN THE KITCHEN WITH DIIIII -- NAH...

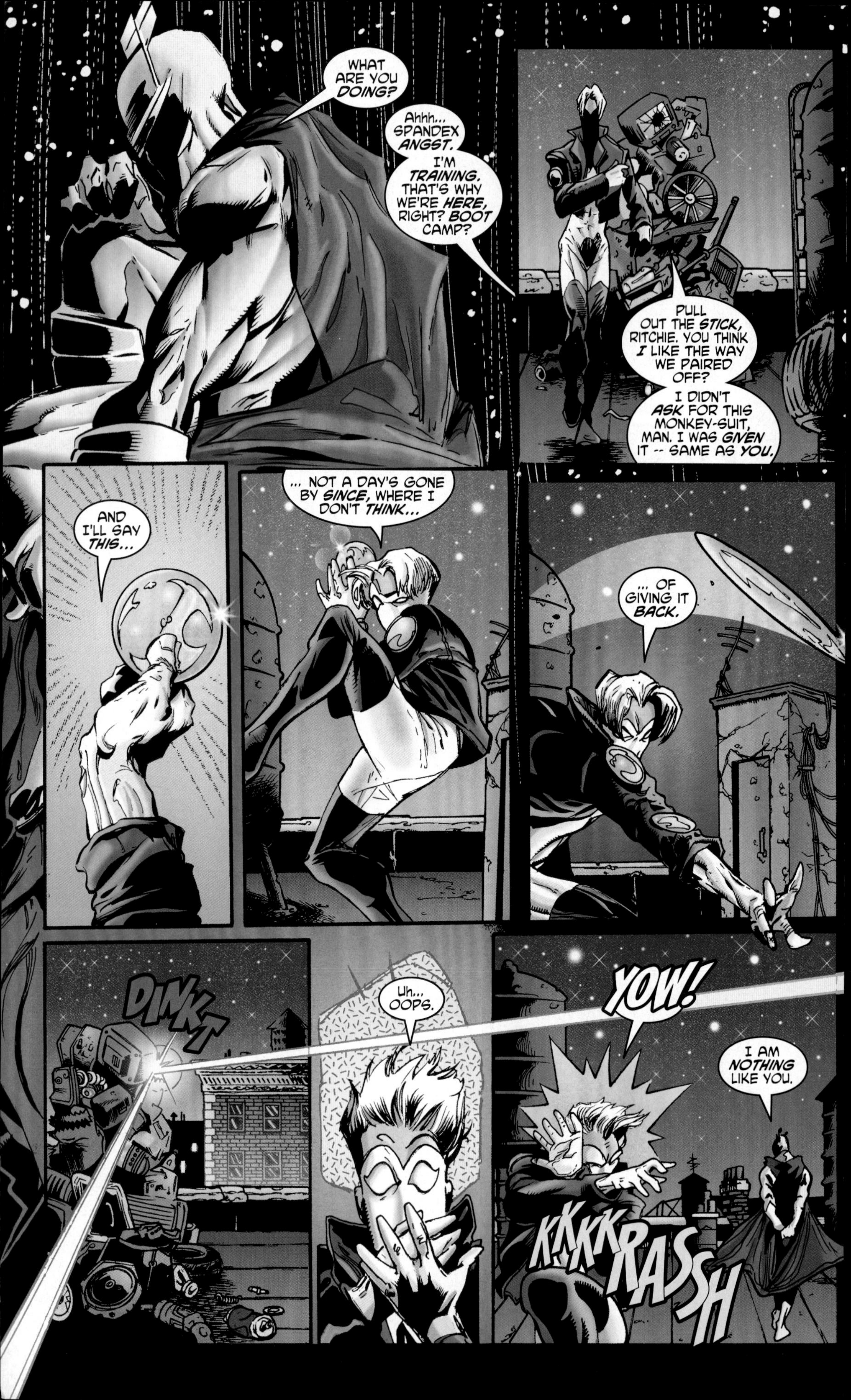
WHAT ARE YOU DOING?
Ahhh... SPANDEX ANGST.
I'M TRAINING. THAT'S WHY WE'RE HERE, RIGHT? BOOT CAMP?
PULL OUT THE STICK, RITCHIE. YOU THINK I LIKE THE WAY WE PAIRED OFF?
I DIDN'T ASK FOR THIS MONKEY-SUIT, MAN. I WAS GIVEN IT -- SAME AS YOU.
AND I'LL SAY THIS...
... NOT A DAY'S GONE BY SINCE, WHERE I DON'T THINK...
... OF GIVING IT BACK.
DINKT
Uh... OOPS.
YOW!
I AM NOTHING LIKE YOU.
KKKKRASSH

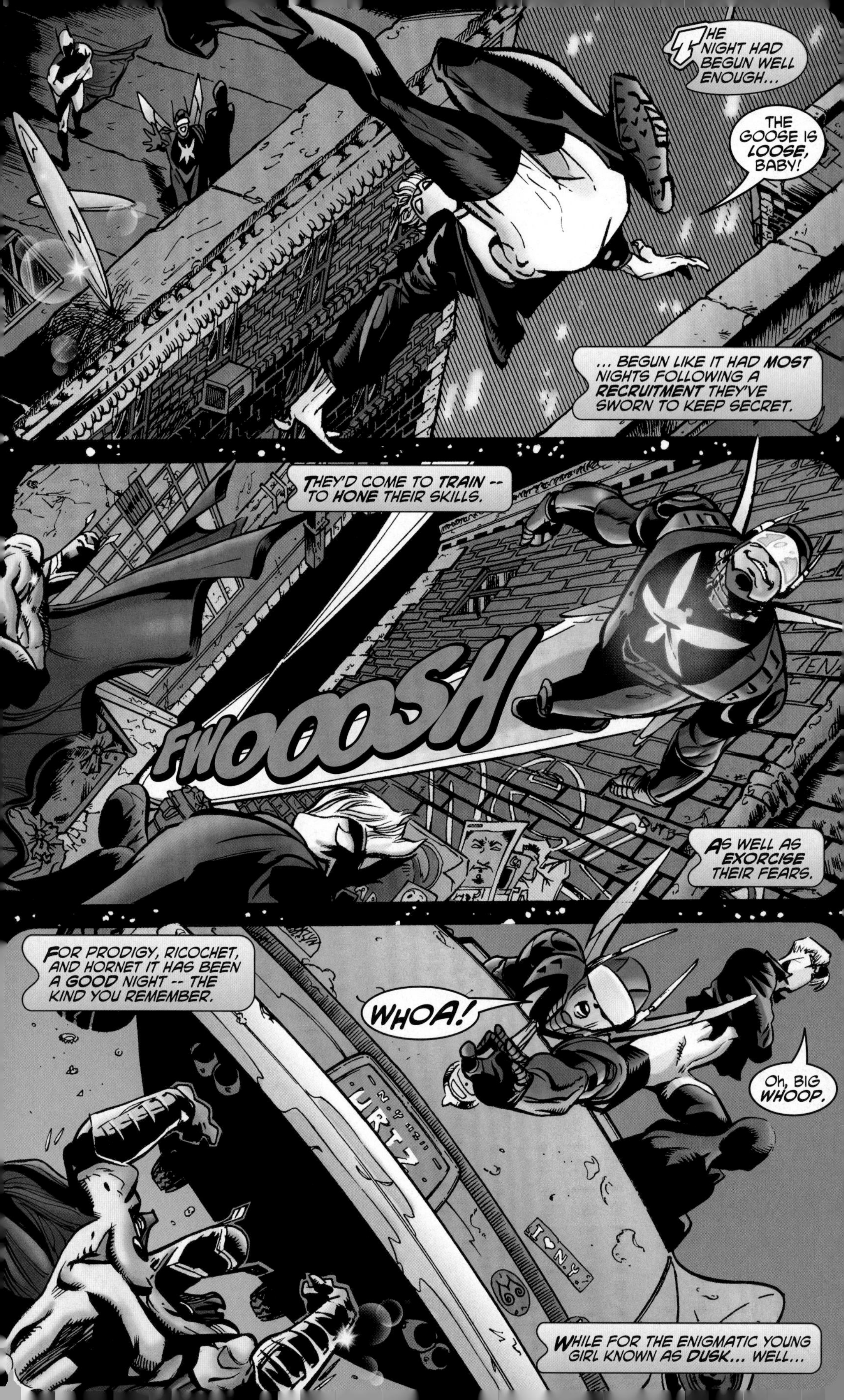
THE NIGHT HAD BEGUN WELL ENOUGH...
THE GOOSE IS LOOSE, BABY!
... BEGUN LIKE IT HAD MOST NIGHTS FOLLOWING A RECRUITMENT THEY'VE SWORN TO KEEP SECRET.
THEY'D COME TO TRAIN -- TO HONE THEIR SKILLS.
FWOOOSH
AS WELL AS EXORCISE THEIR FEARS.
FOR PRODIGY, RICOCHET, AND HORNET IT HAS BEEN A GOOD NIGHT -- THE KIND YOU REMEMBER.
WHOA!
Oh, BIG WHOOP.
WHILE FOR THE ENIGMATIC YOUNG GIRL KNOWN AS DUSK... WELL...

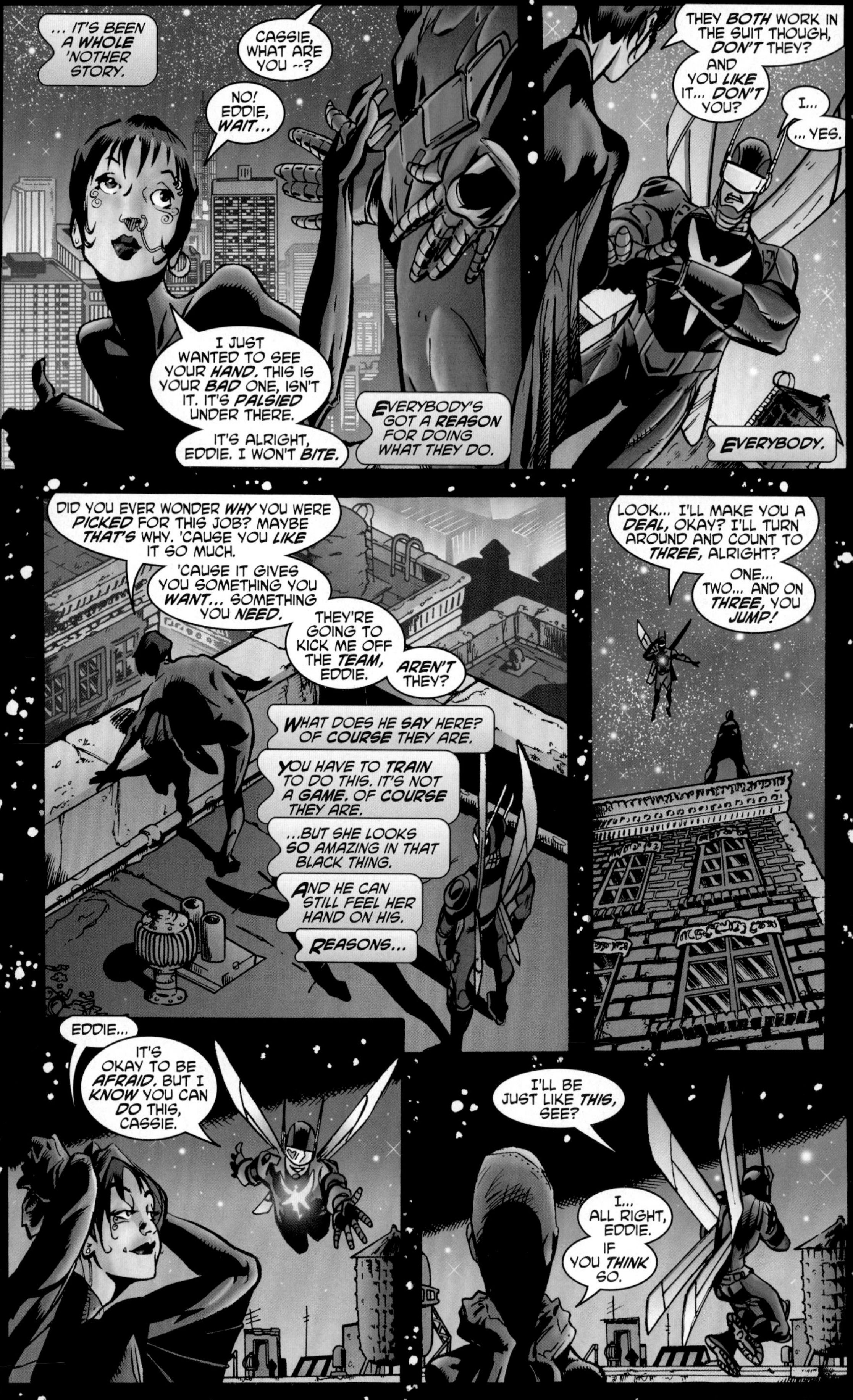

... IT'S BEEN A WHOLE 'NOTHER STORY.
CASSIE, WHAT ARE YOU --?
NO! EDDIE, WAIT...
I JUST WANTED TO SEE YOUR HAND. THIS IS YOUR BAD ONE, ISN'T IT. IT'S PALSIED UNDER THERE.
IT'S ALRIGHT, EDDIE. I WON'T BITE.
EVERYBODY'S GOT A REASON FOR DOING WHAT THEY DO.
THEY BOTH WORK IN THE SUIT THOUGH, DON'T THEY?
AND YOU LIKE IT... DON'T YOU?
I...
... YES.
EVERYBODY.
DID YOU EVER WONDER WHY YOU WERE PICKED FOR THIS JOB? MAYBE THAT'S WHY. 'CAUSE YOU LIKE IT SO MUCH.
'CAUSE IT GIVES YOU SOMETHING YOU WANT... SOMETHING YOU NEED.
THEY'RE GOING TO KICK ME OFF THE TEAM, EDDIE.
AREN'T THEY?
WHAT DOES HE SAY HERE? OF COURSE THEY ARE.
YOU HAVE TO TRAIN TO DO THIS. IT'S NOT A GAME. OF COURSE THEY ARE.
...BUT SHE LOOKS SO AMAZING IN THAT BLACK THING.
AND HE CAN STILL FEEL HER HAND ON HIS.
REASONS...
LOOK... I'LL MAKE YOU A DEAL, OKAY? I'LL TURN AROUND AND COUNT TO THREE, ALRIGHT?
ONE... TWO... AND ON THREE, YOU JUMP!
EDDIE...
IT'S OKAY TO BE AFRAID. BUT I KNOW YOU CAN DO THIS, CASSIE.
I'LL BE JUST LIKE THIS, SEE?
I... ALL RIGHT, EDDIE.
IF YOU THINK SO.

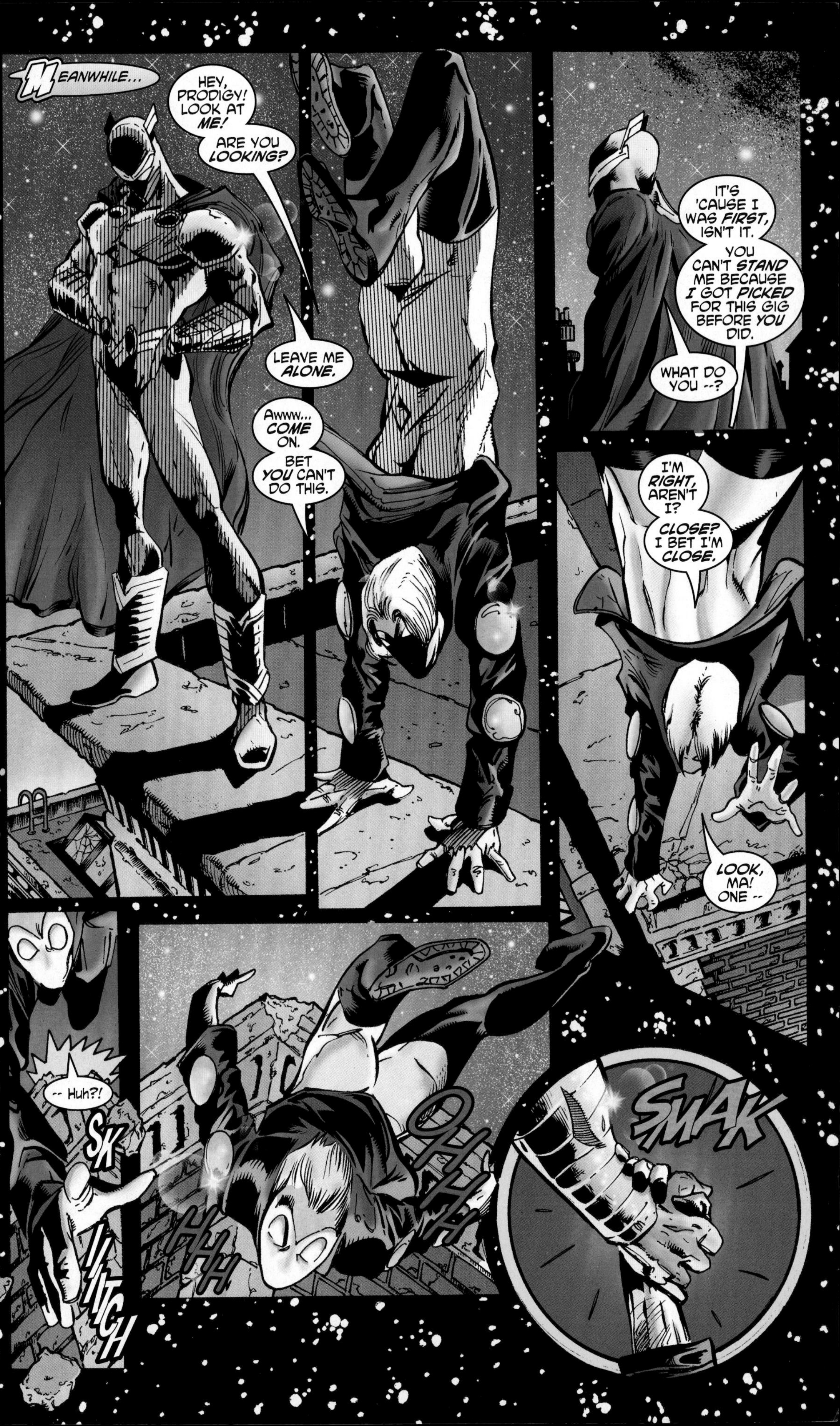

MEANWHILE...
HEY, PRODIGY! LOOK AT ME!
ARE YOU LOOKING?
LEAVE ME ALONE.
AWWW... COME ON.
BET YOU CAN'T DO THIS.
IT'S 'CAUSE I WAS FIRST, ISN'T IT.
YOU CAN'T STAND ME BECAUSE I GOT PICKED FOR THIS GIG BEFORE YOU DID.
WHAT DO YOU --?
I'M RIGHT, AREN'T I?
CLOSE? I BET I'M CLOSE.
LOOK, MA! ONE --
-- Huh?!
SKWITCH
OHHHHHH
SMAK

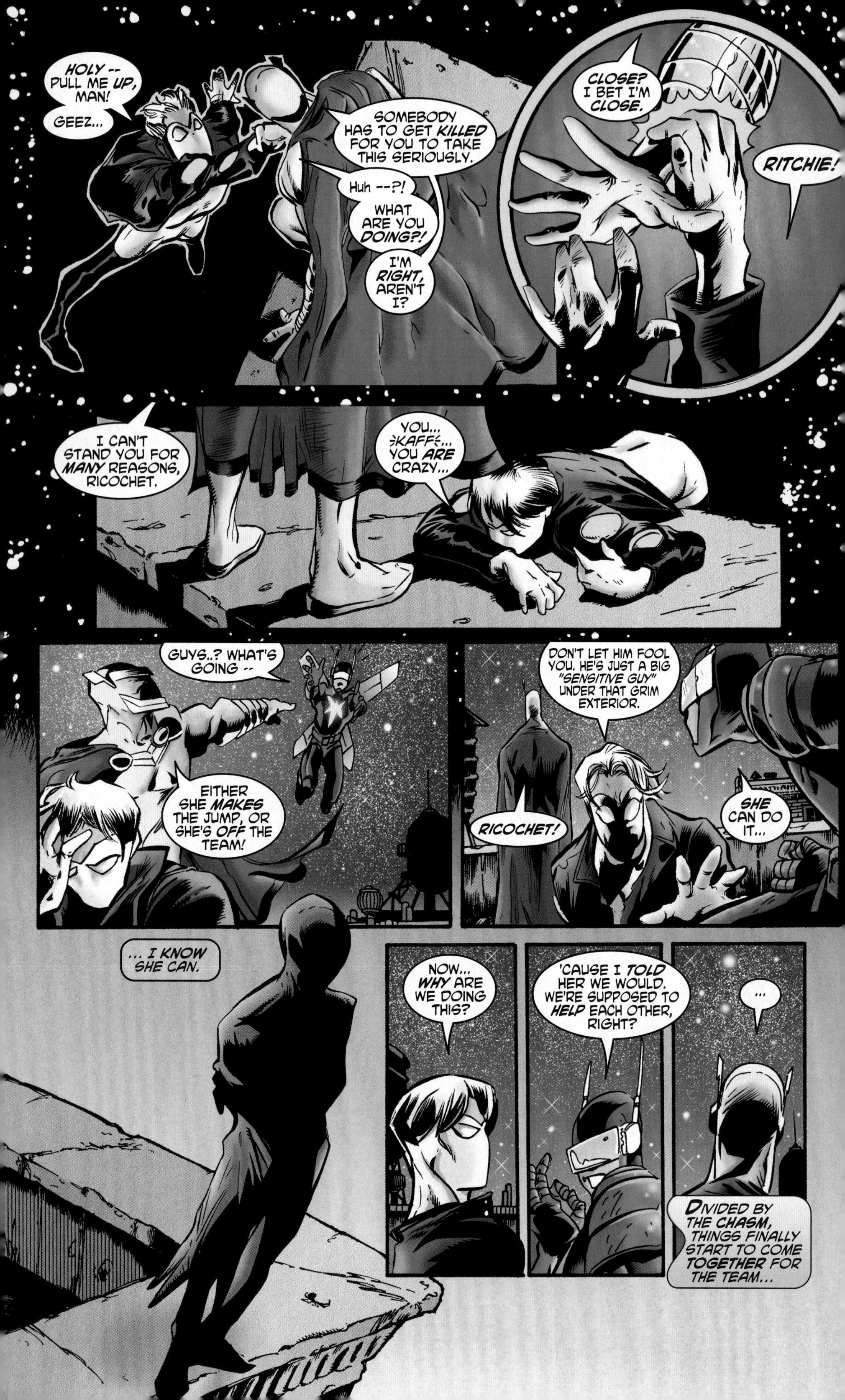

HOLY -- PULL ME UP, MAN!
GEEZ...
SOMEBODY HAS TO GET KILLED FOR YOU TO TAKE THIS SERIOUSLY.
Huh --?!
WHAT ARE YOU DOING?!
I'M RIGHT, AREN'T I?
CLOSE? I BET I'M CLOSE.
RITCHIE!
I CAN'T STAND YOU FOR MANY REASONS, RICOCHET.
YOU... ≯KAFF≮... YOU ARE CRAZY...
GUYS..? WHAT'S GOING --
EITHER SHE MAKES THE JUMP, OR SHE'S OFF THE TEAM!
DON'T LET HIM FOOL YOU. HE'S JUST A BIG "SENSITIVE GUY" UNDER THAT GRIM EXTERIOR.
RICOCHET!
SHE CAN DO IT...
... I KNOW SHE CAN.
NOW... WHY ARE WE DOING THIS?
'CAUSE I TOLD HER WE WOULD. WE'RE SUPPOSED TO HELP EACH OTHER, RIGHT?
...
DIVIDED BY THE CHASM, THINGS FINALLY START TO COME TOGETHER FOR THE TEAM...

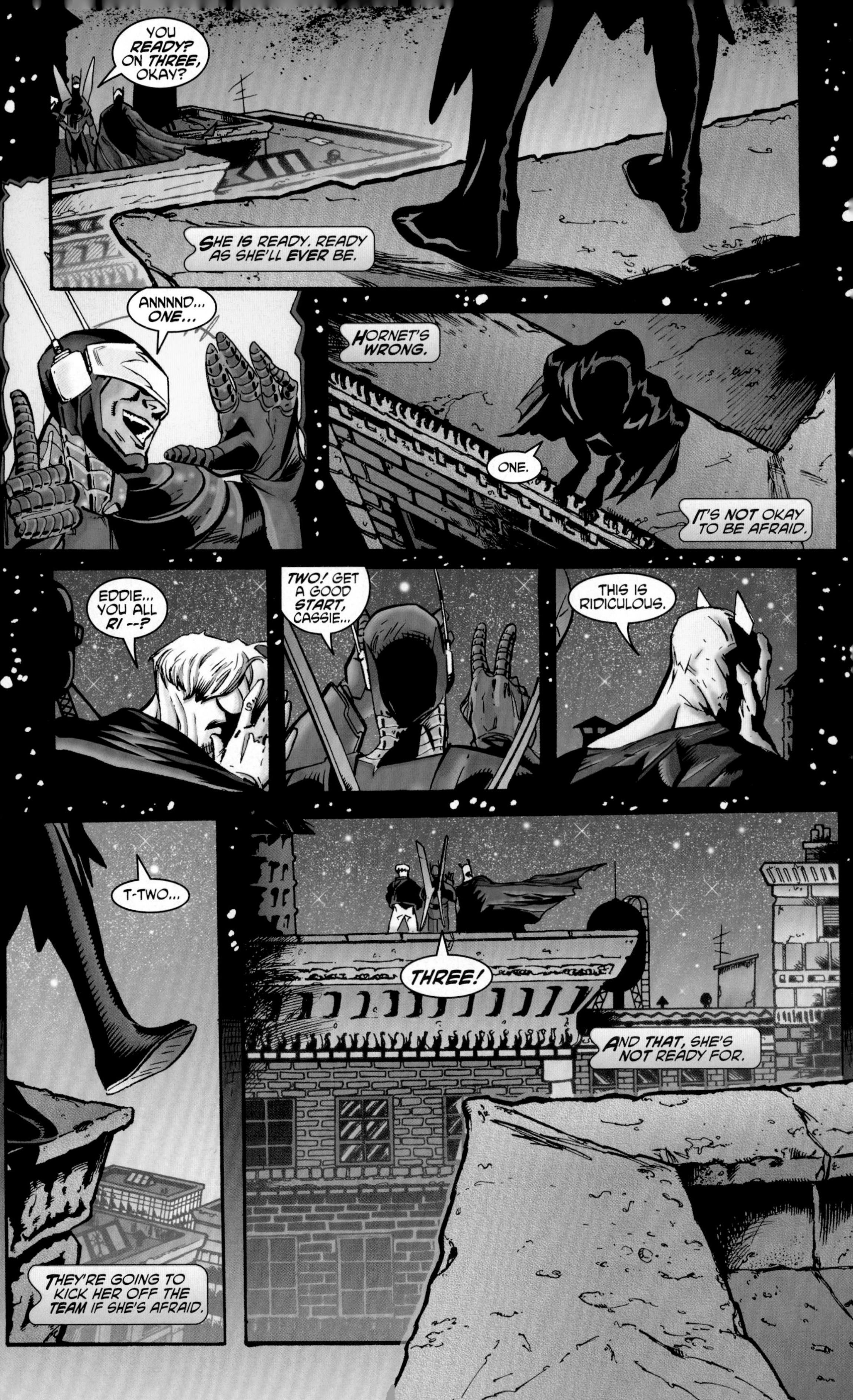
YOU READY? ON THREE, OKAY?
SHE IS READY. READY AS SHE'LL EVER BE.
ANNNND... ONE...
HORNET'S WRONG.
ONE.
IT'S NOT OKAY TO BE AFRAID.
EDDIE... YOU ALL RI --?
TWO! GET A GOOD START, CASSIE...
THIS IS RIDICULOUS.
T-TWO...
THEY'RE GOING TO KICK HER OFF THE TEAM IF SHE'S AFRAID.
THREE!
AND THAT, SHE'S NOT READY FOR.

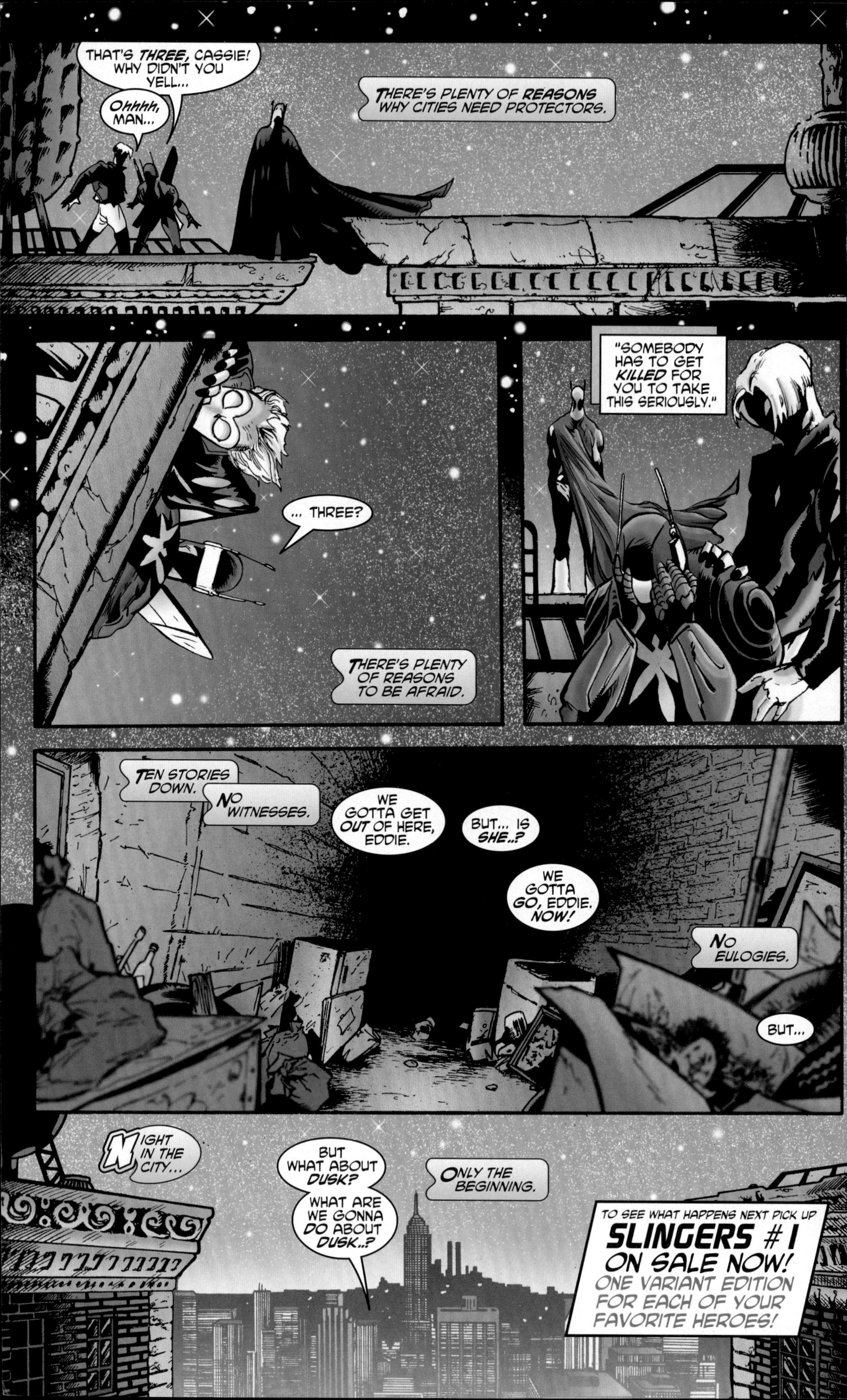
THAT'S THREE, CASSIE! WHY DIDN'T YOU YELL...
Ohhhh, MAN...
THERE'S PLENTY OF REASONS WHY CITIES NEED PROTECTORS.
... THREE?
THERE'S PLENTY OF REASONS TO BE AFRAID.
"SOMEBODY HAS TO GET KILLED FOR YOU TO TAKE THIS SERIOUSLY."
TEN STORIES DOWN.
NO WITNESSES.
WE GOTTA GET OUT OF HERE, EDDIE.
BUT... IS SHE..?
WE GOTTA GO, EDDIE. NOW!
NO EULOGIES.
BUT...
NIGHT IN THE CITY...
BUT WHAT ABOUT DUSK?
WHAT ARE WE GONNA DO ABOUT DUSK..?
ONLY THE BEGINNING.
TO SEE WHAT HAPPENS NEXT PICK UP
SLINGERS #1
ON SALE NOW!
ONE VARIANT EDITION FOR EACH OF YOUR FAVORITE HEROES!

sneak PEEK

BEHIND THE SCENES GOODIES

slingers

Commentary by Slingers writer Joe Harris.

"Ricochet speaks his mind; he's the guy that's going to wind up being leader — not because he wants to, but because people trust him. There's something very honest about Rico."

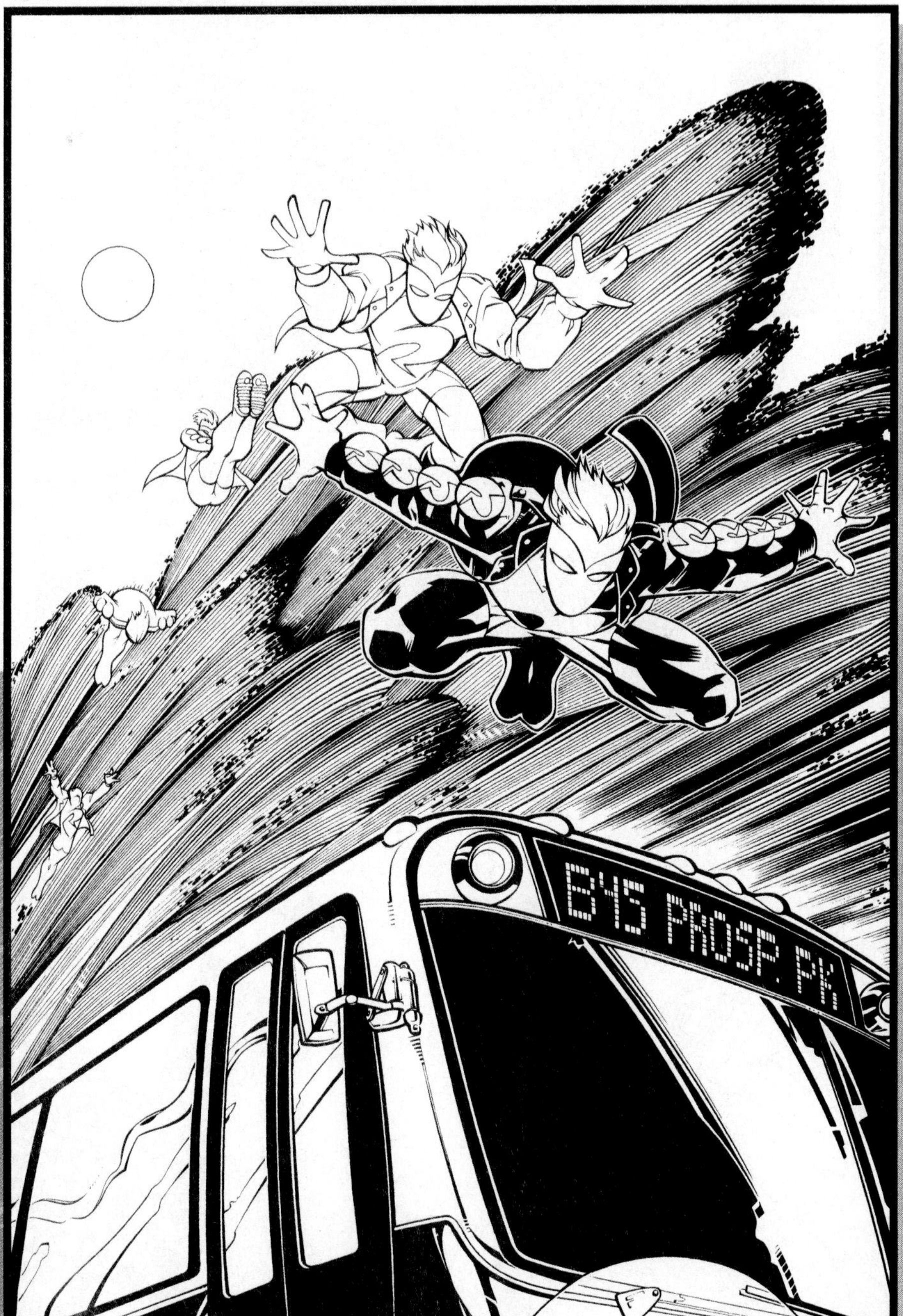
B45 PROSP. PK

SLINGERS

sneak PEEK

"Hornet finds this alter ego can let him be the person he's always wanted to be. He's able to escape from his lonely world and his handicap. But is that what it takes to escape from his prison? That's the thing Hornet worries about."

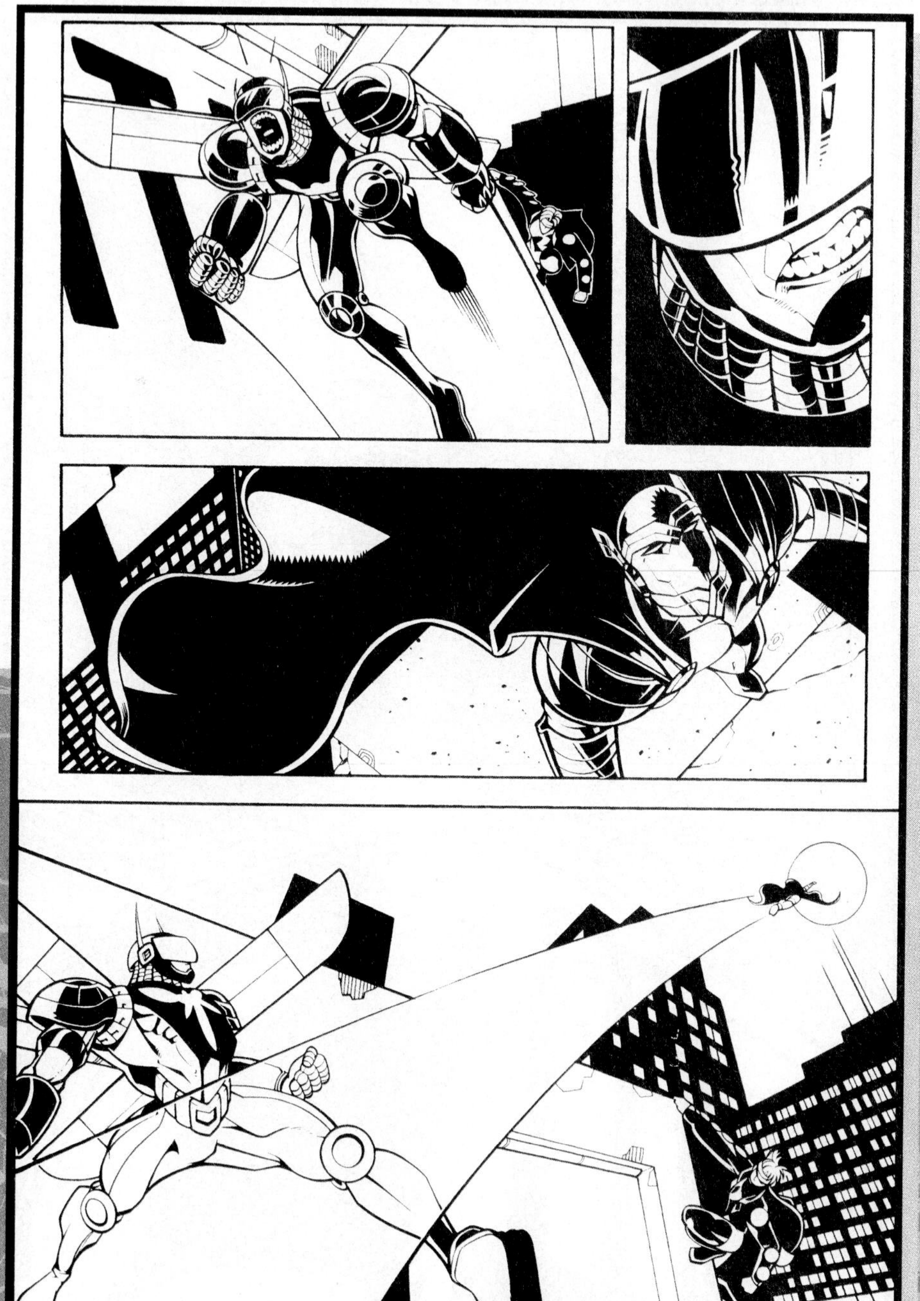

"Prodigy strives to be the best, period. He takes his role very seriously and demands the same from the others. The only problem is: How far can they be pushed without going over the edge?"

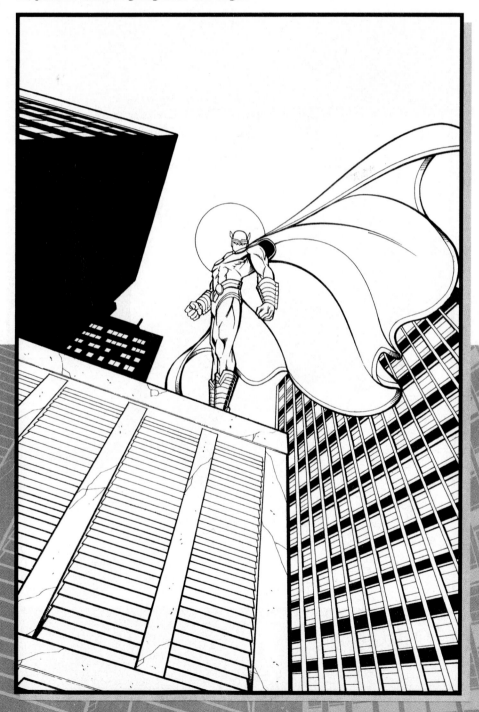

sneak PEEK

"Dusk is like a wild card, nobody knows what to make of her. She was desperately searching for something that led her to this fate. Dusk's a mystery yet to be unraveled—even to herself."

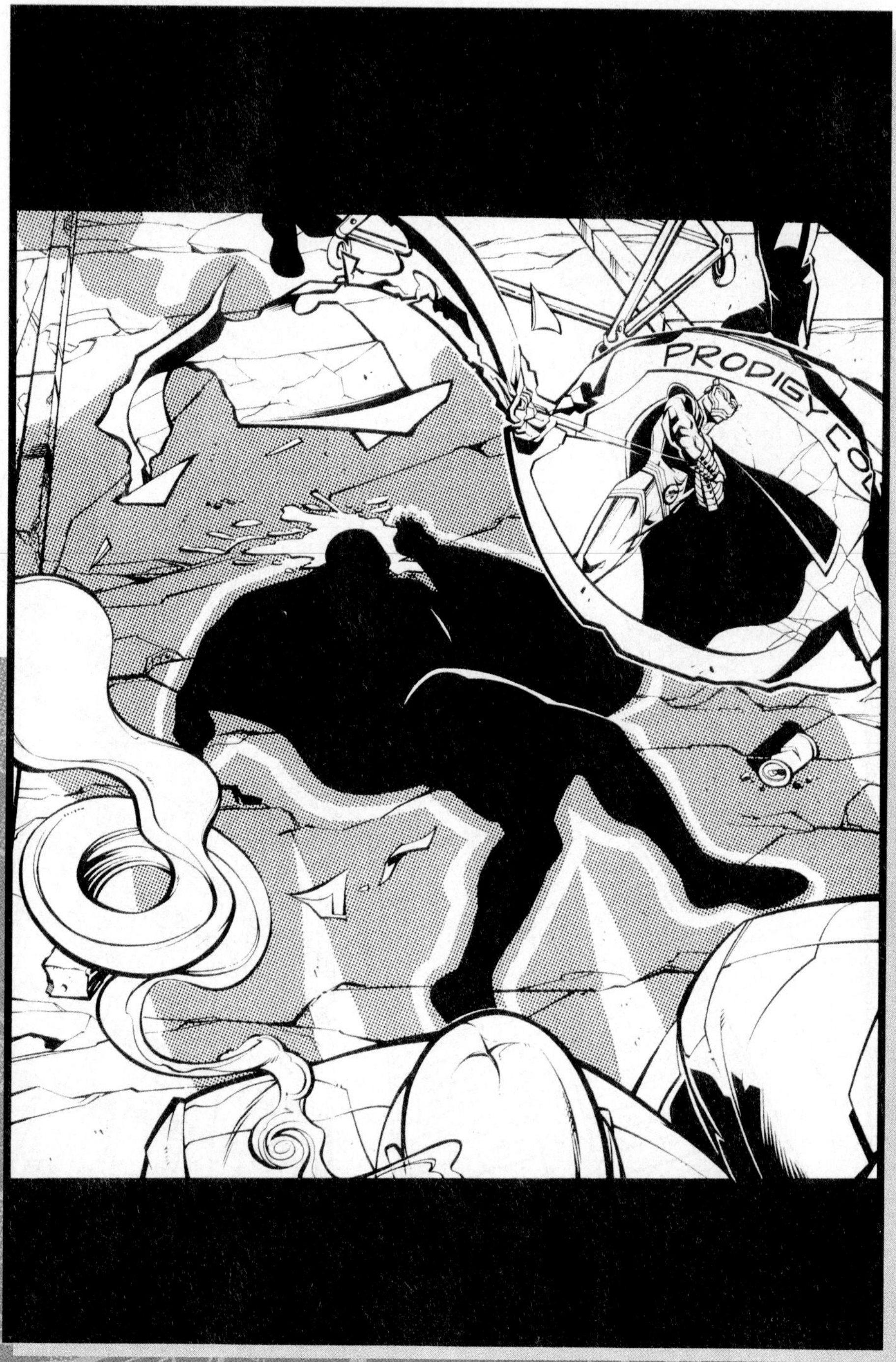
PRODIGY

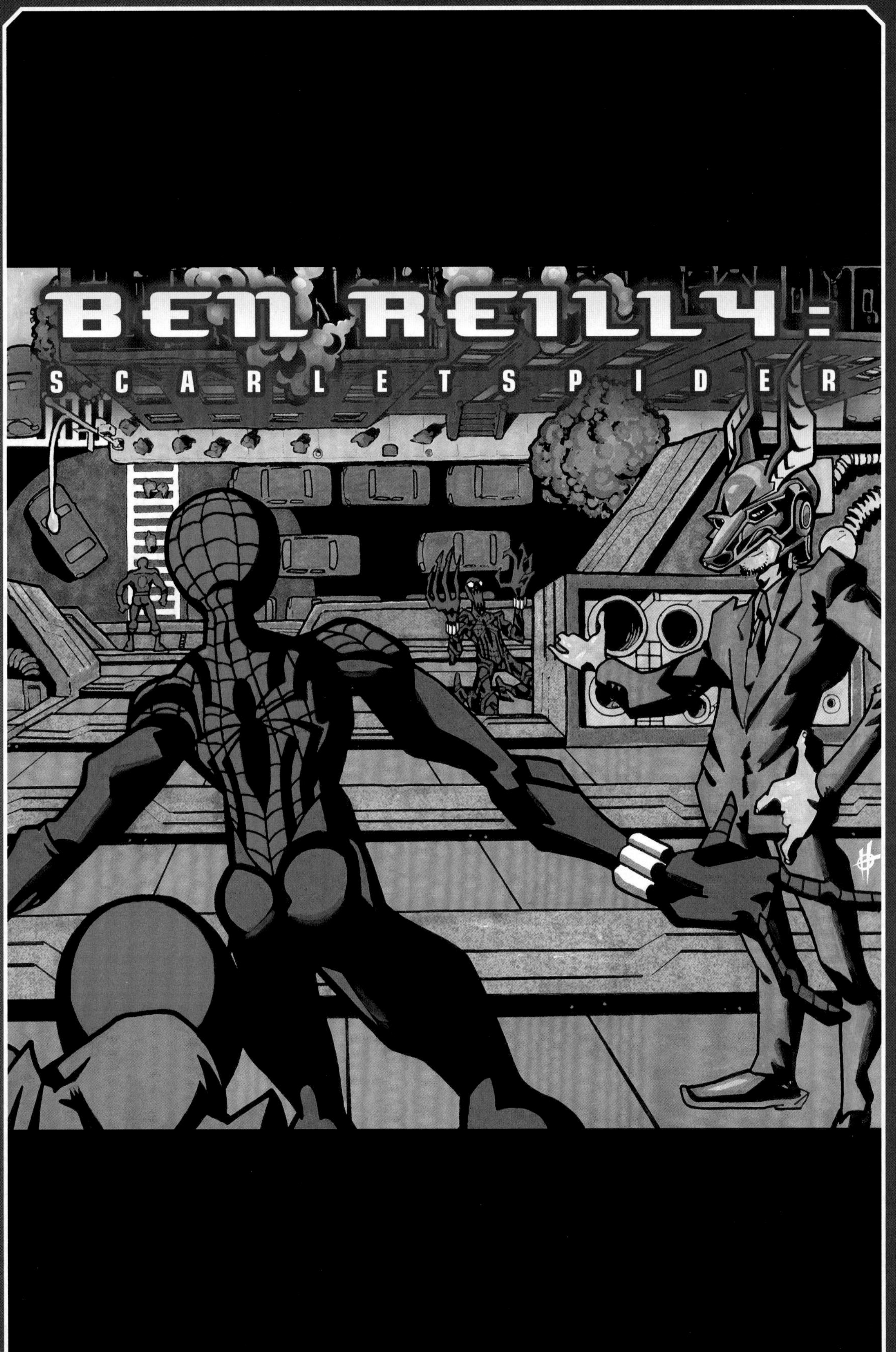
BEN REILLY:
SCARLET SPIDER

Damion Scott

BEN REILLY: SCARLET SPIDER #7 HIP-HOP VARIANT

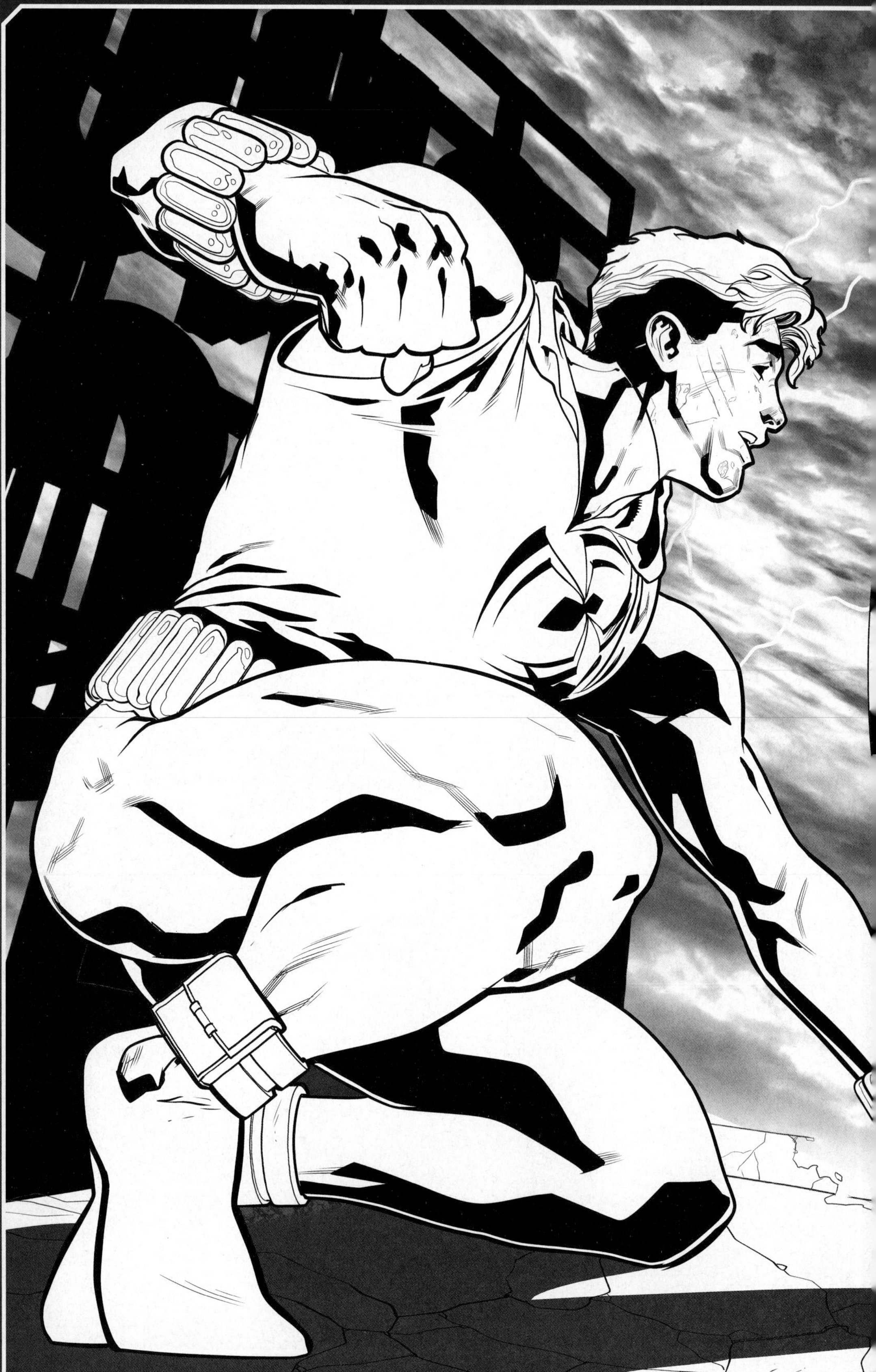

Will Sliney

BEN REILLY: SCARLET SPIDER #7, PAGES 4-5 ART

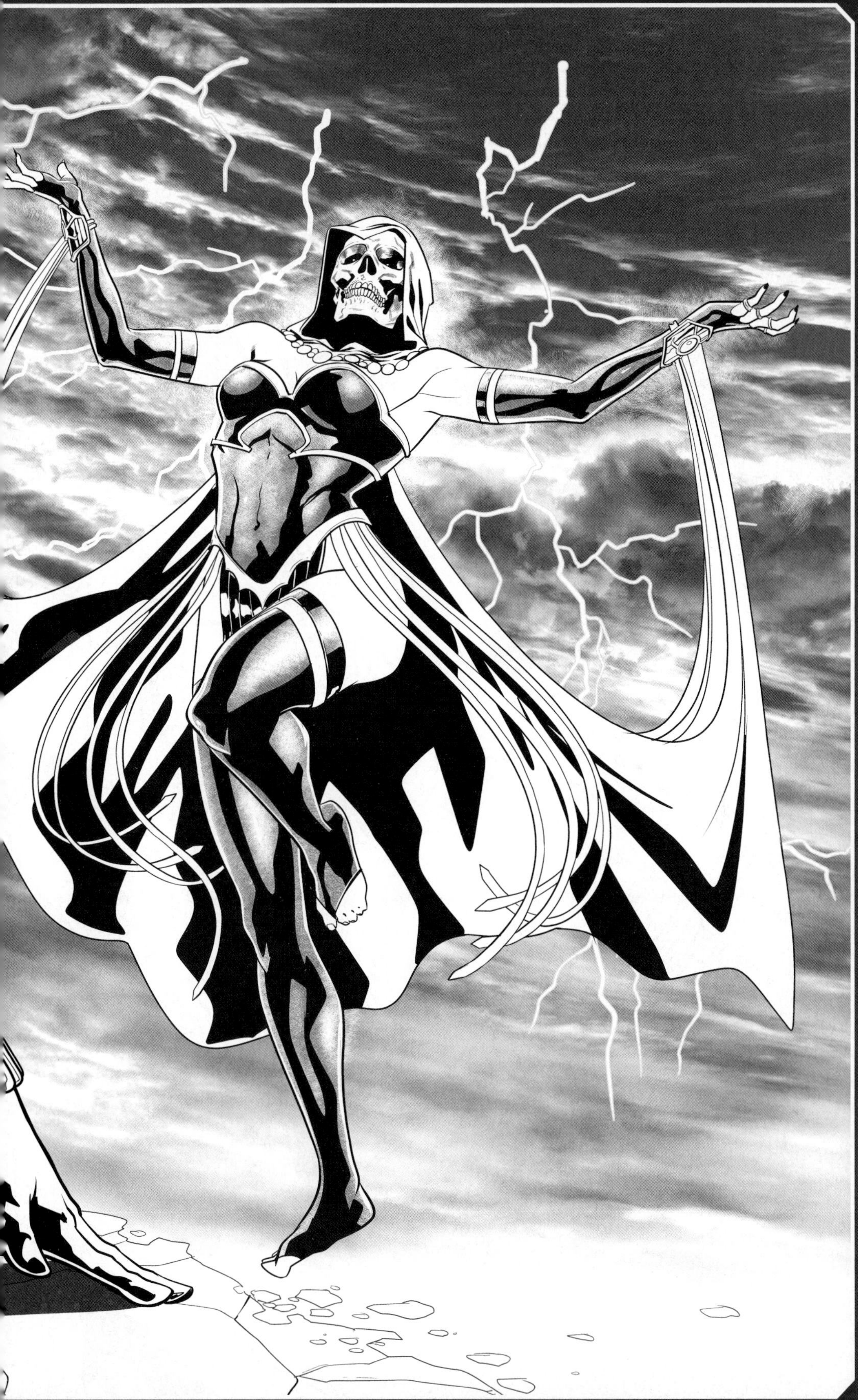

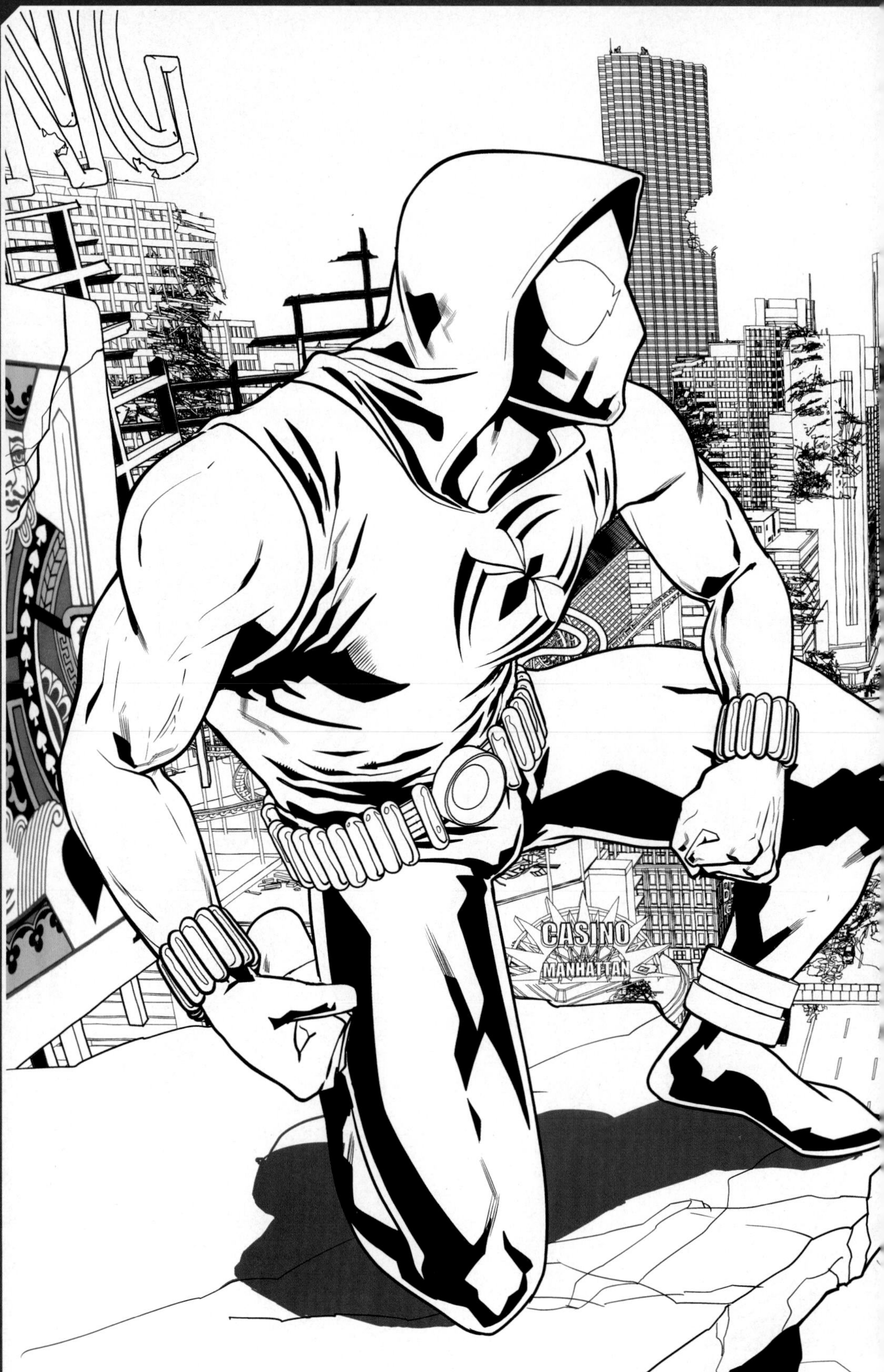
CASINO
MANHATTAN

Will Sliney

BEN REILLY: SCARLET SPIDER #8, PAGES 3-4 ART

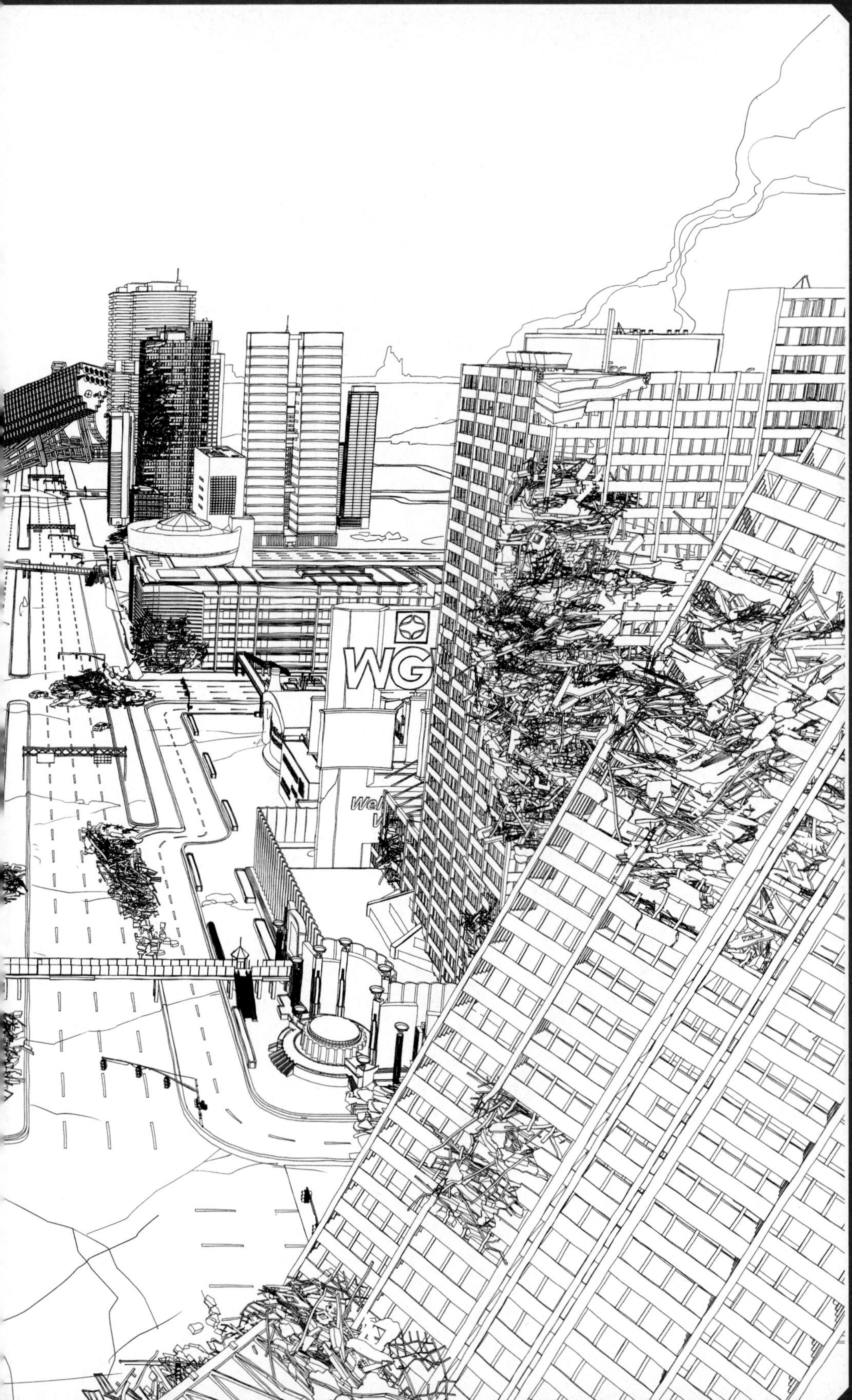
WG

Will Sliney

BEN REILLY: SCARLET SPIDER #8, PAGE 8 ART

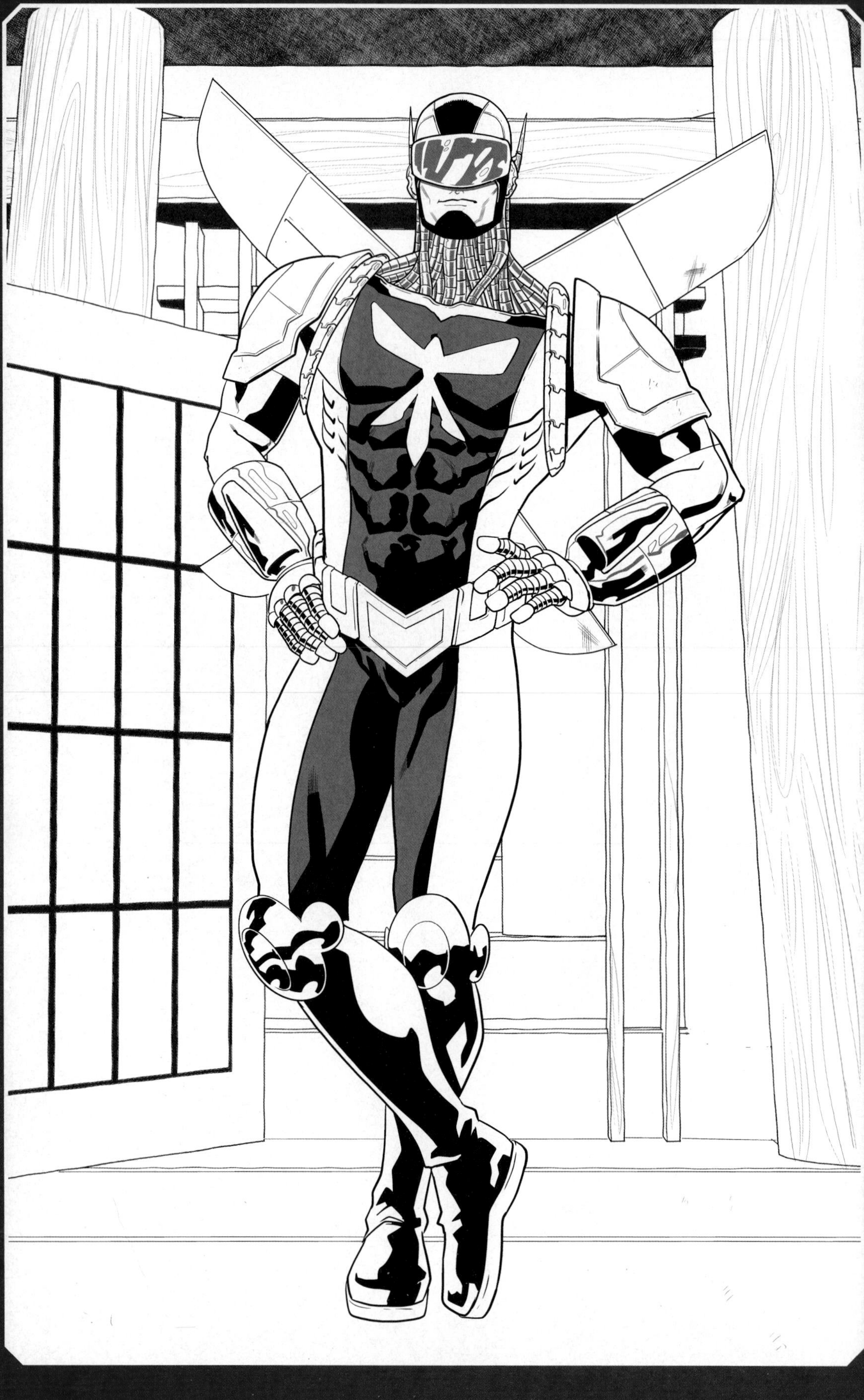